D0223899

The first volume in the series "Cambridge Studies in Philosophy and the Arts" offers a range of responses by distinguished philosophers and art historians to some crucial issues generated by the relationship between the art object and language in art history. Each of the chapters in this volume is a searching response to theoretical and practical questions, in terms accessible to readers of all human science disciplines. The issues they discuss challenge the boundaries to thought that some contemporary theorizing sustains.

The first contributors examine the dissonance of language and art object. Jean-François Lyotard and Stanley Rosen propose that art concerns *presence* and *transcendence*, rather than just *communication*, and thereby render the object always beyond our linguistic reach. The next contributors consider this disparity. Richard Wollheim develops a concept of *projection* to reaffirm our grasp of objects through their expressive qualities. For Michael Baxandall, art criticism is talking about talking about art, a view which Catherine Lord and José Benardete examine critically in their contribution. The exploration of the necessarily figurative qualities of art historical language proceeds vigorously in chapters by Carl Hausman, by Richard Shiff (with a particularly fruitful discussion of catachresis), and by David Summers. Finally, Andrew Harrison determines how we must conceive of the supra-linguistic quality of art objects once all that can be accounted for linguistically has been established.

CAMBRIDGE STUDIES IN PHILOSOPHY AND THE ARTS

Series editors:

SALIM KEMAL AND IVAN GASKELL

The language of art history

CAMBRIDGE STUDIES IN PHILOSOPHY AND THE ARTS

Series editors:

SALIM KEMAL AND IVAN GASKELL

Advisory board:

Stanley Cavell, R. K. Elliott, Stanley E. Fish, David Freedberg, Hans-Georg Gadamer, John Gage, Carl Hausman, Ronald Hepburn, Mary Hesse, Hans-Robert Jauss, Martin Kemp, Jean Michel Massing, Michael Podro, Edward S. Said, Michael Tanner.

"Cambridge Studies in Philosophy and the Arts" is a forum for examining issues common to philosophy and critical disciplines that deal with the history of art, literature, film, music, and drama. In order to inform and advance both critical practice and philosophical approaches, the series analyses the aims, procedures, language, and results of inquiry in the critical fields, and examines philosophical theories by reference to the needs of arts disciplines. This interaction of ideas and findings, and the ensuing discussion, bring into focus new perspectives and expand the terms in which the debate is conducted.

Forthcoming volumes in the series include:

Explanation and value in the literary and visual arts
Authenticity and the performing arts
Landscape, natural beauty, and the arts
Politics, aesthetics and the arts

The language of art history

Edited by

SALIM KEMAL

Pennsylvania State University

and

IVAN GASKELL

Harvard University Art Museums

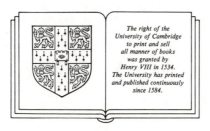

*The right of the
University of Cambridge
to print and sell
all manner of books
was granted by
Henry VIII in 1534.
The University has printed
and published continuously
since 1584.*

CAMBRIDGE UNIVERSITY PRESS

Cambridge   New York   Port Chester

Melbourne   Sydney

Published by the Press Syndicate of the University of Cambridge
The Pitt Building, Trumpington Street, Cambridge CB2 1RP
40 West 20th Street, New York, NY 10011–4211, USA
10 Stamford Road, Oakleigh, Melbourne 3166, Australia

© Cambridge University Press 1991

First published 1991

Printed in Great Britain at the University Press, Cambridge

British Library cataloguing in publication data
The language of art history.
1. Arts. Philosophy
I. Kemal, Salim   II. Gaskell, Ivan
700.1

Library of Congress cataloguing in publication data
The language of art history / edited by Salim Kemal and Ivan Gaskell.
p.   cm. – (Cambridge studies in philosophy and the arts)
Includes index.
ISBN 0–521–35384–x
1. Art – History.   2. Object (Aesthetics).   3. Communication in art.
I. Kemal, Salim.   II. Gaskell, Ivan.   III. Series.
N53–3.024   1991
709 – dc20   90–28256   CIP

ISBN 0 521 35384 x hardback

Contents

Plates

Contributors

MICHAEL BAXANDALL
University of California, Berkeley

JOSÉ A. BENARDETE
Syracuse University

ANDREW HARRISON
University of Bristol

CARL R. HAUSMAN
Pennsylvania State University

CATHERINE LORD
Syracuse University

JEAN-FRANÇOIS LYOTARD
University of California, Irvine

STANLEY ROSEN
Pennsylvania State University

RICHARD SHIFF
University of Texas at Austin

DAVID SUMMERS
University of Virginia, Charlottesville

RICHARD WOLLHEIM
University of California, Berkeley and Davis

Editors' acknowledgments

Several members of the series' Advisory Board have given us help and advice beyond the call of their responsibilities. We should particularly like to thank Carl Hausman and R. W. Hepburn. Other colleagues offered valuable counsel, chief amongst them Emily Grosholz.

Marian Hobson and Tom Cochran kindly undertook the translation of Jean-François Lyotard's chapter at very short notice. This essay, 'Presence', was first published (in French) in his *Que peindre? Adami, Arakawa, Buren* (Editions de la Différence, Paris, 1988).

Michael Baxandall's paper is a revised version of an article originally published in *New Literary History*, 10 (1979). We are grateful to Johns Hopkins University Press for permission to publish it in this collection.

At Cambridge University Press we should like to thank Terence Moore (New York) and Judith Ayling (Cambridge) for their patience and support.

Finally, we both – individually and collectively – owe a great deal to Jane Baston and Jane Whitehead who have borne the brunt of our anxieties since the inception of this volume and the series as a whole.

Art history and language: some issues

SALIM KEMAL AND IVAN GASKELL

The purpose of this volume – the first of a new series – is to offer a range of responses by philosophers and art historians to some crucial issues generated by the relationship between the art object and language in art history.

The choice of "art history" in preference to "art criticism" in this context requires comment. Stephen Bann distinguishes between the two activities: art history "follow[s] the fortunes of an object in time" whereas art criticism "provide[s] an extratemporal evaluation of that object."[1] We might add that art history seeks to define the circumstances in which the art object was initially produced and perceived. Nor should we forget that we construct our art history from a particular stance that borrows from and contributes to a general culture. We should therefore recall that art criticism is inherent in art history. In his paper in this volume Michael Baxandall carefully employs the term "art criticism" rather than "art history," subsuming the latter within the former.[2]

Some academic art historians may prefer to play down the fact of this inter-relation, for art history's concern with historical retrieval – not with criticism – primarily sanctions it as an academic activity. As Norman Bryson points out, art criticism is generally treated as journalism.[3] While we acknowledge the validity of the appraisals by Bann, Baxandall, and Bryson, we have nonetheless chosen to focus on art history as an academic discipline, rather than on art criticism as it is generally perceived. However, the arguments presented by our contributors are significant for art criticism no less than for art history.

The inextricability of criticism from art history is clear from the very first chapters of the collection. These examine the "presence" of art works. This issue also demonstrates the propinquity of art historical and philosophical interests. Some critics, like the late Peter Fuller, have argued that the art object has a distinctive presence because it signals a transcendence of quotidian life.[4] Given "the ever-present absence of God" Fuller proposes that "art and the gamut of aesthetic experience provides the sole remaining glimmer of transcendence." This transcendence depends on a qualitative and evaluative aspect of art, as "every aesthetic response is an act of discrimination which implies a hierarchy of taste."[5] And this hierarchy is the subject of philosophical justification.

While Fuller restricts himself to re-introducing the category of the "spiritual," others are more positive about the philosophical commitments necessary to explaining the "presence" of art. In *The Philosopher on Dover Beach* Roger Scruton argues that any aesthetic experience which lacks a religious dimension remains inadequate.[6] Similarly, George Steiner suggests that great works of art are valuable ultimately because they are "touched by the fire and the ice of God."[7] Both these are responses to the contemporary context in which people have questioned the legitimacy of a single canon and – in Fuller's phrase – "shared symbolic order."[8] In returning to God and the ostensibly shared natural experience of humankind both authors seem to strive for the certainties of a pre-modernist perspective and order.

That regression is not our only choice. The authors of the first two chapters in this volume, Jean-François Lyotard and Stanley Rosen, have explored the nature of this transcendence in recent work, as sublimity and openness to the object.[9] They even flirt with a religious vocabulary in their chapters here; but rather than commit themselves to a religious account to explain the "presence" of art objects, Lyotard and Rosen develop another crucial aspect of the relation between art and philosophy, examining the presence of art objects and their specifically and irreducibly visual aspect.

In "Presence" Lyotard presents his argument in the form of an allusive dialogue appropriate to the constant deferral of the object's presence in our apprehension and reflection in language. He explains that talk of presence points in the direction of the art object, of a pre-conceptual ordering. Even though it emphasizes the particular, this visual presence of art works does not prohibit reflection or commentary. But the latter must seek out the presuppositions of an art object in and through the work itself, rather than by applying some general theory to relate this work to all others.

In "Writing and painting: the soul as hermeneut" Rosen takes up a similar theme. Citing Plato's *Philebus* and its two demiurges of writing and painting, he proposes that any attempt to use language hermeneutically to grasp objects will fail the painter. He draws issues from Kant's *Critique of Pure Reason* in a particular reading to contrast the hermeneutic approach with a direct openness to the object's qualities. Only this openness guarantees the coherence of our thought and experience, he maintains;[10] and his insistence on the irreducibility of painting to writing raises issues of how the two might ever be linked.

In chapter 4, "Correspondence, projective properties, and expression in the arts," Richard Wollheim develops one theory of the link between language and the art object. Some theorists find the art object interesting because it is expressive. Recently, some have argued that such expression is best understood by analogy with language and grammar (for instance, Wollheim's own *Art and its Objects*).[11] However, most theories of this type founder where they fail to explain how we ascribe a psychological property, such as expressiveness, to objects. In his chapter Wollheim provides a mechanism for this ascription by working out a conception of "projective properties."[12] This yields a foundation for theories of expression in the arts and, by implication, will also ground linguistic accounts of expression.

This chapter develops Wollheim's earlier work on painting, expression, and the meaningfulness of objects.[13] His diminution of at least one crucial element of the supposed resistance of art objects to language – by explaining a relation between mind and object – is especially pertinent to the theme of this volume. The use of language to grasp the object is also Michael Baxandall's concern. In his chapter, "The Language of Art Criticism,"[14] he develops a practical, art historical, response to the issue. We should bear in mind that Baxandall's analysis of art historical principles arises from specific art historical problems. His consistent attention to the art object as a physical entity (related to his past experience as a museum curator) enhances his influence among art historians. It encourages many of his colleagues to trust his theoretical judgment more readily than that of others who forbear such attention.

In his chapter Baxandall outlines his conception of the "basic facts of art critical life." These are threefold. First, the language available to those who write about art is culturally limited. Secondly, discourse on art must be demonstrative rather than descriptive, and is therefore predominantly oblique. Thirdly, the linear form of discourse is at odds with its object, which is perceived by scanning and resolution. Baxandall attends most closely to the second matter, analysing art critical language usage by drawing distinctions based on the various implied relationships between the maker, the object, and the beholder. He argues that nearly all this language is metaphorical, even if in many instances the original force of the metaphor has been lost.

A concern with metaphor and figurative language relates Baxandall's chapter to those which follow by Catherine Lord and José Benardete, Carl Hausman, and Richard Shiff. Clearly, the point at which language and the visual become inextricable continues to be central to the concerns of this volume. Philosophers and art historians have related interests in this matter. The quality of art which Lyotard and Rosen identified in their papers as irreducibly visual and which Wollheim made accessible to expression and language, Baxandall wants to grasp by talk of talking of art works. But he realizes that the distinctiveness of art objects – their visual interest – is not straightforwardly grasped in prosaic descriptive language. We need, then, to understand what kind of language is at issue and how it must work in ways particular to visual interest.

In their chapter, "Baxandall and Goodman," Catherine Lord and José Benardete contend that language and the visual inevitably interpenetrate because only the use of language constitutes the art object. This allows them to accept Baxandall's insight that we talk about talking about art. But they also suggest that Baxandall relies on an untenable conception of the language of art history as catachretic. They look to Nelson Goodman's theory about the *Languages of Art*[15] to provide a corrective complement to Baxandall. They propose that Goodman's theory provides a successful conception of meaning that justifies ascribing relevant qualities to art objects.

Carl Hausman also considers the metaphorical nature of art historical language. In "Figurative language in art history" he argues that metaphor is inevitable in art history because works of art, as the results of creativity, are constituted of newly produced meanings. Standard language seeks descriptive precision, and must be repeatable and recognizable. Therefore it cannot fully articulate the novelty intrinsic to the art object. Because it generates new meanings, metaphorical language is peculiarly appropriate to articulating the novelty of art objects.

Talk of metaphor raises the question of what kinds of figurative language suit the language of art history. In both this chapter and his book, *Metaphor and Art*,[16] Hausman relies on an interactionist theory

4

of metaphor. Other kinds of figurative language may also be available to art historians. Richard Shiff examines and applies the metaphorical language of art history in an analysis of works by Cézanne in chapter 8, "Cézanne's physicality: the politics of touch." His emphasis is on catachresis, which he presents as an unavoidable metaphor. Some metaphors depend on substitution or comparison for their meaning; by contrast, catachresis affords no choice of this kind. For instance, as Shiff suggests, when we talk of the arm of a chair, we are not substituting "arm" for something else. This term may allude to the human arm, so some comparison is at work, but we are using it as the usual and only available term for referring to that part of a chair. In their paper, Lord and Benardete questioned the efficacy of catachresis in art history by arguing that a metaphor that dispenses with the assertion of resemblance cannot sustain a genuine predication. However, by appealing to Maurice Merleau-Ponty's analysis of the ambiguity of the relationship between subject and object, self and other, touch and vision, produced by catachresis, Shiff argues that catachresis provides a means of both conceiving the construction of art objects and grasping them in language.

Shiff's essay, then, exemplifies the catachretic language of art history. People have supposed that the issue of the relation between language and art object arises because they are absolutely distinct from each other. Shiff's chapter, like those by Baxandall and Hausman, suggests by contrast that the search for such purity is misguided. The language of art history allows us to grasp art objects only by using technically "impure" language imbued with catachresis and metaphor. The object and language do not exist independently of each other as pure entities.

One approach that gives priority to language over "independent" art objects is central to chapter 9, "Conditions and conventions: on the disanalogy of art and language," by David Summers. Pointing out that the terms are often conflated in art historical writing, Summers draws a clear distinction between conditions, as those factors without which any given work of art could not exist, and conventions, which he argues are closely related to understanding in linguistic terms. For Summers, conventions must be secondary to conditions. In making this distinction he argues that an understanding of conceptual images as iconic – that is, not arbitrary and depending on visual metaphors – underlies western thinking about art. Beginning with the classical account, he goes on to examine two versions of Ferdinand de Saussure's semiology and aspects of Sir

Ernst Gombrich's account of the psychology of the perception of art to show that a purely linguistic understanding is inadequate to art objects. The necessary lack of complete equivalence between image and referent is essential to the image's use and meaning, which is far from exhausted by recognition of the referential aspect of the image. Summers proposes that the real spatial context of the art object – the culturally specific articulation of space within which it exists – constitutes its conditions, forming the basis of the conventional construction of meaning.

If David Summers demonstrates one way in which linguistic analogies for art objects are inadequate, Andrew Harrison, in the last chapter in this volume, "A minimal syntax for the pictorial: the pictorial and the linguistic – analogies and disanalogies." demonstrates another. Harrison reaffirms the peculiarly visual quality of art objects. He argues that art objects have a specifically visual character that remains even after language has articulated all that it can, but which nonetheless can be conceived syntactically – that is, by means of a strictly limited analogy with the linguistic. This visual character prompts our distinctive interest in the art object.

A brief introductory summary far from exhausts the content of these papers. A number of other themes and issues structure and inter-relate them. One issue is the extent to which art objects depend entirely on the communicative intention of the artist. Richard Woll-heim's paper makes this intention crucial to the meanings of works.[17] Others reject this suggestion. Andrew Harrison proposes that the meaningfulness of a work depends on syntax, which may not depend on intentions alone and may even thwart them. The artist's intention lacks authority over the object and its meaning, and communication between viewers around the object can occur because of that syntax, despite the absence of the artist's intention. David Summers's chapter develops the issue of the structure of the art object through the distinction between convention and conditions, while the role Carl Hausman ascribes to metaphor, with the linguistic structure that implies, also ruptures meaning from dependence on the artist's intention alone.

Another theme determining a number of the chapters is the cultural and social context of art. This should not be surprising in a text concerned with art history, but it is a factor that aestheticians can easily ignore for the sake of grasping a pure "aesthetic experience" abstracted from concern with context. David Summers's distinction between conventions and conditions seeks to make room for this historical and social contextualization. Recognizing that conditions emerge from a social and cultural context, his paper affirms the vital inter-relation between art and culture. It reminds us that we construct the conditions and conventions of our art historical analyses of works from a particular stance that *contributes to and forms* culture. Thus we may add to our conception of art history that it not only defines the circumstances in which art objects were initially produced, but also helps to determine the cultural context for our understanding of works of art. Carl Hausman implies a similar point. As art historical language is metaphorical, it generates new meanings in grasping the art object and so contributes to our construction of culture. Jean-François Lyotard and Richard Wollheim also suggest the crucial role of culture. Lyotard's sensitivity to the peculiar associations that constitute the presence of works of art (here specifically recent paintings by Valerio Adami, Shūsaku Arakawa, and Daniel Buren) locates the work in a particular psychological and cultural context, while Richard Wollheim's account of projective properties and expression allows for the conventional nature of producing and appreciating art objects.

The issues raised in this volume are also of consequence for contemporary art practice, where the relationship between philosophy, art history, and art criticism is already important. In his chapter, Andrew Harrison skeptically observes that some modern art "is virtually a form of philosophy." While some contemporary art may indeed be no more than the visual manifestation of degraded theorizing, the work of other contemporary artists can hardly be dismissed so readily. Barbara Kruger and Jenny Holzer, for instance, are among those artists who directly examine the immanence of language in art, employing slogans in imagery apparently appropriated from advertising and proverbial truisms on electronic signboards. Such work reminds us that disciplined explorations by artists of conceptual issues, including the relationship between art object and language, have long been an avenue of inquiry as important as those trodden by academic philosophers.

Another concern of contemporary art practice is the development of means of evading the production of art objects as such. Here, again, the examination of the relationship between language and art is crucial. Most obvious among the strategies followed by artists has been the growth of performance art. A performance cannot be treated in the same terms of display and commerce as an art object. And, as

Henry Sayre has demonstrated, issues raised by performance have been taken up in many other forms of contemporary art practice.[18] There is considerable concern with the relationship of the art object to the gallery, as the principal site of display and hence definition. Two responses have been to use alternative and hence implicitly subversive sites – for instance, advertising hoardings – and to redefine the gallery as total installation space, rather than an ostensibly "natural" setting that validates objects by displaying them as art.

It seems germane to mention developments in the practice of artists, gallery curators, and critics at this juncture because they help to determine contemporary conceptions of earlier art, yet lie largely beyond the bounds of academic discourse. In spite of art training taking place within the framework of educational institutions, making, displaying, and commenting upon new art are scarcely regarded as academic activities. However, we have long become accustomed to a progressive elision of art and its commentary as artists have come to use both visual media and language, sometimes separately, though increasingly in conjunction. Furthermore, many curators hold display to be as important as textual commentary in shaping critical responses to art. In consequence, we should bear in mind that some people engaged in these activities believe that language alone, however richly figurative, will always be inadequate to the task of grasping the art object analytically, or even poetically.

We would argue, nonetheless, that art – however defined – is in some sense amenable to independent examination in language, as the chapters in this volume suggest. This is so even if the "mature inferential vocabulary in full play" favored by Michael Baxandall no longer proves adequate for all purposes. An awareness of philosophical issues may refresh the concern with the application of language to art. We hope that a philosophical approach to these issues will encourage art historians and critics to measure the meaning, accuracy, and coherence of their language, for instance, to question the reliability of concepts imported from semiology and other totemically treated terminologies. Similarly, philosophers may achieve a more accurate understanding of art historians' struggles to reconcile visual experience with language on a day-to-day basis, often in pursuit of answering pressing but intellectually unglamorous questions concerning who made a given art object, by what means, where, and when.

The common interest of all the contributors to this volume is with applying language to the object to account for visual art fully. All who wish to reconsider making and criticizing art will have to face the issue of the relation of the art object to language and we are confident that the issues our contributors raise in the papers that follow are central to any such reconsideration.

NOTES

1 Stephen Bann, *The True Vine: On Visual Representation and the Western Tradition* (Cambridge, 1989), p. 112.

2 Baxandall develops this issue further in *Patterns of Intention: On the Historical Explanation of Pictures* (New Haven and London, 1985). He sees the historical explanation of art objects as in one sense a "special taste" within art critical discourse and art history as an essentially critical endeavor (see especially pp. 135–137).

3 Norman Bryson, *Looking at the Overlooked: Four Essays on Still Life Painting* (London, 1990), pp. 8–10.

4 See Peter Fuller, *Images of God: the Consolations of Lost Illusions* (London, 1985; 2nd edn, London, 1990). In several of the essays collected in *'Wonder' and other Essays: Eight Studies in Aesthetics and Neighbouring Fields* (Edinburgh, 1984), R. W. Hepburn explores transcendence in our appreciation of natural beauty and its representations.

5 Fuller, *Images* (1990 edn), p. xiii.

6 Roger Scruton, *The Philosopher on Dover Beach* (London, 1990).

7 George Steiner, *Real Presences: Is there Anything in What we Say?* (London, 1989), p. 223.

8 Fuller, *Images* (1990 edn), pp. 10–16.

9 See Jean-François Lyotard, *Le Différend* (Paris, 1983; English edn, *The Differend: Phrases in Dispute*, trans. Georges Van Den Abbeele, Manchester, 1989) and Stanley Rosen, *The Quarrel between Philosophy and Poetry: Studies in Ancient Thought* (New York and London, 1988).

10 See Rosen, *Quarrel*, chapters 1 and 10.

11 Richard Wollheim, *Art and its Objects* (New York, 1969; 2nd edn, with six supplementary essays, Cambridge, 1980).

12 "Projection" in this context carries echoes of Sigmund Freud's use of the term in his analysis of the Schreber case of 1911 ("Psycho-Analytical Notes on an Autobiographical Account of a Case of Paranoia (Dementia Paranoides)", trans. Alix and James Strachey, in *The Standard Edition of the Complete Psychological Works of Sigmund Freud*, vol. xii (London, 1958), pp. 3–82, especially pp. 66, 71). For Wollheim's application of it to the experience of art, see Richard Wollheim, *The Thread of Life* (Cambridge, 1984), especially pp. 214–15, and also his *Painting as an Art* (Princeton, N.J., and London, 1987), especially pp. 82–85.

13 Notably *Painting as an Art* (see note 12).

14 The chapter is a revised version of an article originally published in *New Literary History* (10 [1979], pp. 453–465).

15 Nelson Goodman, *Languages of Art: An Approach to a Theory of Symbols* (Indianapolis and New York, 1968; 2nd edn, Indianapolis, 1976).

16 Carl Hausman, *Metaphor and Art: Interactionism and Reference in the Verbal and Nonverbal Arts* (Cambridge, 1989).

17 Wollheim makes the same point in other writings, e.g. *Painting as an Art* (see note 12), especially on p. 96: "The spectator's experience [of the work of art] must concur with the artist's intention, but it does not have to do so through knowledge of it."

18 Henry M. Sayre, *The Object of Performance: The American Avant-Garde since 1970* (Chicago and London, 1989).

2

Presence

JEAN-FRANÇOIS LYOTARD

Translated by MARIAN HOBSON and TOM COCHRAN

YOU

He says that the painter, today as at all times, and whatever means he uses, does nothing but try to apprehend sensible presence. I maintain that presence escapes, whichever bit you think you've caught it by. That it can only be apprehended as deferred. That even if you apprehend it, you defer it. There are many ways of apprehending it in painting. The philosopher knows that it defers itself by itself, any how or any way. It is enough to reflect. On reflection the least glance appears laden with presuppositions, with those undertones that should be called "underseens," leaving out of account the physical, physiological, socio-cultural conditions which make the glance possible. How can painting offer an object to the glance without taking into consideration all the things the gaze is expecting? Immediate presence in one brushstroke of color hides whole worlds of mediations, which the painter who makes it cannot ignore, unless he's a dauber. And today less than in the past. To start with, the painting tradition has got richer in a thousand ways which were unknown even a hundred years ago. Then the scientific and technological context of today is thoroughly shaking up conceptions of space and time, and our experience of them. Painters' skepticism about the givens and the forms of sensible presence can only get worse. "Doubt" is spreading from Paul Cézanne to Daniel Buren, from Marcel Duchamp to Shūsaku Arakawa, from Raphael to Valerio Adami.

I maintain that the history of painting, western of course, can only be a tale of the decline of sensible presence, because the history of painting is a part of the history of the mind's knowledge of itself. In the course of its putting its objective and subjective formations

11

between itself and the sensible, the mind distances and mediates the latter, it weakens its presence. I mean insofar as presence is the object of our reception, at least. The mind has more control over the giving of the visible. What is given becomes what the mind gives itself, and the sensible event becomes what the mind can give itself as something to feel – to its own surprise, eventually, since it will never have finished knowing itself. This event is added to what we know and modifies it. Speculation never stops encroaching on naive reception. The art of presence is dying. The art of deferring presence is growing. If painting were really, as he says, in search of presence above everything else, it would be on its deathbed. Aesthetics, on the contrary, which only comments on the mediations that allow in the immediately sensible, would be in splendid health. In fact, painting today will not stop commenting on itself, and working out its own aesthetics not just through the text, but also through lines and colors. That's how it's so alive, by showing that presence is absent.

If it is figurative, a painting re-presents what it presents but it exhibits its representation. What you see "on" the picture is certainly not the picture you see. Is that to say that you look at a picture, and you see a landscape? Like in a window, the Italians used to say. But the ideal of transparency, of the picture surface giving a view out over the depth of the field, is no longer the key to the organization of figurative painting, if it ever was. The scene's production is advertized "in front of" what is represented. What is represented appears visibly "staged" rather than shown. That's a term from the operational vocabulary of war or the stock exchange, of the theatre or the cinema. Painting as activity does not efface itself in the receptivity of seeing. The artifice, you might say, points to itself, points itself out. The landscape, the "scene" (the action), the face are thus put in a state of reprieve from presence. And, by the same token, from the present. They are still there, to be seen "now," but invoked or evoked, so called back in memory. Simulacra, Pierre Klossowski explains, rather than phantasmata. Figuration, any figuration, is inscribed in narrations which are discourses, from memory. Especially a narration which sketches out, simplifies, complicates, decorates, strips, deconstructs its object, which does "too much" with it. As Adami's drawing does too much. This "too much" distances the "scene" in time. You have to "explain" it, unfold it, reconstruct its before and afterwards. Its story, period. You didn't know that's Cosima? You know who that was? Story of the picture. This becomes a scene in its turn, "staged" by its exhibition. Just small-talk and anecdotes. The

12

first time I saw that Arianne, you know, at the end of the studio ...
The chronicle of the artist. When he painted the Orpheus, he spent
whole days in the Roman collections in the Naples Museum. The
chronology of the work. The picture belongs to Adami's third period,
the one with the mythological tales, which followed the period of the
consumer society and the failed revolution. The genesis of the
picture. At first Medea was represented full-length, then hidden by
the other side of a canvas, then on her knees ... The history of the
title, etc. Narratives come shooting off from the picture and its object;
they spread themselves out upstream, clogging up their downstream
with a growing mass of stories. Derived from the distance representation imposes, narrations repeat it, they extend it into duration. And
with the passing of time, absence hollows itself out. Figuration is
merely a pretext for nostalgia.

Whether abstract or conceptual, painting seems to deny openly that
any presence has a hold over it. It says: this is a supporting medium.
Its surface has been prepared in order for lines to be traced on it, for
words to be written on it. So read then, try to understand, decode the
diagrams, think about it. There's little to see, and a lot to think about.
In that case, it is said, why paint? You could get by with writing, with
tracing out graphics, if sensible presence isn't your thing any longer.
Silliness. Color, even if it's weakened, right down to pure white, line
even if it's simplified into regular curves, canvas, frame, and exhibition, all are indispensable for the proof that presence is lost, just
because it is thought that painting, whose elements these are, is
seeking for presence. It's the opposite case from the figurative
manner. The latter makes sensible presence gangrenous by staging it,
and by narration. Conceptual art and abstract art thumb their noses at
exact learning and understanding by exposing their statements and
their "illustrations" to the conditions of pictorial representation. The
signs of presence, immense as they are with a Robert Ryman or an
Arakawa, are only signs, are still used to take apart the mind's
certainties. There's little to see, there's nothing to understand. It can't
be said, anyway, that these painters are looking for sensible presence
when they only use it to make us sensible of what the mind lacks.
Working thus, whatever they intend, to its continuing development.

Isn't it just the same with the "installer" Buren? With the difference
that he takes exception less to the picture than to its very exhibition.
One step further in the annihilation of the supposedly immediate
visible. Painting is no longer anything more than a mark or a
remarking of what makes "painting" as an institution possible, and

visible in the first place. Here, color and line come out off their supporting surface, the painting, which can be carried around – they are like waste from a sumptuous visual presence, picked up and arranged by the installation "with the intention" of picking out and perhaps denouncing the conditions of aesthetic vision. Of course the alternating colored/colorless bands, vertically attached on the site they thus cause to emerge, are to be seen in the here and now. It remains that their viewing isn't the important thing, their presence in itself, but the "view" which they are destined to become: a view of the mind criticizing itself in that self-conservation that is the place and moment of art, a museum, or a landscape. The mind denounces its blindness when it thinks it sees and enjoys visible beauty. Presence is only being used, and to show the falseness of presence.

After this, how can it be maintained, as he does, that visual presence is the only aim of painters?

HIM

I grant you all that. What you call reflection, in painting itself, is keeping on winning, and that's good. Painting keeps on working out the conditions for painting, and trying to show them by the means which are its own. It includes its own commentary. There is no painting, especially in the last hundred years, which doesn't paint the question: what is painting? and which doesn't sketch out a painted answer to this question. All right.

But admit that something took place; I don't say some one thing, an object, but an event which isn't a thing, but at the least a caesura in space-time and that that's what must be "rendered." It has taken place, since it is true that one paints afterwards, just as one speaks afterwards. And it will have taken place through the witness that painting bears to it. That's what gives, has, and will have given occasion, given the place and the moment, to the reflections you speak of, to Adami's memory, to the paradoxes of Arakawa, to Buren's criticism. That's what they are trying to make present. The place for the "taking place," the *Stattfinden*, the locus for the *"avoir lieu,"* the case of the *accadare*. That, reflection doesn't engender it; speculation receives it. In comparison, reflection comes "too late," always.

It's not reflection that "makes" the woad blue in the east of a summer's morning, which makes this pale silence on rising awaken

14

today, in your still half-asleep mind, a wonderment which you will need minutes, hours, perhaps a lifetime to connect with your first summer departure, when, still a child, you climbed on your bike laden with good things for the journey, accompanied by your big sister, to go, map on the handlebars, to meet school friends on holiday in the area who, a hundred kilometres from there, were likewise starting out to meet you. Now you say, you give a name to it, yes that's the pastel of the Vendée skies on getting up in July, not far from the sea, when the weather was at its best, yes, that's the adventure of cycling all those kilometres, alone for a whole day, space opening out towards an agreed meeting-place, a jubilating mastery over the paths and fields far from your parents, the liveliness of the first time, your life's authority handed over for a day to the circuit of sun and shade, to the ordering of faithful streams, the blue of being given over to the ordinances of the things of the earth, the emotion of a meeting so difficult to arrange (weren't you a bit in love with your friend's sister? and with him?). You place in ironic light the blue, lost and found again, in which the head of the young cyclist was bathed, you observe that the very associations which the blue sets off in your adult soul are like a beginning of the reflexive work, at least they make up a tale taken from memory, and they place as absent, that's just the point, the chromatic timbre of the present morning, which is what caused it all – the painter, who has stayed that child, who will still be it, says to you: laugh, smile, that blue will have got there before you. That is what presence is. The sensible event, if you like.

Yet it is this particular presence, this timbre that the artist wants to render with the picture. Rendering it is to be understood as meaning that the picture in turn should be for someone, I don't know, an event, this blue, this morning. It isn't representation that worries him; presence isn't lost from the mere fact that it is represented, it passes over to the picture. It remains to be seen how his picture "will look at" the scene. But that his picture may be, in the gaze of the gazer, a pastel hue of a dawn sky to the gaze of a child, that will happen or not, and you, the philosopher, like him the painter and like everybody, you'll have to wait for the picture to be there. And if that takes place, only then will you speculate. When that will have taken place. The remembrance can put itself forward with this presence even before being localized, and without that of which it is the remembrance having had this presence. Perhaps presence is always remembrance. "Remembered" Arakawa writes. Souvenir photos from Buren. *Memorandum* feeding the work of Adami.

YOU

He says "picture" out of habit, because his Vendean pastel is a picture. Description and landscape. And a landscape from nature. But that's quite out of date. That's Diderot in front of Claude Lorrain and Vernet. Baudelaire already has only urban scenes to look at. In fact, a squad of obstinate methodical workmen has come and redone the house of our gaze, redone it from top to bottom. Adami puts in blind windows, Arakawa sprays graffiti on entire walls, Buren does installations. They are squabbling over the gaze; they are squabbling among themselves. They are nevertheless all in agreement that it's no longer going to be a "chez nous."

If necessary, I'm willing to admit that Adami's windows are what used to be called pictures. That is his apparent classicism. Especially in the later works, with the hegemony of his landscapes, the historical and mythological scenes losing their importance at the same time as what has been called his retreat becomes more striking. Careful. It's too clear that with his windows on lakes, mountains, Adami is not seeking to offer presence to the gaze but an open space for day-dreaming. With the effect of the severity of his lines, with his midway-colors (as we say mid-season) he is not seeking to show, to get us to see, but to evoke. The here and now drip everywhere with another time and another place. He plunges us in an anamnesis, rather than into an event. His windows open out onto absence. He doesn't believe in the visible any more than Buren or Arakawa. If he shuts up his doubt into an intact, or almost, *quadro*, it's out of delicacy, it's the graceful ways of an Italian from a good family. The sadness made for him by what is called reality needs a classical label, strength from being constructed, chromatic moderation, discipline according to a protocol for the gaze. The *this* which shows itself to our eyes after this cleaning and pressing, meticulously dressed, what is it showing so politely? That *this* is dying, has no life in itself, belongs to somewhere else, and is going back there. Observing precedence brings with it the sweet madness that reality, what are called the events of life, has no importance and is not. He makes me think of Hölderlin gone mad, who called his visitors "Your Royal Majesty." And who said he was seventeen when he was sixty. The crime against presence can clothe itself in an extreme civility.

As for Buren and Arakawa, they don't hide, but they exhibit the little faith they have in presentation, obsessed both of them, quite differently it's true, by the mediations that presentation presupposes and implies. One still tries to paint them; it's enough for the other to mark them. The house walls are pushed back to the cosmological dimensions of energy with one. The other puts up arbitrary signs in insignificant corners, when he's not redoing the whole architecture to shake off the complicity of your gaze with his dwelling-place. One opens space out onto the unending of infinite Ideas; the other reveals the unseen ordering which guides vision and the whole visit of the onlookers in those spaces where painting is conserved – he reveals the gaze that is needed.

We're a long way from that blue. I said that they think a great deal more than they see, that they make use of the eye, theirs and that of the public, not so that it sees complacently, but so that it surprises itself in not finding anything to see and forces itself to wonder how and why this is like this. And even to recognize that they don't know at all. They look as if they are awaiting a commentary from a philosopher in order to know this. They know that none of us knows at all, but that we must seek to know. And in this way they complete their allotted part in the ending of this art of sight which was painting, and its sublating into the thought of what seeing is. They are putting the last touches to the aesthetics of Romanticism, with means that Romanticism certainly didn't have in its sights, but nevertheless according to Romanticism's philosophy, which is reflexive.

HIM

What is dying while painting is turning itself into thought isn't painting or art, which are doing well, but aesthetics. Another name is going to have to be found to designate this commentary on art, on painting and on visual art, which seeks out the presuppositions, the undertones, the *a priori*, but in and through painting, with its means, at the same level as the supporting structure, line, and color. Hegel when he wrote that it is too late for art and that aesthetics' moment has come, has put things back to front, with his usual assumptions in favor of totalizing through the concept.

YOU

As if he didn't know, as we all do, that today commentary on a work is part of that work, in one way or another, whether we show the underside, or the rough drafts, whether the commentary accompanies the work, writing itself directly on the same supporting structure (Arakawa) or through note-books, pamphlets (Adami, Buren), books, (Buren,[1] Arakawa/Gins[2]) and also because the commentary, apparently classically distinct from what ought to be its referent, does stay subordinate to it, in that the commentary's validity is limited to the site where the work takes place (Buren) or again, in that it tries to make itself equal to the work by the way it handles its own material, language, through writing (Arakawa/Gins). Or even it turns out sometimes that the commentary is the whole work, a text whose inscription is moved onto the supporting structure where painting was expected. And again, sometimes (all three) the commentary limits itself to indicating the direction to be taken, by an unexpected title, written or not straight onto the canvas, the paper, or what have you. The commentary spreads into the work from everywhere and supports it when it doesn't replace it. It is for Adami the oldest stories, for Arakawa the most bizarre concepts, for Buren the most concealed situations, which nourish it. I don't say that the commentary is the same type with all three, but that each one's painting would not have existence without this word-work, without this meditation. Although in their different ways, the one or other incite little to visual pleasure and a great deal to reflection. When he pushes it as far as it will go, Buren for instance is ungraspable if the text which gives the reasoning behind the set-up and the purpose of his work isn't there. Arakawa does a book with Madeleine Gins, in which the paradoxical "sense-mechanism" is illustrated. And does he really believe that Adami owes less to language because he appears more restrained, when his titles, his inserts, his *Memorandum* are always referring the intrigued eye to stories of all sorts, for which his pictures are only snapshots?

HIM

Painting has always been enveloped in thousands of phrases, which were always reflexive, even if they weren't always critical. You seem confused by this situation, even though it's commonplace today, which puts the commentary on the work in part onto the workload of the artist. You are paying too much attention to the distribution of social roles. Do you really want the painter to paint and the critic to criticize, and everyone to stay in his rightful place when it is clear that these artists, like many others, are questioning what is happening to place? Are you one of those who are of the opinion that a painter must not philosophize, nor a philosopher get mixed up in doing a painting, an exhibition? And then, above all, you are mixing the terms of the question. You believe that in showing up that there is not much reality these painters are turning away from presence and are criticizing it. But reality isn't presence, it is representation. And maybe works belong to representation, but their destiny is presence. And that is true of our painters, however "gossipy" they seem to you. The figures of Altamira and Lascaux were also points of emphasis, so to speak, illustrations for the legendary narrative, which is the first commentary, and stopping-places in that first visit–pilgrimage in the subterranean sanctuary. We don't know at all whether the narrator was someone other than the painter, and that has no importance except social – that is to say, pragmatic. The relation between *dictum* and *pictum* had hardly changed in the Catalan monasteries in the middle of the eleventh century AD. During meals, the lector reads the commentary of Beatus on the Apocalypse from a pulpit. The figure of the Beast, on the folio which he has just turned and which hangs over the tables where the monks are eating, illustrates his word, suspends it, deepens it. The figures evidently have come out of the narration like so many tableaux vivants, immobilized moments, made strong by this hiatus, or weak, as you like, overburdened with possible meanings, or disburdened of actual meanings from the mere fact that they interrupt the thread of the narrative, and that they allow with this suspension many more links, that is, other commentaries, which the course of the story, whether it is legendary or not, can only neglect in order to obey its own finality. These silent scenes, stopped short turn out to be wordy, filled with ambiguity, empty; they incite reflections already; they demand that minds free themselves from the direction that the narrative wants, which is its destination. Contrary to, separate from, this they trace out paths with no destiny and thus they trace out nothing. By *destination* I mean that arrangement of time which makes it rhyme with itself.

YOU

He's been reading Hölderlin. Destiny: the end of the story is in agreement with its beginning. An event has taken place, whose making good, whose reparation the narration is unfolding. Mythical, tragical or comical, epic or novel-like, a making good in any case, since the end solves the puzzle of the beginning, whether the listener knew it or not: whether as an oracle which destines, as a character who propels everything along, as a primal scene whose constraint

strikes and strikes again, as an unmasked criminal, the inevitable –
funny or cruel – comes to pass. We knew it, even if we didn't know
how, and at the end things are in order, time is effaced and collected,
a framed space held open, available edge-to-edge for saying it again,
with all the variants one could wish for. Narration opens this area of
availability of time out into time, which is of its nature what is
unavailable, because narration destines the story's heroes and, in this
way, those who listen to its telling. Who is not ready to sacrifice life
and time to achieve this destination? The most adventurous will in
the end have best served to rein in the event, by extending the area
offered to the telling of it, by giving a destination to what didn't
already have one in the narrations of the community, and thanks to
this extension, by destining the community more to its own narration.

Stories are made to be repeated, in a thousand different ways,
including that of the historian, because they have in them that
principle of reparation or of resolution which is destination. That is
their didactic force. They attach the whole world, everything that
happens, to a time which has rhyme. They rhyme one with another
because each rhymes with itself. What they say has little impact.
They teach that time makes up a cycle. I'd like to show him that this
arrangement is that of desire, that it is a result of that final causality
which works, *a fine ad initium*, taking succession backwards and
only selecting among events those which can enter into this composition. That this is a whole hegemony of the faculty of desire which
is exercized on time by narration. Yet desire does not know presence.
It only knows destination and plot.

HIM

What I provisionally call the figure escapes like a snapshot in this
duration, whose course will infallibly bend back to its source, and
which imparts its rhythm both to recitation and to diegesis. Figure
opens out another space-time which isn't yet, not already, caught up
in the rhythmic rule of before and afterwards. It doesn't matter if it is,
as they say, figurative, or abstract, "good," or bizarre. The figure is
there now, and it blocks the course of the tale by putting a sort of sigh
in its way, something between breathing in and breathing out. It is not
the presence *of* the figure itself. Here, generally, people bring up
"form." They go digging in the visual field. The figure, they say,
"presents itself," but it is the "form," its secret organization which in
reality presents it, without presenting itself. Which hides itself in the

figure. Any artist knows that. Visual isn't visible, as sonorous isn't audible. From its retreat in the exposition of the figure informed by "form," a space-time which isn't destined puts itself on loan. We are getting closer to the unnarratable.

Side-tales, grafted onto the one suspended by the figure, perhaps soon to be grown-up and right for getting it forgotten, can indeed take it over and imbue it with destiny once again. The story of this, the story of that. Isn't that what happens even to those figures which are the most neutralized from the narrative point of view, to those which were imagined as challenges to any organization, to any organism, to any rendering symmetrical by discourse? The white square, that absolute, can at least be got to talk in a history of Suprematism and of modern painting. "Art historian," you know, there's a whole pre-destined destining in the title of this competence. But the figures, or rather the "forms" which cling to them like gossamer, laugh at any historicization. People ask, I hear, how today in Europe we can be sensitive to the bas-relief of Nectanebo II which decorated the vestibule of the exhibition *Les Immatériaux*[3] and which is 2,500 years old. That question gives away the depths to which the thought of art has sunk when it is given over to historicism, that is precisely to the hegemony of narrative closure and of the making absent. In the middle of the thousands of narrative plots knotted between the last Egyptian-born Pharoah and us, a stele of silence, modest, not to be captured, is there and stays there. It does not provide us with material for reparation. The space-time it gives off, its "form" if you want, stays non-destined, indeterminate. To be subject to this silence, that is seeing. You just have to be blind with a certain sort of blindness, to make yourself slow on the uptake about plots. About 2,500 years of plots.

YOU

I hear his protesting scarequotes around the word "form." Having slid from figure to form, he's getting ready for another sidestep. To what in the end is he going to impute presentation?

HIM

It would be futile to pretend that form isn't destined. Perhaps it only is destination. But this must be separated from presentation. The whole of the philosophy of taste is built on the affinity of form with what Kant called a state of mind, aesthetic pleasure, good "propor-tion," that is his word, between the faculty of feeling and that of conceiving. A proportion that isn't rule-given, and is indeed indeter-minable, and thus an affinity which isn't foreseeable, "inexponible"[4] he said, we would say not articulatable. Nevertheless, the beautiful isn't beautiful, except to the extent that the form, at work secretly in the object from which the occasion arises, engenders this free harmony in us. And it has really to be supposed, even if the hypothesis has to stay as a simple analogy, that it is as if the forms were deferred messages addressed to our faculty of feeling, as if the latter were able to "decode" them immediately, transforming, without the aid of a concept, a spatio-temporal manifold into euphoria.

If you continue obstinately to back form, then you will have to argue for this affinity, this complicity, as an immediate pre-reflexive transitivity, as Merleau-Ponty called it – when describing the enigma of perception, it's true, but whose model, anyway according to him, was given by the experience of the beautiful. He thought that by "exhibiting" the structure of the ontological "chiasmus," ungraspa-ble, a relative of Arakawa's focus, he would make us understand how the felt sensible changes into the feeling sensible, into perceptual awareness, and into aesthetic feeling. More than an affinity, it was the same deep homogeneity, the belonging together of the world of the pastel blue and of the soul of the child.

YOU

But the blue isn't form; he's losing track.

HIM

Merleau-Ponty showed that chromatic "matter" awakens in our body, in the preconceptual subject, as well or at first, sketches of movement, dispositions, and thus bits of experience – you would say feelings – which are quite different according to whether one sees in blue or in red. And in this way the blue makes form, don't you agree? Because it makes a feeling, a sense before the mind does. In this philosophy we only have feeling to guide us towards the form which is, the philosophers say, its "reason." I don't say, and Merleau-Ponty especially wouldn't have said, that that is already in Kant. But grant me that the gap between the "prose of the world" of the one, his "indirect language," his "voices of silence," and the "cypher writing" of the other, the *Chiffrenschrift* in which nature is supposed to send you its messages of beauty, is only the gap which separates transcendental criticism, sketching out a metaphysics of nature, from phenomenology which is developing the project of an ontology of the world.

YOU

And what is wrong with this affinity of form for mind? Why are we supposed to do without it? How would any art be possible if there was not this complicity of space-time with feeling? The philosopher can hardly go further in making concessions to the inexplicable. If he doesn't close himself into the serene realm of the concept, he will have to give a *de jure* recognition to form. I grant you that the metaphysical career of his thought, "nature," prose of the world, begins with this recognition. One only needs to look at the case of Kant: the immense effort of his critique ending up in natural theology and soon in the official, almost arrogant reconstitution of idealist metaphysics. Back to re-established harmony, under other titles. All that because of forms, it's true. But is that a sin against art? And were that to be the case, can it be avoided, when you think about it? What does he want? That we shouldn't think? And after all, the metaphysics of nature, of the work, isn't that the confession that there is a beyond for thought, which is inevitable in philosophical thought itself? Doesn't this "beyond" afford art sufficient reserves, sufficient shelter?

HIM

Beneath form, it is perhaps nothing other than the interdict which is at stake in what worries me under the name of presence. I took the case of narrations because they are thought to be very archaic. And also because it is this organization of time which we have received, under the name of novel (*roman*), from Romanticism as the fulfilled form of all *Dichtung*, all "writing" – and which controls the speculative dialectic, that dialectic which dares assert that time is concept. But it is, I think, all articulated thought which presence interrupts. Even Wittgenstein suggests that, when he writes that logical thought is only concerned about the *quid* and leaves the *quod* to other types of thought. I grant that presence isn't there from the start, that it presupposes all the a priori of language and that it implies all the idioms from the individual and cultural past, and that it is better to speak of it as a break in the middle of the thousands of discourses, rather than as of their source, for that would be to begin once more to include it in that rhymed history, perhaps a cosmology, in any case a teleology. Presence, that interstitial space which, I repeat, isn't the "presence of being," is what is necessarily invoked by painters even when painters, as you say, are busy getting us to have doubts about it, getting us to think about the little reality there is and engaging the mind of the viewer in meditation rather than in aesthetic pleasure. This effect of reflection, on what cannot be presented, they are looking for it in the way artists must, by means of presence, and if they didn't, they would simply not be painters but thinkers.

I would even say that the more they question presence, the more they challenge commentary, including their own, just by doing that, and the more they invoke presence against commentary and force the mind to guide the eye towards it. This is how painting is doing all right, and aesthetics is dying off.

Interruption, intercession, and secession as well, figure, "form," something brings to a halt, arouses expectations.

YOU

But these expectations are those of a continuation of the tale, the waiting for the inevitable. We are waiting for what has already been linked on. It feeds off jubilation and terror. Schlegel wrote of *Hamlet*: "Through its decelerated [retarding] nature [*seinem retardierendem Character*], it is to the novel, whose essence is precisely that, that the play seems most closely related." Like good storytellers, who make you wait by slowing down the course of things. The child, his sheet tucked under his chin, impatiently hangs on for the repeat which the mother or father puts off at bedtime. Luster, luxury of the variants, contrary currents in the stream of the massive river, whose mouth the child knows, that source onto the ocean of his sleep. A good wait, that is to say good form, because one knows what to expect. One just keeps on for the metre, even if it is badly kept up. Because it can be smartened up into a rhythm, and that is not to be winked at. It hints that the mastery of time can still show itself in a piece of calculated negligence. Let's wait up a bit. Naive homage to "form" even in the use of what deforms it, but without touching on what he calls plot. This minor delaying makes us feel the way out more. The Romantics called it irony. Everyone knows how Freud attributes this delay, as opposed to the ending, to the life drives. It can clearly be seen that all this belongs to the faculty of desiring.

HIM

Is this a waiting which arises in spacing, in interdict? This suspense, is it due to the synchrony of things in space, to the *tota simul* which would put a stop to the diachrony of business for one moment, at least? Space versus time, the art of vision, which takes things in, interrupting the art of speech, which unfurls? I don't really believe in this; I don't believe really in this separation which Lessing intro-duced: space and time are not dissociable, though they are distin-guishable. In the suspense of which I am speaking, space-time unravels completely. You do not know what to tell. Nothing to say, too much to say. No desire to say. But to stay. Amazing number of markers for destination. A space-time not distributed, inexploitable, one moment here, through language. Or a language, a phrase, which would not situate the universe which one or other spreads out, which would not imply anything about who is talking nor to whom, nor about what, nor how, in what code, on what supporting material. All these relations staying waiting for their determinations, which are stupid.

I am not talking about fascination. The mind isn't all tied up. It is not a stop by being hindered. It would be before mind, if the mind has given itself over to intriguing plot, to concept, and to will. It would be the annunciation of mind, forgotten otherwise, dissipated into link-ages, put on stage by narrations, slipping past its reserve to the advantage of drama, of expenditure and receipts. I am talking about a non-action, where the mind cannot but miss itself, where it announces to itself its own dependency, lingers behind with itself. I am not talking about evidence, not at all. Let's say that it's a question of the soul. Usually it is the soul which is seen as giving life to the work. I don't understand it like that. I would like to remove the notion from any vitalism, from any dialectic. I don't believe the soul to be immanent in visible (or audible) forms. You won't find it by proceed-ing to the analysis of structures, of manifest figures, of linkages. It isn't thematizable straight from the works, nor schematizable. There is no method leading to it, or linking on from it. Literary or art criticism isn't its fulfillment, even its unfinished completion, what-ever Romanticism thought, and Hegel in his own way. Soul is the mind's poverty, the zero degree of its reflexivity, its aptitude for presence. Perhaps mind won't make anything of the soul. The soul doesn't engender anything. I should like to disconnect it from every operation, from every work construction, and criticism of a work, even if it is true that it is on the work, and in the work, that afterwards the mind of the reader, the looker, the listener, and probably of what we call its author, can find that it has been touched by presence. This touch's effect, or rather this touch itself, that is what the soul would be. The word "effect" is pretty bad, you know that. It belongs, precisely, to discourse, to links, to the mind in its busy activity. The effect comes late. It is the expectation which has paid off. But the word has the merit of suggesting that the work is a *retouching*. Something which tries to retain and to render the touch, and which never manages to, because the touch makes the place and moment of another space-time than the one of the maintaining-now and the rendering. My commentary is also something of a retouching. Impossible evidence. You can laugh, you can laugh. Laughing is a good protection against the edifying in all that.

In short, I want to say: there is an occasion. Work and criticism are forbidden, speechless. In your countable time, in a picosecond, perhaps, in mensurable space, a micron. Or, on the contrary, a very big interval. But when the word "incommensurable" is uttered, one has to know what one is saying. You have to give up measuring. Something happens. Color is a good example, in painting of this deal of the cards. It can't be deduced. You can hope to move it down a class, towards matter, that's how it's usually done, and Kant did. As is done with music and timbre.

YOU

He said *form* and now its supposed to be *matter*? *Matter* to mean presence?

HIM

I imagine that every painter was and will be mind given over to this thing, this something which owes nothing to form, which is, let us say, color. A mind which gives up its own self for color. It would like to render color in its absolute degree. You can conceive of it as being what's left over from any formal analysis. Inevitable. In another way, you could deposit in it the secret which is at the source of the picture. You would be wrong in both cases. Your intelligence will trick you.

Presence

You need to be more intelligent, or less. The pastel blue of the young biker, no one has chosen it on a shade chart and applied it to the horizon of his journey. It fell upon him. The mind pulls itself together, tells the stories about this blue. But then, back there, he was changed in the soul, and dumbfounded by the blue occurrence. Sensation is occurrence through its matter. Proust wrote books to try to make the mind the equal of a former presence in sound or in taste, or in sight. What is called matter in the arts, it isn't firstly what form is caught in, what it can be applied to. It is what dumbfounds form, and summons it, the occasion, the touch.

YOU

Novalis writes: "Reflection on oneself, isn't that the nature of consonants?" On which Benjamin, quoting this, comments in a note: "A consonant, understood in opposition to a vowel as a principle of deceleration, is an expression of meditation." And he quotes Novalis again: "When the novel has a decelerated nature, it is really prosaic poetics, it is consonant." I don't see how one can say of presence that it is at the same time pure occasion, like color, and reflection, even of the lowest degree.

HIM

I understand[5] presence like a vowel. Vowel without voice, but which sounds before or after any consonant, any plot in sound, including your vocalization. And the reflection I'm trying to talk about has nothing to do with the *Retardieren* of novels, and minor suspense, nor with sublation; it is like a thunderbolt, immediate. And the same with color, which is the painter's vowel, his timbre. I know one doesn't talk with vowels. But neither just with consonants. The Hebrews knew that: such a respect for color, for presence and the soul, for the voice that they forced themselves to bend in silence over the consonants alone. Condemning themselves to reading and writing. Knowing that the spirit in its activity cannot sound or voice. The timbre belongs to the Lord. The Lord delivers the occasion from the consonants. What I call matter is this afterbirth or this deliverance. I am talking here about the occasion.

It was always a cloud, a fire. Presence darkens the day and lightens the night of the way. Presence is lighting, nuance. It demands exodus, which is not the road out, but the way out off the road. The path traces itself in consonants, and that's good. He who dares voice in presence, render the timbre of God's voice and the color of his countenance, is lost. Imposture, speculation, expression. He is condemned to lack soul, to seduction. The child on his bike in the morning escaped too from Egyptian plots. His cloud and his flame were that blue. You go out, you aren't guided, no. You go out, here, now. You have been got out, then, back there. You get out of the mediations. They stop. The desert of the timbre, the desert of the blue. Presence: you go out towards it. You aren't there any more, you are absenting yourself towards it. That is the expectation which is also in question in painting. Buren, Arakawa, or Adami know perfectly well that they can only rhyme, harmonize in the space-time of plots. That is not a question of keeping the promise, but at the very least of bearing witness that it has happened. By being off the road.

YOU

He says *absenting* when it is a question of presence? And on the other hand, his exodus, that's an ethical problem, not an aesthetic one.

HIM

One absents oneself from the representation of mediate forms, from narrative textures and others. A hole forms in the continuum of phrases, of perceptions. One of them, a word, a sound, a color, has gone missing in the prepared linking.

YOU

Mystical? Irrationalist delirium.

HIM

That is very small, modest, impalpable. You aren't on the top of Sinai every day. Little fires, little clouds, little breezes, little streams, a line, an air, a smell, the soul deepens itself into the mind. A pebble on the road. Occasion, I said. And matter. Not matter in the sense of physics, nor in the sense of the materialist philosophers. The vacuum, if you want, where the *clinamen* takes place, and with it the formation of objects. The *clinamen* is the elementary plot, the plot at the level of the elements. But this place that it generates, it generates it from a non-place, this object from a non-object. I say it negatively, as in theology or in ethics. But in art this "not-that" touches. When the mind is touched by that, it is soul.

YOU

A fine absurdity. His presence is presence of nothing.

HIM

It has no complement. It is nothing or everything because it doesn't call for completion. Who says the little brother's blue in the Vendée needs a complementary color? The theory of colors, the spirit of orders and forms, the distribution of matter and content with a view to plots. It isn't even the presence *of* blue; blue is presence. You will not conceive it. I can only get you to understand it by the obliquity of saying "without that." Without this lapse in the textures, you would have no idea of color, of timbre, of line, which are, have been, there. There would be no art, even, but the craze for reproducing, repairing, and conserving.

YOU

About reflection. And to come to the aid of the cyclist. In 1840, written down by Bettina von Arnim, you find these observations that Hölderlin (seventy years old, and mad) is supposed to have made to Sainclair, and which the latter reported to her:

In order that the mind become poetry, it must bear within itself the mystery of an inborn rhythm. It is only in that rhythm that it can live and become visible. For rhythm is the mind's soul. And all works of art are only one and the same rhythm, of which the caesura is the moment of reflection; the mind rears up; and then, carried forward by the divine, it rushes to its end. Thus the god-poet reveals himself. The caesura for the human mind is the point where it stays suspended, and on which the divine light beams.

Before this, according to the same sources, Hölderlin is said to have taken care to distinguish rhythm from "metrical accent," from the "vain and insipid search for rhyme," which cannot in any way make poetry. But as for the caesura, the same that directs the *Remarks* he wrote in 1803 on *Oedipus Tyrannus and Antigone*, this caesura, "die gegenrhytmische Unterbrechung" ("the antirhythmical suspension" ["suspension antirythmique"], as Beaufret translates it) is

29

perhaps not unrelated to what he is trying to say by the name of presence or of dumbfounded interdiction. The divine light beaming on to the mind, changing it into soul, forcing it to reflect, that is, to rear up against the course of destiny into which it will nevertheless still throw itself. Hölderlin is trying to find where in the thread of each of the two tragedies this caesura takes place. Let's leave aside this difficult problem of localizing what gives place, what causes. The caesura is the instant where the divine touches the human mind, precisely where it turns "away from it quite categorically." It announces to the mind that nothing which sense is hiding and is asking for. Then – the end of the story, the fulfillment of the rhythm in the tragic telling – they enact themselves in the retreating of the godhead. They throw themselves forward because of this retreating. They are the abridged effecting of what has already been said. The matter is expedited and cobbled together in breathlessness. It's no longer the matter of the god, that times are coming and have come. Times come in representation. But the caesura is the event, he would say a space-time that is an exit point, a line of lightning which shatters the space-time of plots.

HIM

Plot only has time and duration in the forgetting of stripes (what Barnett Newman called "zip") in the making-whole of presence half-perceived. The reflection I am talking about is quickly burnt out. As soon as it is put into the steamer, in scenes.

Reflection, you need to imagine it without mind. "Rear up," said Hölderlin. But it is still Oedipus' mind for plotting that can rear up at the declaration of the obscure Tiresias. More than a rebuff, the donkey's whim.[6] It lets things hang in the balance. There is really no obstacle, the mind tells itself. It gives a blow, to speed up motion. In the mind's cosiness, the pause opens out a desertlike endurance. The donkey is waiting on the path. Insensible, that is, aware of something quite different. It is blind to things. It is itself Tiresias. Then it "sees" at last. A pebble. There is no obstacle, that "means" that there is no edge to his pause. Because if there was one, one would have to find a common measure for walking and for stopping. Say how much time and what space the pause takes up. Space and duration which necessarily would be counted in the unities which serve to measure its motion, the relation of the distance that the donkey covers to the time he takes to cover it. This edge would determine an interval.

Well, I don't mind you saying "interval," as I say "interruption," "interdiction," "inter"-something. But that will be because there's nothing better. Because the donkey's rest isn't caught inside his movement. It has mind as long as it keeps going. Its soul stops him when it comes. But when and where the stop begins, it is not there nor then that the walking finishes. Reflection is not joined into narration. It isn't the donkey's story which flows back on itself to become fixed in a picture which it might then contemplate obstinately.

I am sure it doesn't contemplate anything. It is blue like a biker in the rising sun. It might continue to walk, anyway, and that wouldn't change anything. The soul can be hidden inside the mind, rest inside movement, silence in music and presence in representation. It can be learned. Donkeys know how to. To learn as well to tell when the other pretends to walk, but his soul isn't in it. Isn't in the steps he gets through. Mechanically, as the saying goes.

Note that moving mechanically may not make sure the mind has its freedom of movement, but may make it so that soul and presence stay possible, unmoving, right into the movement of things. The lover of painting learns to distinguish soul in a picture. Skill, yes. Daring, originality, perhaps. But when these qualities are equal, then between one painter and another, between one work and another by the same painter, the difference lurks in the secret stupidity which is hidden by talent in order to bear witness to it. It is this stupidity I call reflection. Just as Kleist maintained that more grace is permitted and promised by the mechanical movements of marionnettes than can be obtained by the purest intention of the mind: stupefaction against plot. The soul of Clairon the actress, it too, Diderot says, wraps itself up in a "great mannequin." And what is translating, says she who translates, if it is not to empty one's mind like the actor and let the text come to the soul. But mannequins, marionnettes, mechanics, are not witness to soul. Nor the pause. There is no recipe to obtain presence which indicates soul. But when there is presence, reflection suspends the matters of the mind.

YOU

What he wants with *presence* is: no links. Clearly, that's lifting oneself up with one's own bootlaces. First any work is linked to others, in the never-ending transporting of sensibilities which is called culture: Adami to Poussin and Blake, and the Italians,

Arakawa to Duchamp, Buren to Cézanne, I just give the names as they come. And any gaze, even that of a someone who can't read, is loaded with the already-seen. (He himself, isn't he in the process of comparing three works?). And anyway, commenting on presence! that's to link what is linkless. There is nothing more given over to plotting than commentary.

HIM

I'd like to be able, it seems to me it would be enough, to write some words, a few words, which would be the panting of presence in my text on presence, do you understand? That would be enough. You would feel it. A few words on the matter (in the manner) of matter, not to signify. Of them, none would "get rid of everything." Arakawa found *blank* like that, for that. Which chimes with *black* and *flank*. Very close to the *gray* of Klee. Arakawa is helped by the Zen tradition, of course, a big advantage over his fellows who are westerners, bound to links, for saying "way out." The moment and the place of the interruption of places and moments. The cut and the breaking-up. I found *intimity*, the paroxysm of the *intus*. This is a sense of *in* which isn't *inside*, since it has gone out. *Mumonkan*, a collection of *koān*, little stories of the Zen sect Rinzai, means "passage without a door." The way into the most extreme way out. An installation (what a word) of Buren at Weber's in New York was called *Exit*. Buren too looks for words to use as titles. With "intimity" I hear "intimation." About music, I had found *obedience: gehorchen, gehören, zuhören*. It is the intimation of hearing by timbre. Now it is the timbre which is the matter that I mean here. Certainly it is always caught up in the measurable coordinates of sound and in the harmonic and melodic plots, a well-tempered composition. Usually it is described as the brute *tone*, what is left after analysis. I'd like to chase away this idea of residue, of bruteness. Old western idea of the *prima materia*, primal matter. Stuff. A technical and reasoning idea. Timbre and color of themselves intimate stupefaction. The blue of the cyclist, the chromatics of Gesualdo's *Responsoria*, the yellow of Vermeer's wall which suspends the mind of Marcel, the man of the world, and makes it jump into soul. As a child, untaught, inquisitive, I used to go to the Louvre on my own to "try out" this suspense, in front of the matt *décolleté* of a virgin by Baldovinetti. A very poor painter. The case is rather a bad one. But this material stopping, completely material, which even the most searching eyes must find incontestable, the

32

Piero della Francesca frescoes at Arezzo will have intimated it to you. I leave you to discuss his drawing. But what is called his light! It has that faculty which Scelsi asks for in music: it would make the walls of Jericho tumble down. That fall is presence. And Scelsi is right a thousand times when he says that you don't get it through formalism. There is a *tenuto* on the violins at the end of Schönberg's *Verklärte Nacht* which makes the walls of Jericho tumble down, like the *Quartets* of Scelsi. I would like to say as well: *le soûl*, to be sold on, to have one's soul-full. To let it be understood that, with it, that's always enough, immediately saturated, full. Full of matter, like pure soul, without degree. Achieved form, said Cézanne (like the old workman of the material soul that he was), when color is at perfection.

That's not to bring drawing down a peg. Otherwise, what would Adami be doing here? Who is, it is known, a bold draughtsman. Drawing can be taken like matter, instead of limiting it to this miserable function of organizing, of structuring space, the architectonics inflicted on it out of the custom of builders and conceivers. They say: forms descending into matter to inscribe meaning, mind, etc. in it. That's anthropocentric, phallocentric, logocentric. Drawing is supposed already to "write" matter, to make chaos readable. But a line can saturate the soul as well as a color, and can leave one stupid, with an intimation of something. I remember a great canvas of Matisse, I believe, or Mirò, no, Mirò, apple-green, which only bore one extended stroke, closed on itself in the outline of an apple. The stroke was done with a punch in the wet paint, I imagine, its oat-white being that of the canvas or the priming. Infallibility of this stroke. Infallible that presence, in which nothing is lacking. The painter showed here that drawing is as good as color if it is right that the mind "jumps" into soul. "Jump," *chō*, is Dōgen's word to mean "waking." You cannot jump out of events. If the bird jumped out of the air, says Dōgen, it would die. Waking occurs right up against matter. You go in with the same movement as you come out. It does not emancipate mind from the sensible. When the mind "jumps" into soul, in this jump, in this stopping, the eye of the body is sanctified. *Shin-shin*, it is *body-heart*. I like in Dōgen this attempt to slide out of the mysticism of the other Zen schools. To uphold the modesty of an "aesthetics." The soul-body is sanctified in and by the *aisthesis*. Six domains, he writes: color, voice, smell, taste, touch, and the event (*ho*). What the artist is looking for is the event in the five domains. The stopping, the intimation, the dumbfounding are the names of the *quod*, that is of the *ho*. No death in that, no sentence of death nor stopping of death. Death is with plots. In the infinite intricacy of deaths and lives, the intimation comes like the texture of the skin or the voice, Barthes said, time, "tenuto" of Adami, not a gesture, akinematic, "site" of Buren, lightning of blank. This "aesthetics" does not know death. Because it isn't referred to an "I." The art of presence. Another name should be found for it. And it isn't parousia.

NOTES

1 D. Buren, Legend I, Legend II (2 vols., London, 1974).
2 S. Arakawa and M. H. Gins, The Mechanism of Meaning (New York, 1979).
3 Les Immatériaux was the title of an exhibition organized by J.-F. Lyotard with Thierry Chaput at the Centre Pompidou, Paris, in 1986.
4 I. Kant, Critique of Judgement (trans. James Creed Meredith, Oxford, 1952), paragraph 57.
5 "Entendre," which in French also means "to hear."
6 Ame – soul – and âne – donkey – are nearly homonyms in French.

3

Writing and painting: the soul as hermeneut

STANLEY ROSEN

I

My title is derived from Plato's *Philebus*. At 38a6ff., Socrates introduces a striking image of two demiurges, a writer and a painter, who
are themselves generated within the soul by the activity of perceptual
judgment. The identity or form of the perceived thing is mediated by
two kinds of interpretation, discursive and visual. Yet that form is
not, in accord with the traditional account of Platonism, produced by
its double hermeneutical mediation.

It is frequently said that modern philosophy enters its decisive
stage with the Kantian transcendental doctrine, according to which
the cognized object, but not of course the sensuous content of that
object, is produced by the activity of cognition itself. But what of the
object of perception? Is it independent of cognition and furnished to
the conceptual spontaneity of the understanding by intuition?

Kant says that "thinking, taken in itself, is nothing but the logical
function or pure spontaneity of the combination [*Verbindung*] of the
manifold of a merely possible intuition" (B428/29).[1] Making allowance for Kant's variable terminology, we can understand him to say
that the content of intuition is supplied by sensation, which is
passive, but that these sensations must conform to the pure forms of
space-time, which are therefore not receptive but active, and indeed,
spontaneous functions of the mind (*das Gemüt*).

If we put to one side the obscure question of the difference and
relation between synthesis and unification, as not relevant to my
present concern, we may make two points. First: the intuited content
of the actual object of perception is synthesized by the same functions
of the mind that unite intuition to concepts (B104/05). Second: there
is a fundamental ambiguity here with which I am indeed concerned.

If the object of perception is actually an object, then it must be fully determined, and hence there can be no erroneous perceptions, because there is no real difference between perceiving and conceiving. To state this point in the terms of my title, Kant would accordingly have reduced perception, or painting in the soul, to conception, or writing.

These questions, together with that of the Platonist alternative to Kantianism, provide the focus of this chapter. The problem of the object of perception lies at the intersection of hermeneutics and ontology. I scarcely need to emphasize the importance of a thesis, which I shall attribute here to Kant, that it is not merely the *sense*, but as we may say the *being*, of perception, which is discursive. I begin with some preliminary remarks. In everyday life, we take it for granted that, with full allowance for the distortion imposed by differing perspectives, when we perceive something, say a dog or a tree, we do not ourselves produce that being.

Subsequent analysis of perception reveals that what we take to be a dog is a locus of many interpretations, which vary according to whether our analysis is philosophical, artistic, or, if scientific, whether we are physicists, physiologists, chemists, and so forth. All these interpretations, however, take their bearings by the dog, which is not transformed by reference to the so-called "myth of the given" into a tree, an elephant, or whatever we like.

The scientific analysis does not produce the perception of a dog from the correct analysis of the conceptual structure of the act of perception. It begins with the perception of the dog, and then provides us with the ostensibly correct analysis of the conceptual structure underlying that perception. There are interpretations of the perception of a dog, but the perception of a dog is not itself an interpretation.

To this one may object that whereas simple sensations like color and smell are incorrigible, a dog may in fact be taken for a wolf, if not an elephant. Or what we take to be a dog may be a play of shadows, and not an animal at all. "Perceiving," the objection goes, is "taking to be," or grasping something *as* something; and this is already interpretation.

This objection, which can only be postponed by recourse to further acts of perception, poses a difficulty for Platonists and Kantians alike. The Platonist (or the Aristotelian, for that matter) must explain how, if what we actually cognize is the pure form, errors of perceptual judgment are possible. That is, the form is what defines or determines the instance. If I intuit the form in the act of perception, then there is no difference between cognition and perception. If I do not intuit the form, then in what sense am I perceiving anything in particular? How could I misidentify a Platonic Idea or Aristotelian *eidos*, either of which is either grasped or not, but if grasped, is grasped veridically? But the Kantian faces the same problem: if to think the dog is to produce it, how could we possibly mistake a dog for a wolf?

I will say very briefly that "Platonism," in the general rather than the philological sense, requires a doctrine of the perception of form as antecedent to interpretation, whether by the writer or the painter. The minimum thesis of Platonism as I understand it is not that we perceive an eternal form underlying the changing instances of genesis, but that the perception of each instance of genesis is of something that is definite in itself, however muddled our perception of it may be. Kantianism, in response to the same problem, requires a distinction between perception of an "indeterminate" object that is not fully determined by concepts, yet is predisposed toward or in conformity with such determination. Both responses are awkward; let us try to see which response poses the greater difficulties.

I turn now to a condensed but I hope paradigmatic exposition of the situation in Kantianism. It is often noted that Kant intends his account of experience to explain, not how we perceive dogs and trees, but how we acquire scientific, and hence synthetic a priori, knowledge about possible objects of experience. To employ the terminology of Gerold Prauss, to whom I shall return later, perception combines with cognition to supply an "interpretation" of appearances or empirical objects.[2] It follows from this reading that "production" or "constitution" is synonymous in Kant with "interpretation." Prauss does not put it so, but we may say that the "being" of the empirical world is hermeneutical.

There is a paradigmatic text to illustrate the hermeneutical nature of Kant's doctrine in the *First Critique*, B128/29. Kant explains there that the function of the categorical judgment is to relate the subject to the predicate. From a logical standpoint, it is undetermined which concept is the subject and which is the predicate. For example, "all bodies are divisible" and "all divisible things are bodies" are equally legitimate. Whether "body" is a subject or predicate depends upon whether we subsume its concept under the category of substance or of inherence. The relation of substance and inherence is a transcendental structure of two variables, the values of which we decide as an interpretation of experience.

Experience cannot determine the decision as to what will count as a substance because there are no natural substances. Furthermore, experience is constituted by judgment, and judgment decides the identity of the substance in each context. If this decision is relative to human intention, or, as one might almost dare to say, the will, then the soundness of Kant's metaphilosophy as a justification of synthetic a priori knowledge depends upon the stability of the empirical object, as well as upon its independence from the activity of judgment.

If Kant is providing us with a metaphilosophical account of scientific language about experience, then he must be able to explain our experience of actual objects, or our actual experience of objects. It is in fact imprecise to say that Kant explains knowledge about possible objects of experience, because no one experiences possible objects. "Possible object" must be shorthand for "conditions for perceiving actual objects," and these objects are discovered empirically, not by reading the First Critique.

I repeat: possible objects are those which can actualize. Actual objects are those like dogs and elephants. They are directly determined, not by schematized categories, which underwrite judgments about objects, but by "empirical concepts."[3] These concepts can never be fully defined, but only continuously redefined as our experience grows.[4] Once these concepts enter into judgments, they must be determined by the schematized categories as well. Since the process of continuous redefinition is obviously one of formulating predicative judgments, it is plain that Kant will have difficulty in enforcing the distinction between non-scientific and scientific experience. This amounts to the difficulty of distinguishing between perception and judgment.

The experience of objects is a flux of interpretations or perspectives, not a discontinuous perceiving of actualized or self-presenting forms with continuity supplied by the subsequent activity of interpretation. Strictly speaking, there are no actual empirical objects in Kantian experience; the only actuality is transcendental activity. The corollary to the problem of distinguishing between judgment and perception is that of guaranteeing synthetic a priori knowledge about actual objects of experience. Even if we grant the a priori nature of the conditions for knowledge of possible objects, how can there be scientific knowledge of experience itself? In sum, either actual objects of experience are indeterminate and hence not even perceivable as anything in particular, or else they are fully determinate, and perception is indistinguishable from judgment.

I submit that this is not a satisfactory account of our actual experience. Kant owes us an explanation of how we perceive a dog. At B180, in the chapter on the transcendental schematism, Kant has the following to say: "the concept of dog signifies a rule in accord with which my imagination can draw [*verzeichnet*] in general the form of a four-footed animal, without being restricted to any particular form that experience furnishes me, or to any possible image that I can exhibit *in concreto*."

In other words, the empirical concept is not the form of the perceived dog *in concreto*. We have already seen that the empirical concept is a rule in flux. Furthermore the schema is not an image or perception of a definitely formed empirical object, but "the representation of a method" whereby a category may be represented in an image in conformity with a certain concept (B179). As to the categories, these allow us to think objects in general, not to perceive them in particular.

Are we to suppose then that the form of the perceived dog is supplied by the image? Since this cannot be derived from the categories, the empirical concept or rule, or the schematism, it can only come from intuition. But intuition must be either purely formal (space-time), in which case it supplies us with formal relations of extension and figure (B35), with location and motion, and with laws determining changes of motion (moving forces: B67f). Or else intuition consists of *Empfindungen*, or the content of the perceived object, not its form.

It should now be obvious that Kant has no explanation of how we perceive a dog. How could one derive an image of a definite three-dimensional body from a discursive rule? Kant does in fact transform painting into writing. But what set of written instructions will give us the Mona Lisa? The empirical object "dog" is an interpretation, via a discursive rule, of a manifold of intuition. Is not the "shape of a four-footed animal in general" as applicable to an elephant or to an aardvark as it is to a dog?

Let us look at the same difficulty from a slightly different perspective. At B104–105, Kant says: "the same function which gives unity to the various representations in a *judgment* also gives unity to the various representations in an *intuition*; and this unity, in its most general expression, we entitle the pure concept of the understanding."

Understanding is the capacity to think, that is, to know through concepts (B93), and hence, the capacity of rule-formation (106,

B171). As we have already seen, this capacity is exercized spontaneously as combination, synthesis, or unification: "Knowledge consists in the determinate relation of given representations to an object. An object is that in the concept of which the manifold of given intuition is unified" (B137). Accordingly the perception of a determinate object must be the same as the conceiving or knowing of that object. False judgments must be of indeterminate objects. But allowing for the possibility of the perception of indeterminate objects, how can there be *judgments*, true or false, of indeterminate objects, when judgment determines objects?[5]

It should be mentioned that Kant occasionally contradicts the canonical thesis that objects are produced by a synthesis which *at once* unifies the perceptual and the conceptual dimensions, as for example at B122: "objects may therefore appear to us without their being under the necessity of being related to the functions of understanding; and understanding need not, therefore, contain their a priori conditions." More generally, Kant often speaks as though intuition furnishes the "object" to the concepts of the understanding. In so doing, he reverts, no doubt unconsciously, to the pre-Copernican or "Platonist" stance.

In noting the contradiction at B122 of the "authentic critical doctrine," de Vleeschauwer offers a possible escape: Kant may be referring here to "a not yet unified grouping of perceptions."[6] De Vleeschauwer does not explain how a not yet unified grouping can constitute an object. But if we adopt his suggestion, the quasi-objective grouping must have a propensity to be subsumed under an empirical concept (not to mention the categories).

De Vleeschauwer's pre-object is also appealed to by Bernard Rousset in the guise of the "indeterminate object."[7] In my view it underlies Gerold Prauss's influential distinction between judgments of perception and judgments of experience. Kant himself refers to the indeterminate object at B94 as the pre-predicative object. I have already stated that I deny the meaningfulness, on Kantian premises, of a pre-predicative object. This does not preclude pre-predicative perceptions or awarenesses of objects, provided that they are indeed "given" to perception, as cannot be the case for Kant.

Prauss, like other commentators,[8] sees a problem for Kant in distinguishing between true and false judgments. An objectively valid judgment both determines or constitutes the object and expresses synthetic a priori knowledge, that is, truth, about the object. If there are to be false judgments, then there must be perceptions, that is, judgments about perceptions, which are neither objectively true nor false, but which can be subsumed correctly or incorrectly under concepts.[9] Since these perceptions are not objectively true or false, they must be perceptions of indeterminate objects.

This is further borne out by Prauss's claim that judgments of perception are neither true nor false intersubjectively but are subjectively valid for the perceiver only.[10] "Valid" does not mean "true" here, because it is impossible to be mistaken about one's own appearances (Erscheinungen as distinguished from phenomena). What appears to me, on Prauss's account, is that "it seems to be x," where x stands for some perceptual situation, such as "raining." By analogy, it would be a judgment of perception to say to oneself, "It seems to be a dog."[11]

I must restrict myself to the essential points in my criticism of Prauss's interpretation. It is highly significant for my own thesis that Prauss asks us to treat the Erscheinungen as letters with which the categories "spell out" or achieve the unification of objects of scientific experience (Erfahrung) as opposed to perception (Wahrnehmung).[12] The "experiences" are accordingly "determinable" or "interpretable" as objective (i.e. determinate) Gegenstände.[13] This metaphor is in my opinion faithful to Kant's doctrine, but it also makes evident the unsatisfactoriness of that doctrine. Not only are the letters of an alphabet conventional but, in spelling, the letters do not play a functional role in determining the structure of the sense, whereas perceptions do play a functional role in determining the structure of the object.

More important, however, is the following objection. How can intuitions be designated, with Prauss, as "conformable to"[14] a given concept unless they are predisposed to it? Are we to assume that intuitions are conformable to conceptualization in general, but in such a way that any intuition can be subsumed under any concept whatsoever? Can I erroneously produce a rose bush out of the same intuitions or perceptions which, when correctly subsumed, yield a dog?

If this is so, then on Prauss's theory, intuitions contribute nothing in particular to concepts of objects, but therefore nothing in particular to "experiential" or objective perception of them. Accordingly, they serve as a quasi-Aristotelian prime matter, capable of becoming anything under the imprint of concepts, which now, contrary to Kant's doctrine, must contribute sensible properties and determinate perceptual form. Conversely, if intuitions are in fact "conformable to" in the sense of "capable of being subsumed under" a correct concept (with the corollary that "objective validity" means "capable of being true"), then these intuitions are *potentially the form*. Aristotelianism is once more reinstated.

II

I call attention to the following consequence of Kant's transcendental philosophy. Objects of knowledge are produced as well as known by the spontaneity of thinking. But, contrary to Kant's claim, intuition is not purely receptive, since sensations are produced by the conformity of things in themselves to the pure forms of space and time. Since these forms are as spontaneous as the concepts, whether Kant admits it or not, and since, as Prauss puts it, perceptions serve as letters to be spelled into words or senses by the understanding, it follows that Kant goes very far towards defining the being of an object as the spontaneous and discursive product of the mind (*das Gemüt*).[15]

In addition, since "being" or "existence" is for Kant not a real predicate, but the "position" of a thing as indicated by the logical use of the copula of a judgment (B626), or a logical predicate, Kant also prepares a new sense of ontology as distinct from the ontology of real predication. This sense is developed both by logically oriented philosophers via the doctrine of linguistic horizons, rules, axioms, modal logics, and the like; but it is also developed by Nietzsche in his doctrine of interpretation (*Auslegung*) and by Heidegger, as is initially visible in the distinction between the ontological and the ontic.

Kant thus seems to be the grandfather, if not the father, of linguistic philosophy; in this sense, I regard him as the grandfather of contemporary hermeneutics. We may summarize this result as the consequence of the transformation of painting into writing. It is not, however, enough to insist that perception is a kind of painting. And this brings me to Plato.

As we recall, the previously cited passage from the *Philebus* (38a6ff.) identifies painting too as a kind of demiurgy. Socrates offers a likeness (*proseoikenai*: 38e12) of how the soul appears or shows itself (*phainetai*: 38e9). This terminology is in accord with Socrates' assertion in the *Phaedrus* (246a3–6) that it is a divine and long task to describe the form (*idea*) of the soul, but that mortals may accomplish the shorter task of saying what it is like (*ho de eoiken*).

Demiurgy plays no role in the *Phaedrus*, which is concerned with the silent apprehension of pure hyperuranian beings. We may infer that writing and painting produce artifacts of interpretations of what has been antecedently and silently apprehended. Silent noetic apprehension is a faculty of the noble soul and the mark of its divinity. As such, it makes an awkward theme for discursive analyses of knowing and being. It is not difficult to see why Kant rejects noetic intuition. Nevertheless, I believe it will be helpful to persevere in the difficult task of defending at least a modified version of the traditional Platonist *noēsis*.

The Platonic Socrates and Kant are in agreement in the attempt to regulate interpretations by paradigmatic forms in the one case and transcendental rules in the other. Their attempts are compromised by opposite flaws; Platonic forms seem to elude speech, whereas Kantian rules, as discursive, seem to be unable to specify form. Speech, and by extension writing, runs the risk in Plato of becoming autonomous, just as, in Kant, spontaneity threatens to compromise transcendental necessity.

In the *Sophist*, the Eleatic Stranger introduces two arts, painting and sophistry, each of which "makes and does all things by a single technique," namely, mimesis or image-making (233d1ff.). Whereas images are bounded by originals, the distinction between accurate and inaccurate images depends upon access to the originals themselves. It is patently circular to attribute such access to the analysis of images; but this is the direct result of replacing, or attempting to replace, noetic intuition by discursive analysis. Things are not words, and neither are they logical sets or rules.

The passage in the *Philebus*, to which I now return, provides us with an indication of how Socrates deals with this problem at the level of perception. Protarchus has just agreed that false *doksa* may associate itself with pain or pleasure. We may translate the word *doksa* as belief, opinion, or judgment, depending upon the context. Protarchus denies that anyone would call a pleasure itself false (37e12ff.).[16] He has no doubt at all that *doksa* may be true or false (38b66f.).

Socrates turns from pleasure and pain to *doksa* and asks whether it does not come from memory and perception. Protarchus agrees that this is so. Socrates then employs the device of a dialogue within the dialogue to illustrate how we are disposed to memory and perception. In his talking picture, a person is presented as viewing something at a distance and then interrogating himself: "what is that fantasm [*to . . . phantazomenon*] standing there next to the rock under the tree?" (38c12–d1).

The dramatic enactment of our problem helps to prevent it from disappearing into verbal abstractions. We see ourselves in the act of perception, as that which both underlies and circumscribes the mediating function of writing and painting. Also critical to our understanding of this passage is how we translate *to . . . phantazomenon*. I take it to mean here, not a false or inaccurate image, but a *phainomenon* in the sense of that which shows itself, not yet as this or that specific thing, but as a thing inviting identification.[17]

Once we form an opinion as to the identity of the *phainomenon*, it is interpreted *as* something, and the result is an image, visual, verbal, or more likely, both. We shift mentally from the being that presents itself to the judgment, a predicative statement that *what* appears is a such-and-such. There is then an ontological distinction between *to phantazomenon* as presence and *to phantazomenon* as a judgment or image of what is present.

To say that this distinction is ontological means that we must engage in discursive labor in order to secure it. But *what* we are securing is not a product of that labor: as a presence, it is presented or given to us. Unfortunately, the gift may not be possessed without mediation that compromises its integrity. We should also note that the fantasm does not appear in isolation, but next to a rock under a tree. It is not a "sense-datum" but an element in a pattern of perception.

Let me use the terms "presence" and "representation" to distinguish between the being that appears and our perception of its appearance. One might point to an analogous distinction in Kant between intuition (*Anschauung*) and concept; unfortunately, Kant blurs this distinction by employing the term *Vorstellung* to cover both terms, and indeed, all mental modifications. *Vorstellung* can mean "presentation" or "representation," and either translation could be justified in Kant. The mind "presents" modifications of inner sense to itself because it produces them via spontaneous acts. On the other hand, these presentations, as resulting in objective experience, are representations of things in themselves.

Accordingly, Kant refers even to the judgment, "the mediate knowledge of an object," as "die Vorstellung einer Vorstellung" (B93). I myself would be prepared to translate this expression as "the interpretation of an interpretation." The key point is not so much the translation we employ as this: if *Vorstellung* means "presentation," then the mind discursively produces its own objects. But if it means "representation," the objects are discursive images of things in themselves. The practical result is the same in either case.

To come back now to Plato, Socrates asks whether it is possible to have a false *doksa* or erroneous judgment, namely, about what is standing next to the rock under the tree. In judging, we must answer to ourselves: Socrates uses the participle *apokrinomenos* (38d5), to answer in the sense of choosing between two complementary responses and so judging. Socrates thus takes it for granted that the thing perceived is given to the writer and painter rather than produced by them. A being presents itself to us, regardless of whether we subsequently represent it correctly or incorrectly.

It is entirely in accord with the problematic of the Platonic corpus in general, and the *Sophist* in particular, to say that the distinction between presentation and representation is crucial for the distinction between true and false judgments concerning what we perceive. This has the following further consequence. The painter as well as the writer are both relegated to *doksa*, not to *aisthesis*, taking the latter term to designate not merely sense-perception, but the apprehending of a present being.

To put the same point in another way, for Socrates, the statement "there is something standing next to the rock under the tree" is in its primary meaning an existential rather than a predicative statement. It refers to the presence of the thing waiting to be identified. Let us give this thing the identity of a man. In post-Fregean logic, we would represent the logical structure of the resulting statement most directly and simply as follows: "there exists an x such that it is next to a rock and under a tree and it is a man."

This translation has important ontological consequences. The concept of existence is expressed by the quantifier, and so by the instantiation of a compound concept. Exactly as in the Kantian analysis, the being (Kant's "object") of perception is no longer treated as an independent entity that presents itself to the predicative judgment. It is constructed from concepts. I remind you that for Kant, "to be" or "to exist" is to be posed; but this means either to be posed as a possible object of experience, or if as actual, then as determined by the structure of predicative judgment.

In short: for Kant, "being" is a logical, not a real predicate. "— is a man" is a real predicate, but not "is" or "exists." For Socrates, on the other hand, anachronistic as it sounds, it makes sense to say that existence is a real predicate. I mean by this that what we perceive and conceive presents itself to the mind as independent of its operations yet as apprehended and awaiting identification. The being is what we identify; if it were not independent, there would be no difference between correct and incorrect identifications. If it were not apprehended, there would be no identifications at all.

We arrive at the curious result that Platonism can be defended against Kantianism only by the employment of a Kantian or "transcendental" argument. The apprehension of an independent being is a necessary condition for the possibility of perceptual judgment. This is unavoidable, given the disjunction between noetic intuition and the constructive nature of painting and writing.

Thus far we have been able to make only negative statements about the nature of the *phainomenon* or independent being. Briefly stated, it is neither a synthesis of sense-data nor a conceptual construction. If we say of the thing or being anything more definite than "there is something next to the rock under a tree," we are already interpreting it or replacing it by a surrogate linguistic artifact. Socrates says that the observer "sees something manifested to himself" (38d2–3: "katidon phantasthenta hauto pote"). If what he sees is the fully present and determinate entity "man," then he can never be mistaken about perception; to employ Prauss's circumlocution, when he seems to see a man, he does in fact see a man. On the other hand, if what he sees is an indeterminate something, how can this serve as the criterion for distinguishing between correct and incorrect identifying statements?

Platonism, on the point at issue, seems to come down to this: the commonsensical impression that we discover rather than produce objects of perception must be right, because otherwise there is no difference between truth and falsehood with respect to objects. Yet if we attempt to give a positive determination to the identity of these discovered beings, we immediately produce interpretations that prevent us from certifying the soundness of our identifications.

As I have already noted, the modern epoch begins with the rejection of the Platonist dilemma. We may imagine someone like Descartes saying to himself: "Who cares what things are, independently of perception? We can replace appearances, even if they are almost completely deceptive, with theoretical constructions that enable us to solve problems and fulfil our desires." This is a very tempting alternative, but it has the same difficulty that we already discerned in Kant. What counts as a problem is determined finally by desire and will. Hence so too are our technical surrogates for beings. To summarize a long story in one sentence, spontaneity cannot sustain necessity; the transcendental is inevitably replaced by history.

What I call a difficulty would be welcomed by many today as the solution to our problems. I must leave it at this in this present discussion: how can we seriously accept a doctrine of radical perspectivism as a satisfactory account of our actual experience? In my opinion, the true strength of Platonism is not in elaborate technical analyses of formal structure, but in the orientation to the much-maligned "given," an orientation which one might almost dare to call "pragmatism" if that word did not have so many opposing connotations.

We need to follow our passage in the *Philebus* one step farther before reaching our conclusion. It is true that the visual image of a man is the basis for a discursive account of a man. But a visual image, namely, a painting, is also a perspective or interpretation. Socrates must accordingly distinguish the joint efforts of his two demiurges from some other faculty of apprehension. He provides us with a clue to this distinction at 38b9–13 when he identifies the writer in the soul with the affections (*pathemata*) arising from the unification of memory and perception.

The affections write true or false words in "the book of the soul" (38e12), which is then illustrated by the painter with "icons of what has been judged and said" (39b3–c1). Writing and painting are therefore both posterior to memory and *aisthesis*, which are themselves the faculties by which we apprehend the independent being. The writer in the soul is not spontaneous, as in Kant, but reactive. Socrates does not spell out his metaphor for us. I must therefore leave it at a suggestion, but one that follows from the text, that perception grasps the original presence whereas memory anticipates its identity. I am suggesting, in other words, that perception is both intentional and itself illuminated or directed by the intelligibility of the form.

There is no mention of the doctrine of Ideas in the *Philebus*. The passage we have been considering does allow us to suggest an alternative to Kant, namely, that what we perceive, whereas it may not be an eternal, hyperuranian Idea, is certainly a determinate form that we have not ourselves produced. I close my inspection of this text by calling attention to Socrates' assertion that the words and paintings of the soul refer to the past and present, but primarily to the future (39d7–e6). What is elsewhere in Plato called "recollection" is also anticipation. We remember, so to speak, what we are about to understand.

This process is closely related to psychic pleasures and pains, and especially to their anticipation (39d1–6), but more generally to what

Socrates calls, in a rather Kantian expression, the hope that fills up human life (39e4–6). Philosophy is the expression and unification of hope; consequently, it, and it alone, unites the past and the present with the future. So at least I understand Socrates' indications.

My purpose in this chapter has been neither to refute Kant nor to demonstrate the truth of Platonism. I wanted rather to show something about the status of perception as a problem for both thinkers. This problem cannot in my opinion be resolved by technical constructions, each of which is rather an enactment of a hope. Neither is it my view that we have no basis for preferring one treatment of the problem or the other. The horizon of hope encompasses the technical, but we cannot hope rationally without an exact analysis of the technical difficulties intrinsic to philosophical problems.

From a somewhat broader perspective, I have tried to present evidence to sustain a thesis made by me elsewhere, namely, that Kant is the critical ancestor of the subsequent dominance of the philosophy of language, and accordingly, that he prepares the way for the emergence of late- and post-modern hermeneutics. Hermeneutics is by no means restricted to the so-called "continental" thinkers who follow Nietzsche and Heidegger. It also predominates among those analytical philosophers, and in particular those philosophers of science, who take their bearings by the later Wittgenstein.

In this chapter, I have raised a question that seems to me to require an answer by the new hermeneutical thinking. Attractive as it may be to enrich our linguistic resources and our scientific theories, if we are finally talking about talking, or if, in other words, we are ourselves infinitely transformable sentences in a text with no extra-linguistic reference, who is reading us, to whom, and to what purpose? If to read is to interpret, then reading is in fact writing. But this is to say that reading is impossible.

NOTES

1 Numbers preceded by "A" or "B" will refer to the first (1781) and second (1787) editions of *The Critique of Pure Reason*, respectively. Translations are my own, or modifications of the Kemp Smith translation (*Immanuel Kant's Critique of Pure Reason*, trans. Norman Kemp Smith [2nd impression with corrections, London, 1933]) in which references to the page numbers of the first and second editions are given in the margins.

2 See Gerold Prauss, *Erscheinung bei Kant* (Berlin, 1971). As will be plain from my text, I deny that Prauss's solution to the problem of erroneous perception is successful.

3 *First Critique*, B64, B116, A109, B794.

4 B755: "an empirical concept can never be defined at all, but only made *explicit*"; i.e., it can never be completely defined: "we make use of certain characteristics only so long as they are adequate for the purpose of making distinctions; new observations remove some properties and add others; and thus the limits of the concept are never assured."

5 The same result follows from the brief discussion at B161/62 of the perception of a house. This occurs when, at the same time as I perform a synthesis of apprehension upon space, I sketch [*zeichne*] the form [*Gestalt*] of the house "in conformity with this synthetic unity of the manifold in space." In a note to this passage, Kant says that the empirical synthesis of apprehension is one and the same spontaneity as the intellectual synthesis of apperception which is contained a priori entirely in the category.

6 H. J. de Vleeschauwer, *La Déduction transcendentale dans l'œuvre de Kant* (3 vols., Paris, 1934–1937), vol. II, pp. 173, 177.

7 In *La doctrine kantienne de l'objectivité* (Paris, 1967), p. 305.

8 E.g., Henry Allison, *Kant's Transcendental Idealism* (New Haven, 1983), pp. 72ff. Allison, in commenting on B142, where Kant attributes objective validity to judgments, says: "if this claim is to make any sense, it is obvious that objective validity cannot be equated with truth (otherwise Kant would be committed to the absurdity that every judgment is true). Thus it seems reasonable to follow Prauss on this point, who suggests that 'objective validity' for Kant means simply the capacity to be true or false." How simple philosophical interpretation would be if we were allowed to acquit our favorite authors of absurdity by changing their explicit words. This apart, we still require an explanation of the possibility of falsity. A possibly false objectively valid judgment makes no more sense than an actually false objective judgment, because the former would refer to a possible object, not to an actual one.

9 Prauss, *Erscheinung*, p. 67.

10 *Ibid*, pp. 170, 212.

11 *Ibid*, pp. 202ff. 239.

12 *Ibid*, pp. 95ff.

13 *Ibid*, pp. 123ff.

14 *Ibid*, pp. 123–25, 143, 166.

15 Kant's refutation of Idealism turns upon the claim that all determination of time (i.e., of inner sense) presupposes something enduring in perception that is not just an intuition in me, since these are in time, whereas what determines time must be outside it (B275ff.). Given the Idealist implications of the constitution of the object, this "outside" could reasonably be interpreted along Fichtean lines as the not-I, which results from the very act by which the I posits itself.

16 He does not make a similar denial concerning pain, no doubt because of his hedonism.
17 *Phaino*-words are often used by Plato to designate the "presence" or visibility of the Ideas. For discussion, see "Antiplatonism" in my *The Ancients and the Moderns: Rethinking Modernity* (New Haven, 1989), chapter 3.

4

Correspondence, projective properties, and expression in the arts

RICHARD WOLLHEIM

I

I start with a phenomenon that is familiar to us all.[1] I illustrate it from my own experience, but the phenomenon itself, or that which the illustrations exemplify, is of wider significance. It has a lot to tell us about expression in the arts. It lies at its core. Or such is the claim of this chapter. In point of fact, though I believe this claim is true for all the arts, here I shall develop it solely for the visual arts.

So for the examples:

Autumn rain has been falling throughout the early afternoon. It stops abruptly, and the sun breaks through. Drops of water sparkle on the leaves and on the grey slates, and they drip down onto the pavement, which glistens with a hard sheen. The sky is blue, but streaked with black, suggesting distant rain. This is a melancholy scene.

The narrow road rises and falls. Along the verge on either side there are apple-trees in blossom. The fields as they slope away from the road are a brilliant green, dotted with the blue, yellow, and white of wild flowers. A few miles away the mountains rise up sharply from the rolling landscape. They are grey rising to blue, cut by the silver lines of mountain torrents. Patches of snow persist on the rock face. The air is fresh, and there is the sound of cowbells. At the foot of the mountains, beyond the rich orchards, there are large half-timbered farmhouses forming villages. It is a happy countryside.

What each of these passages has to tell us can be recorded in one or other of two ways. We can, in Rudolf Carnap's distinction, use the material mode of speech or the formal mode of speech. Using the material mode of speech, we would say that sunlight after rain is melancholy, that the Bavarian landscape is happy. Using the formal mode of speech, we would say that the sunlit scene is called "melancholy," or that the predicate "happy" is applied to the landscape. We can say how certain things are, or we can say how they are described.

There are philosophers who on metaphysical grounds would hold that the formal mode of speech is invariably more fundamental: it shows what is basic. But there are other philosophers, who don't have such general views, but who nevertheless maintain that in the sort of case I have just cited resort to the formal mode of speech is better. It is more perspicuous. Their reasoning would go as follows: neither the suburban scene nor the Bavarian landscape has a psychology. In consequence neither can have a psychological property. Neither can actually be melancholy or sad. That being so, we cannot in cases like this explain our saying that the suburban scene is melancholy or that the landscape is happy, by appealing to the fact that this is how they are. In consequence explanation has to go the other way round, and we must explain our thinking that the suburban scene is melancholy (which it couldn't be), or that the landscape is happy (which it couldn't be), by appeal to the practice of calling the suburban scene "melancholy" or calling the landscape "happy." In these particular cases, the reasoning runs, the formal mode of speech does indeed reveal what is basic.

Let me call the phenomenon that my examples illustrate "correspondence": a word that derives from the visionary Swedenborg, and was made familiar by a poem of Baudelaire's. In my examples the suburban scene *corresponds to* melancholy, the landscape *corresponds to* happiness, and correspondence is, it must be recognized, one way, just one way, in which we can correlate parts of nature with psychological phenomena. I shall call the view that we can explain correspondence by reference to a special use of psychological predicates the Predication view. The Predication view holds that, when we think that some part of nature corresponds to a psychological phenomenon, this is because we have the habit of applying to that part of nature the predicate that we normally reserve for persons who are in the grip of that phenomenon. Of course, it might be thought that, for the Predication view to be cogent, it has to give an account of the otherwise mysterious predications that it takes as basic. Without such a further account its diagnosis of correspondence seems incomplete.[2] With this further account, correspondence is explained away.

II

In this section I want to argue against the Predication view. It can, I believe, be faulted on two counts. There are two assumptions it makes, neither of which is well founded. The effect of these assumptions is to obscure from us the real nature of correspondence, and so the real nature of expression in the arts. It makes us look in the wrong direction.

The first assumption is that, in each case of correspondence, or whenever we think that some part of nature corresponds to a psychological phenomenon, the predicate that is ordinarily applied to persons exhibiting this phenomenon can be correctly applied to this part of nature. If there is no such widespread practice, the Predication view lapses. That which it cites in order to explain what it wishes to explain is a myth. Let us call the practice whereby a psychological predicate has this dual application – to persons in a certain condition and to nature insofar as it corresponds to this condition – the "doubling-up" of the predicate, and it seems to me clear that correspondence does not universally correlate with doubling-up of the predicate. There are cases where the two go together and cases where there is one without the other, and as important as this fact is the further fact that there seems no principled way of accounting for the two kinds of case.[3] For instance, nature can be found to correspond to depression and to terror as well as to melancholy and to happiness, but, though we can call nature "melancholy" and "happy," we cannot call it "depressed" or "terrified" – or, more precisely, we cannot call it "depressed" or "terrified" for the reason that it corresponds to depression or terror – and there is no apparent explanation why this should be so. Of course, once we do think that some part of nature corresponds to depression or terror, we can cobble up some predicate that will do the work that the inapplicable predicate cannot take on. But it is obvious that any such improvisation cannot give the Predication view any support. Once improvisation is called for, it must be the case that what we say follows on from what we think, not vice versa.

The second assumption that the Predication view makes, also erroneously, is that, when we apply to corresponding nature a psychological predicate, there is no property of the object to which we thereby refer. What is given as a reason for this, and what is undoubtedly true, is surely irrelevant. This is that there is no *psychological* property of the object to which we thereby refer: we do not, in this kind of predication, refer to a property that could be possessed only by the possessor of a psychology. That is true, but it is irrelevant, because it is perfectly possible that the psychological predicates that we apply to corresponding nature refer to properties, but not to the properties that they refer to in their standard use. In other words, we could hold the view that there is what philosophers call "a fact of the matter" to correspondence without believing in animism or committing the Pathetic Fallacy. In fact I believe that such a view is right, even though it does require invoking a notion that I believe we should in general try to avoid: ambiguity. Psychological predicates that double up *are* ambiguous.

Let us consider for a moment an alternative strategy to which a supporter of the Predication view might incline, since it would allow him to deny that psychological predicates applied to corresponding nature pick out properties. It also has an independent plausibility. This strategy consists in maintaining that such predicates are used metaphorically.[4] The supporter of the Predication view would claim, in other words, that it is metaphorical to say of the suburban scene that it is melancholy, or of the Bavarian landscape that it is happy.

Let me hasten to add that, when I credit this view of the matter to an upholder of the Predication view, I am for the purposes of the present argument assuming him also to hold a certain recently espoused view of metaphor.[5] This is a view which I find wholly plausible, though I dare say not everyone does, and it makes the following sense of his words: when the suburban scene is called "melancholy" or the landscape "happy," the two predicates retain their standard meaning, even though this results in the sentences to which they contribute being false; but the speaker is indifferent to their truth value, for the point of metaphor is not to convey information, but to get the hearer to see what is being talked about in a new light, and this effect can be achieved variously by banalities, implausibilities, and arrant falsehoods. Such a view of metaphor makes metaphor a genuine alternative to ambiguity in explaining our thoughts about correspondence. Is it a convincing alternative?

Metaphorical assertions about nature may be thought of as falling into two rough groups. There are those metaphors which try to capture a transient aspect of nature, or an aspect that is dependent upon the mood we are in. And there are those metaphors which try to capture aspects of nature that are independent of our mood and that endure until nature itself changes. Now it is only the second kind of metaphorical assertion that could be relevant to correspondence. Correspondence is not dependent on mood, though, where correspondence is with a certain mood, being in that mood may help us discern it. However I contend that it would be wrong to identify attributions of correspondence with any kind of metaphorical assertion: with the second kind no less than with the first. Metaphor and attribution of correspondence are different, in that they do different things. The difference between them may be brought out like this: what attributions of correspondence do is that they refer to, or pick out, those properties of nature of which related metaphorical asser- tions are intended to heighten our awareness. Attributions of corres- pondence do what some advocates of the theory of metaphor I have been supporting tell us is impossible: they give us directly what metaphor aims at by indirection. (In claiming that the direct approach is impossible, such philosophers, I should claim, overlook attri- butions of correspondence.)

If I am right, a grasp of the real difference between metaphorical assertion and attribution of correspondence supports the view that correspondence is a matter of the properties that nature possesses, and in this regard it undercuts the attempt to explain – or, as we might say, to explain away – correspondence by appeal to certain things that in certain circumstances we say about nature. In other words, it undercuts the Predication view. But once we turn round the direction of explanation and attempt to explain the practice we have of, say, calling the landscape "happy" by appeal to its being so, the issue arises of what kind of property this involves. If correspondence does rest on the properties of nature, they are certainly not ordinary properties: they are properties of an unusual kind. Thinking about what they must be like can drive us back, in desperation, into the Predication view. It can convince us, if against the grain, that the phenomenon of correspondence is, after all, best characterized in the formal mode of speech. This is a temptation to resist.

If the Predication view is misguided, then correspondence survives as a genuine phenomenon, which, as we shall see, can play its part in a broad account of expression in the arts. But, first, some refinements, and then a deepening of the topic.

III

I have already implied that psychological predicates can be applied to parts of nature for various reasons: correspondence to psychologi- cal phenomena is only one such reason. When I say that a slope is gentle, or a province of the empire is peaceful, or that the lake is treacherous, that has nothing to do with correspondence. In the first case, I am saying something about how easy the slope is to negotiate: in the second case I am transferring to a tract of land the character of the people who inhabit it: in the third case, not an uncommon kind of case, I am thinking of the lake as some faceless creature and attributing to it a personality. However, when psychological predicates are applied to nature for reasons of correspondence, what they refer to I call *projective properties*. (It follows from what I said earlier that some projective properties cannot be referred to by psychological predicates. In such cases, we have to resort to some improvised locution.)

What then are projective properties?

In the first place, projective properties are properties that we identify through experiences that we have: experiences that are both caused by those properties and of them. In this regard projective properties resemble secondary properties, such as color.[6]

If however we ask what is distinctive about projective properties, the answer lies with the nature of the experience through which we identify them. The experience has a special complexity. It has a complexity we don't find in the experience of secondary properties.

There are two aspects to this experience which account for its complexity. For, on the one hand, though the experience is a perceptual experience, it is not a wholly perceptual experience. It is a partly affective experience, but the affect that attaches to the experience is not affect directed towards the property itself. It is affect directed towards older or more dominant objects. When a fearful object strikes fear into an observer, as it does, it is not fear of that object. On the other hand, the experience reveals or intimates a history. It is not so much that each individual experience intimates narrowly *its own* history: that is true only of the formative experiences in the life-history of the person. What later experiences do is to intimate how the sort of experience they exemplify comes about. Such experiences occur originally in the aftermath of projection, and the fact that later experiences intimate this origin, and do so even when they do not themselves originate in this way, is the reason why I call them experiences of "projective" properties.

The nature of projection apart, this last claim may still seem obscure. An experience can be of its history, certainly, but how can it reveal or intimate either its history or the history of experiences of the sort to which it belongs?

A comparison may help. Let us take experiential memory, or the capacity we have not just of remembering that certain events occurred in our life but of remembering those very events.[7] Now any particular experience of this kind that a person has is always of an event in his life. But there is a further feature of experiential memory, and this feature might be characterized by saying that the memory intimates that it originated in the event that it is of. This is a further feature, for we might have had experiences which carried true beliefs about past events in our lives but, just because they didn't intimate that they originated in these events, they would be experiences which played a different role in our lives. For instance, we would not instinctively trust them.

However, if this comparison with experiential memory does something to illuminate the notion of intimation, it does little to make plausible the broader claim that I make about experiences of projective properties. For I claimed that when such experiences do not – and most do not – intimate how *they* came about, they do intimate how experiences of the sort that they exemplify come about in general. A different comparison may help to clarify this claim. The comparison is with pain. Most experiences of bodily pain intimate specifically how they originate, that is, in damage to that part of the body where they are felt. But there are some individual pains that do not arise in this way: the part of the body where they are felt is undamaged or has been amputated. But such pains, which are in the minority, nevertheless intimate how pain in general arises. It arises, they tell us, from damage to the body.

The next question to ask is, What is projection, and how can it have this afterlife?

IV

Projection is an internal act that we carry out under instinctual guidance, when there is either a mental condition of ours that we value (like love or curiosity) and that we find threatened, or one that we dread (like cruelty or melancholy) and by which we find ourselves threatened. Anxiety alerts us to this situation, and projection alters it. I shall not in this chapter investigate the nature of projection itself, except to suggest that it is bound up with phantasies that we entertain and that represent mental processes as bodily processes. I have elaborated this elsewhere.[8] Instead I shall concentrate on the consequences of projection. The only danger to this tactic is that an unwary reader might identify projection itself with what are just the consequences of projection. I can only warn against that.

In order to spell out the consequences of projection, I must first distinguish, as the literature on the topic tends not to, between two kinds of projection. I shall call them simple projection and complex projection, though the differences between them are greater than this might suggest.

I start with somewhat schematic examples.

For the sake of both examples we assume a person who is melancholy, but who can no longer tolerate his melancholy. Instinct compels him to project it. If this is a case of simple projection, the upshot will be this: (one) the person will now believe that some figure in the environment other than himself is melancholy, and (two) there will be some remission in his own interior condition. However, if this is a case of complex projection, the upshot will be this: (one) the person will come to look upon, and respond to, some part, of the environment as melancholy, and (two) there will be a change for the better in his interior condition.

These schematic examples allow us to see straight off certain differences between the two forms of projection. Three differences need detain us.

In the first place, in the case of simple projection, projection is onto a figure in the environment, or something which possesses a psychology, or, at any rate onto something which is treated as though it had a psychology. With complex projection, projection is onto some natural part of the environment, or something which does not, and is not held to, possess a psychology.

Secondly, in the case of simple projection, it is basically the person's beliefs that are changed as the result of the internal act, whereas with complex projection, though the person's beliefs will certainly change, what is fundamental is a new attitude towards the environment, a new way of experiencing it, which is cemented by the new beliefs he acquires.

Thirdly, in the case of simple projection, the property that the figure in the environment is believed to have is the very same property as the person himself originally had. One is held now to be what the other was: melancholy. With complex projection, the property that some natural part of the environment is experienced as having is not the same as the property the person himself originally had. How could it be, given that nature has no psychology? A blanket-phrase, a made-up locution, for saying how the two properties are related would be this: that nature, in its relevant parts, is felt to be, not actually melancholy, but *of a piece with* the man's melancholy. A deceptive feature, which could misguidedly be seized on as an instructive feature, is that though, in the case of complex projection, the two properties involved are different, in certain circumstances someone might use the same predicate to pick out both (as indeed I did, a few moments ago, in introducing complex projection).

We can now put simple projection out of our minds, for, of the two forms of projection, only complex projection could be capable of generating new properties, let alone properties of a new kind. But does complex projection have such a capacity? Can it alter the world? Does it have the after-life I attributed to it? There are deep metaphysical issues which I shall not probe. But I shall try to set out the situation as I see it.

V

I start a little way back with a point on which so far I have said nothing, and that is whether, when complex projection is activated, there must be an affinity between the inner condition of the person that is projected and the part of nature that it is projected onto. Must nature have features that encourage and sustain the projection? Or is this unnecessary? What seems certain is that, unless there is some such substrate, there can be no justification for saying that what the person experiences in the aftermath of projection is a *property* of nature.

This question cannot be answered without taking stock of the inherently developmental nature of projection. At the beginning of life, projection most likely occurs in a totally haphazard fashion. The infant projects feelings, welcome and unwelcome, onto random parts of the environment without any concern for what the environment is like. But, as a corollary, projection at this stage of development has only a transient effect. It may momentarily relieve anxiety but it has no enduring influence upon the way in which the infant continues to perceive the environment. However, as the psychology matures, projection becomes more orderly, and those parts of the environment upon which feelings are projected are now selected because of their affinity to these feelings. And in consequence they can continue to be experienced as of a piece with these feelings. What I have called the formative instances of projection can occur only after this developmental stage has been reached.

The next question to ask is, Granted that some affinity between the internal condition that is projected onto nature and the part of nature onto which it is projected is necessary if the latter is to be perceived in some enduring fashion as of a piece with the former, why is this affinity not sufficient for the perception to occur? It obviously isn't: otherwise projection itself would not make any real contribution to our perception of projective properties, or (for that matter) to projective properties themselves.

But why is this so, and what is required over and above affinity?

To see what the requirement is, I propose that we return to the claim that I made in introducing projective properties and how they are experienced. That claim, it will be recalled, fell into two parts. Both parts of the claim are currently relevant.

The first part of the claim was that a number of such experiences intimate their own actual history: they intimate, in other words, that they derive from an instance of projection. Consider then the case of someone who has just projected his feelings onto the environment: say, melancholy. Now if this person perceives the relevant part of nature as of a piece with his melancholy, what will lead him to do this is, in addition to the affinity of one to the other, a memory of the projection. This memory will organize or structure the perception in a way that should be familiar to us from analogous cases. So, for instance, a person's pain in his thumb might well be stabilized by the memory that he has just grazed his thumb in the course of paring a carrot.

However, as things stand, this account of projective properties and our perception of them is uselessly narrow. For it confines that which can be explained to perceptions that occur in the immediate aftermath of projection. That is evidently too restrictive, for we can and do perceive nature as of a piece with our feelings in cases where we can no longer recall having projected those feelings onto it, and, indeed, to innumerable cases where we have not done so.

This brings us to the second part of the claim I made about our experience of projective properties. This was that those experiences of projective properties which do not intimate their own history nevertheless intimate how experiences of this sort originate: they intimate that they originate in projection. But how does this intimation make itself felt?

A natural suggestion is that this intimation takes the form of a recognitional capacity we have. In other words, we recognize parts of nature as those into which we might have, or could have, projected this or that kind of feeling. Indeed we might think that such a recognitional capacity is part and parcel of the ability to project. If we do, then, have such a capacity, it seems fully competent to extend the explanation of our perception of projective properties beyond the narrow base provided by what I have called the aftermath of projection.

It might seem a lacuna in this account that I have said nothing informative about the affinity between mental conditions and parts of nature on to which we are inclined to project them. But is this a lacuna?[9] It depends on what kind of information we look for. If what is wanted is knowledge of how nature must look in particular cases if it is to be apt for the projection of this rather than that feeling, then this demand must surely go unsatisfied. For how could we convincingly describe what it is about some aspect of nature that makes it suitable for the projection of some particular feeling without upgrading the mere affinity into the projective properties of which it is – at any rate, on my view – the mere substrate?

I hope I have said enough to suggest how the phenomenon of correspondence fits within the framework provided by projection and projective properties. The idea, briefly, is this: when some part of nature is held to correspond to a psychological phenomenon, this is because it is perceptible as being of a piece with that state or as something onto which we might have or could have projected the state. That it is perceptible in this way comes about through two factors which make their independent contributions to this result: an affinity in nature, and our capacity to project internal conditions.

VI

Correspondence has now received the refinement and the deepening that I promised, and I now turn to the central topic of this chapter: expression in the arts. Correspondence is interesting in itself, but it is fundamental because of the contribution it makes to the concept of artistic expression.

Let me first say that I am not confident that expression, specifically artistic expression, is one of those concepts of which we have such a strong pre-theoretical grasp that, when a theoretical elucidation is produced, it can be assessed by seeing how far it fits and explains what we originally took expression to be. Some of what philosophers will say on this subject must be stipulative. And I shall start by stipulating, *contra* Nelson Goodman, that artistic expression is invariably expression of an internal or psychological condition. The topic is thus returned to its tradition.

My central claim is that a work of art expresses an internal

61

condition by corresponding to, or being of a piece with, it. Furthermore the perceptible property in virtue of which it does so is a property it has intentionally: the property is due to the intentions of the artist. The artist intended the work to have this property so that it can express some internal condition that he had in mind.

VII

An initial trouble with this claim is that, as it stands, it is not merely compatible with, it seems positively to encourage, a counter-intuitive view of the matter. The view comes to this: when an artist who is engaged in making a work expressive of some internal condition judges that his work is complete because it now, in virtue of how it looks, expresses that condition, he arrives at this judgment in just the same way as a spectator would when he judges that some part of nature corresponds, in virtue of how it looks, to a particular internal condition; exactly the same evidence counts in the two cases. Now I certainly believe that the judgment in the two cases has the same content, but how the judgment is reached in the two cases is surely different. And what gives rise to the difference is the fact that, in one case, correspondence arises out of a creative act whereas, in the other case, it doesn't. In one case the correspondence is *made*; in the other case it is *found*. How what is judged comes to look as it does makes a difference.[10]

Ordinarily we recognize that history of production makes such a difference, or that it distinguishes correspondence in art from correspondence in nature. This comes out clearly if we adopt for a moment the epistemological perspective, or consider how we come to the conclusion that a work of art expresses this emotion or that feeling. (In certain respects accounts of expression go astray just because they over-emphasize the epistemological perspective. Consider, for instance, Gombrich's account.[11] But this is not one of those respects.) When we assign expressive value to a work of art, we invariably draw upon our knowledge of, or our beliefs about, the artistic processes involved. For instance, within the oeuvre of a given painter, we are likely to make different expressive assignments as we move from passages with broken brush strokes to passages with long fluent strokes. Knowledge of the technique influences our judgment. Such a judgment has still to do with the look of the picture, but it is an essential fact that the look that a picture has comes about through the processes of art.

One striking way of putting the counter-intuitive view that my account of artistic expression appears to foster would be to say that it denies the creative act, in that it refuses to discriminate between the process of making an object and a process of selecting an object out of a large, perhaps an indefinite, range of pre-made objects. It assimilates the act of making to the act of choosing.[12]

But I must emphasize that, though there is this crucial difference between the way in which correspondence is established outside art, and the way in which it is achieved inside it, this does not mean – as a number of theorists have claimed – that in the domain of art correspondence is less dependent upon perception than it is in the domain of nature. It does not mean that correspondence in art is (dreaded word) conventional. In both domains, correspondence, being concerned with projective properties, is concerned with properties that are identified through our experience of them. The difference is that, in the case of art, the experience that is evidential for the projective property is based on a larger body of background knowledge, a larger cognitive stock, than is required for the perception of correspondence in nature. The background knowledge must include beliefs about a work's history of production and the specific processes of art that went to its making.

That expression in art, though it derives from a creative act, is nevertheless borne by strictly perceptible properties receives confirmation from an impeccable source: that is, the nature of the creative act itself, regarded as a piece of behavior.[13] For across the visual arts the creative act always finds physical realization in a posture that allows, that encourages, the artist to attend to his work even as he makes it. It ensures that the artist is the original spectator of his work. But, if this is what he is, it is important to see why. He is so, not just in order to discover what he has made, but, crucially, in order to make it. The painter paints (partly) with his eyes; the sculptor carves or models (partly) with his eyes; the draughtsman draws (partly) with his eyes. In other words, if, as I have contended, correspondence in art derives from the artistic process, the process itself anticipates this through its physical or behavioral realization. For, by compelling the artist to take stock of the work as it comes into being, it permits him to see if it corresponds to the inner condition that he all the while has had in mind. He can, while making the work, note the experience that it causes in him and he can then regulate, by what he does to the work, the experience it may be expected to cause in others. And there are two other things that can be hoped for from the conventional posture. In the first place, by repeating this process of what Gombrich would call "making and matching" over and over again, not merely within the making of one work, but across the making of different works, the artist can refine his sense of what it is for a work to correspond to a psychological condition. Secondly, as he makes each individual work, he can expect to acquire a better, a sharper, sense of just what psychological condition it is that he has in mind and is endeavoring to express.

VIII

There are two well-entrenched or traditional theories of expression in the arts, which, just because I have not mentioned them, I might be thought to be out of sympathy with. This is not the case.[14] And, if I have delayed mentioning them, this is because I believe that my own account of artistic expression, couched in terms of intentional correspondence, can do better justice to the considerable truth that each theory, once it is properly amplified and articulated, can be seen to embody. Amplification is not the usual fate of either theory.[15]

According to the first theory, a work of art expresses a certain psychological condition just in case it was that psychological condition which caused the artist to make the work. According to the second theory, a work of art expresses a certain psychological condition just in case it is that psychological condition which perception of the work causes in the mind of the spectator.

Each theory as it stands, or as it is usually formulated, suffers from two faults. Each theory has one feature too many, and one too few, and they are the same features in both cases. The adjustments required to remove one and to add the other are minor. They are not surgical.

As to the feature too many, both theories go wrong in requiring that the emotion that the work of art expresses is actually *felt*, whether this be (as our theory claims) by the artist or (as the other theory claims) by the spectator. This is not a sustainable requirement. What is enough is that (as I have been putting it) the emotion is something that the artist or spectator has in mind, or (perhaps better) it is something with which they are put in touch, or (perhaps best) it is something upon which, or upon memory of which, they can draw. These are not easy ideas, there is more to be said about them, but none of it will require us to revive what Nelson Goodman has named the Tingle-Immersion theory.[16]

64

As to the other fault, or the feature too few, both theories go wrong in failing to require that the work of art expressive of a certain emotion should *look* any one particular way. Yet surely it must. Expressiveness cannot be independent of appearance. What is necessary can however readily be written in by insisting that the causal chain that runs from the artist to the work of art (alternatively from the work of art to the spectator) should pass through a perception of the work as corresponding to the emotion that is expressed. This perception should, either way round, have its special causal weight to pull.

The two theories thus amplified, thus rectified, seem to me to fit in well with, perhaps to be constitutive parts of, the theory I have been urging.

Let me in conclusion refer to yet another traditional theory. It is often called the Local Quality theory, because it equates the expressiveness of a work with some sensible property that the work has.[17] If that is what the theory says, then I am, as far as I can see, in favor of it. But traditionally, this traditional theory has been presented in such a sparse fashion, without the genetic psychology that I regard as crucial, that it lacks any clear claim upon our support. The greater part of what I have been saying in this essay may be regarded as an attempt to put this right.[18]

NOTES

1 This chapter deepens the view of expression to be found in Richard Wollheim, *Painting as an Art* (Princeton, N.J., and London, 1987).

2 A philosopher who offers such a further account, though exiguous, is Nelson Goodman, *Languages of Art: An Approach to a Theory of Symbols* (New York and Indianapolis, 1968; 2nd edn, Indianapolis, 1976).

3 This argument derives from Anthony Savile, "Nelson Goodman's *Languages of Art*," *British Journal of Aesthetics*, 2:1 (Winter 1971), pp. 3–27. See also Richard Wollheim, *The Sheep and the Ceremony* (Cambridge, 1979).

4 This position is upheld in Nelson Goodman, *Languages of Art*.

5 See Donald Davidson, "What Metaphors Mean," in his *Inquiries into Truth and Interpretation* (Oxford, 1984).

6 Cf. John McDowell, "Values and Secondary Qualities," in *Morality and Objectivity: A Tribute to J. L. Mackie*, ed. T. Honderich (London, 1985).

7 This view of experiential memory is expounded at greater length in Richard Wollheim, *The Thread of Life* (Cambridge, 1984).

8 On projection and its two forms, see *The Thread of Life* (see note 7).

9 In trying to think about this issue, and elsewhere in writing this chapter, I have benefited, or at least had the opportunity to do so, from conversations with Malcolm Budd, who has an unrivaled understanding of the arguments.

10 Recognition of this point is central to the argument of John Dewey, *Art as Experience* (New York, 1934).

11 See E. H. Gombrich, *Meditations on a Hobby Horse and Other Essays on the Theory of Art* (London, 1963).

12 This error permeates so-called experimental aesthetics. Some writers have falsely concluded that an account of expression that appeals to correspondence is inevitably committed to this error, e.g., L. D. Ettlinger, *Kandinsky's "At Rest"* (Oxford, 1961).

13 I have developed this point in Richard Wollheim, *Painting as an Art*, chapter 1.

14 I have anticipated this point in Richard Wollheim, *Art and its Objects* (2nd edn, Cambridge, 1980), secs. 15–18.

15 For "unamplified" versions of the first view, see Leo Tolstoy, *What is Art?* (Moscow and London, 1898), and Harold Rosenberg, *The Tradition of the New* (New York, 1959), and for "unamplified" versions of the second view, see I. A. Richards, *Principles of Literary Criticism* (London, 1925), and Deryck Cooke, *The Language of Music* (London, 1959).

16 See Nelson Goodman, *Problems and Projects* (Indianapolis and New York, 1972) p. 94, where the theory is attributed to "Immanuel Tingle and Joseph Immersion (ca. 1880)." It proposes that "the proper behavior on encountering a work of art is to strip ourselves of all the vestments of knowledge and experience (since they might blunt the immediacy of our enjoyment), then submerge ourselves completely and gauge the aesthetic potency of the work by the intensity and duration of the resulting tingle."

17 See, for instance, Monroe Beardsley, *Aesthetics* (New York, 1958).

18 In writing and revising this essay, I have tried to do justice to comments from Malcolm Budd, David Hills, Kendall Walton, and David Wiggins.

5

The language of art criticism

MICHAEL BAXANDALL

... it is very difficult to say a great deal about a painting, except by talking about its relationship to something else, whether to other paintings, other arts, contemporary social movements, contemporary beliefs, or contemporary ideas.[1]

LIMITATIONS OF THE LEXICON

The specific interest of the visual arts is visual, and one of the art historian's specific faculties is to find words to indicate the character of shapes, colors, and organizations of them. But these words are not so much descriptive as demonstrative: I am not sure how firmly we have grasped the implications of this. Unlike a travel writer or the man who writes about exhibitions in a newspaper, we are not primarily concerned to evoke the visual character of something never seen by our audience. The work of art we discourse on is to some extent present or available, if only in reproduction or in the memory or even more marginally as a visualization derived from knowledge of other objects of the same class, and though the form of our language may be informative – "there is a flow of movement from the left towards the center" – its action is likely to be a sort of verbal pointing. What distinguishes it from manual pointing is mainly that along with direction ("left to center") goes a category of visual interest ("flow of movement"). We are proposing that our audience compare the one with the other.

It is this that goes some way towards extenuating the crudeness of our language. If I apply half-a-dozen simple terms of visual interest (a phrase I am not going to define) to the pencil I am writing with – "long," "thin," "shiny," "green," "of hexagonal section," "with one conical end" – that is a quite inadequate description: to someone who did not have experience of pencils it would not carry an accurate image, and equally to someone who did have such experience some of the terms would be otiose. But if my purpose is not to describe but rather to indicate (a) to someone who has seen it (b) such kinds of visual interest as I am finding in it, then the half-dozen terms do cover some of what I have to offer. My blunt words (e.g., "green") are sharpened for me because what I have done is to instigate, or offer to instigate, a guided act of inspection of the particular object by the hearer, and he knows really that that was my intention. Neither of us expects him to think, if he does elect to follow my prompting, "Oh, not red then": rather, he will elaborate and refine my category "green" for himself. Of course the matter is more complicated than this, but the immediate point is that the art historian's use of language invites the receiver to supply a degree of precision to broad categories by a reciprocal reference between the word and the available object. It is ostensive.

But my pencil is an untypically simple object, which is why I could cover so much of its visual interest with so few words. If I try to do the same even to my typewriter ("square," "mat," "gray," and so on), I get less far: the words cover less of what I find interesting in it. If I try to do it with a painting or a sculpture, I will hardly get anywhere at all: direct descriptive terms can cover very little of the interest one wishes to indicate. I can use them – it is not vacuous to point to Michelangelo's *Moses* as "square" – but the fit between sense and reference is now becoming very loose, and I can only use them by assuming that my hearer will interpret them in a sophisticated and specialized way: he must supply a great deal in the way of mental comparison with other works of art, of experience of the previous use of such words in art criticism,[2] and of general interpretative tact. The words have become things of a rather different kind.

Indeed, if one is not careful, the lack of the right, or adequately determinate, word reduces one to someone just making an emphatic noise; it becomes quite unclear why one should be taking it on oneself to address other people about the picture at all. A thing the practice of art criticism quickly teaches one is that the European languages discriminate very finely in some areas (e.g., underlying Euclidean form) and very coarsely in others (e.g., seen surface texture): this has its own fascination as an object of study, but it also sets a practical problem because there is a limit to how much one can enlarge the lexicon by coining and borrowing. It is not so much that one wants to avoid academic jargon as that novel coinages and loanwords are cultural orphans, not properly part of the collective framework of our thinking. Thus, I might like to have genuine access to the Nigerian Yoruba critical term dídón,[3] which indicates a degree of smooth but not glossy luminosity in the surfaces of sculpture, closely related to the contrast of these with sharp shadows and edges: it would cover much of an interest I find important in some European sculpture. But dídón is a fragment of a complex of Yoruba critical concepts and takes its rich meaning from just this set of relations. Even for my private exploratory purposes I cannot possess it except in a crude and shallow, a dissociated way.

THREE KINDS OF INDIRECTNESS

But in fact most art critical language is not of such direct descriptive background as "green" or "square"; rather, it is variously oblique or tropical. And while there seems nothing to be said for working out any very crisp or general classification of the types of indirect art critical words, it will suit my purpose here to group them in three rough divisions or moods.

(I) Some words seem to point to a kind of visual interest by making a comparison of some sort, often by metaphor: "rhythmic," "fugal," "dovetailing," "a forest of verticals," "striplike" – these words used of a picture work comparatively. Among them I will also include words like "square" in the extended use involved in calling Michelangelo's *Moses* "square": thus, "Apollo and two of the Muses ... forming a broad triangle." And a special class of comparative words (I *bis*, let us say) refers to representational works of art as if the things or persons represented were actual: "agitated" figures or "calm" or "spirited" figures. (II) Some words characterize the work of art in terms of the action or agent that would have produced them: "tentative," "calculated," "sensitive," "elaborate," "difficult," "skilled," this or that "treatment" or "development" or "virtuosity." (III) Some words characterize a work of art by describing its action on the beholder or his reaction to it: "imposing," "unexpected," "striking," "disturbing," "unpleasant," this or that "effect," "a feeling of crowding." One could refer loosely to these moods as (I) comparative or metaphorical, (II) causal or inferential, and (III) subject or ego words, and might visualize them in a field something like Fig. 1 (on page 70). But of course they are all projections of the subject, the speaking beholder, as we all know perfectly well. Equally they are nearly all in a weak sense metaphorical, though some of the metaphors are more educated than others.

Michael Baxandall

Similia
(I)
.
.
.
.
.
.
.

The maker ⇌ [The object] ⇌ The beholder
(II)   .   (III)
.
.
.
.
.

Matter of representation
(I *bis*)

Fig. 1

There is much that could be said in a softening way about this. Clearly a history of use will loosen the relation of a word to its original basis: "monumental," say, is a moribund metaphor that has left monuments some way behind, and it would be foolish to make a thing of "interesting" being an ego word. Clearly, too, many words partake of more than one type: "dry," for instance, can be used in comparative, I *bis*, causal (*secco* rather than *fresco* handling), and subjective ways, sometimes equivocally, and is a tricky word all round. It is also clear that roughly the same general area can often be pointed to with different types of words: say, (I) stormy, (I *bis*) excited, (II) excited, (III) exciting. (The example, by the way, alerts us to the verbal affinity between I *bis* and II, which has much to do with our vulnerability to the "physiognomic fallacy"[4] or Winckelmann syndrome.) Above all, there is the point that in any piece of actual art criticism all this is going on on several tiers. My examples were mainly single words, but sentences are framed within one type or another, and paragraphs and books are weighted overall towards one or another. All the examples in the last paragraph were taken from Heinrich Wölfflin's account in *Classic Art* of Raphael's Camera della Segnatura. If anyone looks at those pages he will find, I think, that their character is determined by an overall dominance of types I *bis* and II. Within this general character all the kinds of language I have mentioned, including what I have rather simply called "direct" language ("round," "large in proportion," "surrounded," "profile"), are in play. It is the pattern of this hierarchy that gives the individual critic a physiognomy. It is a trait of Wölfflin's, for instance, that within a sentence of Type III, reporting an impression, there is often a Type II word as core: he tends to have an impression of a cause, honest man. I am not sensitive, I should say here, to the suggestion that the differences in words are purely formal and that somewhere between sense and reference their origins are sloughed off, words becoming denatured from their class once they are presented within continuous discourse. When reading art criticism, I do not find this to be so. On the contrary, I am pleasurably conscious of the constantly veering orientations in the good critic's dance towards a sufficiently determinate demonstrative act. But what does strike me is that his need to string his words into discourse raises a problem of another kind.

THE PROBLEM OF LINEARITY: WORDS ABOUT WORDS AND WORDS ABOUT SHAPES

The art critical lexicon is normally assembled into consecutive language of some sort. (Notionally, I suppose, one could assemble single categories of visual interest, presyntactical ejaculations, in a non-sequential, galactic pattern on the page, but this would be affected.) This raises problems that I can best accent here by pointing to the contrast with literary criticism. Literary criticism is words about words where art criticism, as has often been pointed out, is words about shapes. Many differences – the dissimilarities between art criticism and literary criticism seem much more interesting than the similarities – follow from this, but one comes out of the shape of language, its dependence on syntagmatic muscle, the fact that words have to be assembled in a linear progression.

A piece of literature, being language, is itself a linear affair led from here to there, or from now to later. A poem or story has a beginning and an end and an authentic sequence in between. We may perceive many non-linear patterns underlying either a sentence or the whole, antithetical syntax or narrative symmetries; there are also likely to be many retracing moments of rereading and referring back. But the linear progress of the text is comprehended in these excursions and withstands them. If a critic's account of *Wuthering Heights*, or *Sarrasine* involves him in pointing to bits of it out of order, this is all right because the directional movement of the book is strong enough for his activity not to be misunderstood. He is emerging here and there from the stream, walking back along the bank, and getting in again to float alertly down a particular stretch once more. When the literary critic does engage with a particular stretch of a text, his language can pace its language, each linearly progressive. My point is weakened here by the failure of many literary critics to make athletic use of their advantage, no fault of mine, but the possibility is there and is used in the literary criticism I most envy from over the fence – to offer a hostage, William Empson on Donne's "A Valediction of Weeping." And in any case I think the point is not so much that the literary critic can work in parallel with his text as that the text and our reception of it have a robust syntagmatic progression of their own which the linear sequence of an exposition cannot greatly harm. The language of the descriptive critic can run with, run away and back, run round the firmly progressing language of the text, like an active dog on a walk with a man.

A picture on the other hand, or rather our perception of it, has no such inherent progression to withstand the sequence of language applied to it. An extended description of a painting is committed by the structure of language to be a progressive violation of the pattern of perceiving a painting. We do not see linearly. We perceive a picture by a temporal sequence of scanning, but within the first second or so of this scanning we have an impression of the whole – that it is a Mother and Child sitting in a hall, say, or a sort of geometricized guitar on a table. What follows is the sharpening of detail, noting of relationships, perception of orders, and so on. And though the sequence of our scanning is influenced as to pattern by both general scanning habits and particular cues in the picture, it is not comparable in regularity and control with progress through a piece of language. One consequence of this is that no consecutive piece of verbal ostension, linear language, can match the pace and gait of seeing a picture as it can match the pace of a text: the read text is majestically progressive, the perception of a picture a rapid irregular darting about and around on a field. There are various ways of meeting the problem. One can work the ostensiveness of one's language hard, so as to draw the hearer sufficiently into his own active act of perception for his attention to shift away from one's own. One can also shun expository sequences that look like representations of perceiving, e.g., descriptions, in favor of ones that assimilate themselves to thinking. The history of art history offers other techniques, too.

INFERENTIAL CRITICISM

I have been making three kinds of suggestion: first, that the art critical lexicon is strongly ostensive; second, that art critical language is largely and variously oblique, and at more than one level; third, that the linear form of our discourse is curiously at odds with the form of its object, whether this is considered to be the work of art itself or our experience of it. These seem to me basic facts of art critical life, and one would like to come to some sort of constructive terms with them. Four hundred years of good and very diverse European art criticism certainly suggest that there are ways of doing so. It seems characteristic of the best art critics that they have developed their own ways of meeting the basic absurdity of verbalizing about pictures: they have embraced its ostensive and oblique character positively, as it were, as well as bouncing their discourse out of the pseudodescriptive register that carries the worst linear threat. I repeat that they have done this in many different ways; about all Vasari and Baudelaire have in common is conspicuous success. This seems something to insist on in the present climate of discussion: the linguistic facts of our life may be general and pressing, preliminary conditions one may well want to take account of in working out a way of doing whatever it is one wants to do, but they do not direct us to one kind of art history.

For instance, I am anxious not to suggest that there is a simple affinity between the orientation of a critic's overt interest and the orientation of a mood of language – between, say, those of us who like occupying ourselves with the circumstances in which works of art are made, on the one hand, and inferential language on the other. What worries me about much criticism that offers itself as social-historical analysis of art is precisely an un-self-aware Type III quality at the lowest verbal level marshaled at a higher level in large a priori Type II patterns – soft impressions sloshing about in hard causal schedules. For contrast one can read the early books of Adrian Stokes[5] for *local* inferential muscle, however subject-assertive the total manner and effect.

Words inferential about cause are the main vehicle of demonstrative precision in art criticism. They are active in two distinct senses. Where ego words are formally and often substantially passive, reporting something done by the work of art to the speaker as patient, causal words deal in inferred actions and agents. At the same time they involve the speaker in the activity of inferring and the hearer in the activity of reconstructing and assessing the pattern of implication. For my taste, I will say, all this activity is cheerful and absolutely more wholesome than a lot of comparing of impressions, but the real point is that it seems to yield adequately determinate and properly stimulating ostensive words. One of the details my description of the pencil on p. 67 omitted was the sort of scalloped edge of the green paint at the point where it meets the conical end. If I wanted to, I could register this quite sharply and economically by inferring cause – the blade of a sharpener revolving circularly at an angle of 15° to a hexagonal cylinder. I do not think I could register it with ego language at all: I am too uncertain a quality to my hearers for my reaction to a scalloped edge to register the scalloped edge or its visual interest – unless my share is indeed to infer the revolving blade. In a more complex way the same is true of art criticism, where a mature inferential vocabulary in full play can have formidable demonstrative precision and punch. The eighteenth-century critic Shen Tsung-hsien[6] – to dramatize the matter with something exotic – gives a glimpse of the resources classical Chinese criticism had for inferential characterization of the painter's brush marks: among much else he distinguishes between wrist-dominant and finger-dominant strokes; between dead and live strokes, in the sense that there is variation of power within the single live stroke; between dragged marks and slippery marks, splashed-ink ones and broken-ink ones, between the marks of a straight brush and those of a slanting one, between cutting strokes and led strokes; he can speak of an individual brush stroke having a center or core and opening and closing phases, and he could wonder how far the closing phase of a stroke carries the suggestion of further development; he could even characterize a brush mark by the noise the stroke would have made, as a "sousing" noise. Of course, there are reasons for the activeness of this language: both Shen Tsung-hsien and his readers were themselves active users of the calligraphic brush so that there was a firm background of reference in everyone's experience. But still it is enviable language: to find anything comparable in Europe, one must go to things like Delacroix's occasional remarks in his journals on the technique of Rubens – remarks addressed by a painter to a painter. We cannot compete with it in this area, but there are other areas of inference we can work towards, including – to twist John Passmore's remark a little – "relationships ... to ... other arts, contemporary social movements, contemporary beliefs, [and] contemporary ideas."

NOTES

This paper is an abbreviated version of "The Language of Art History," published in New Literary History, 10 (1979), pp. 453–465.

1 John Passmore, "History of Art and History of Literature: A Commentary," New Literary History, 3 (Spring, 1972), pp. 575–587.

2 "Square" has a splendid history ; its use in Greek and Latin art criticism has been investigated in an ingenious paper by Silvio Ferri, "Nuovi contributi esegetici al 'Canone' della scultura greca," Revista del R. Istituto d'Archeologia e Storia dell'Arte, 7 (1940), pp. 117–139.

3 For dídón and its context, see Robert Farris Thompson, "Yoruba Artistic Criticism," in The Traditional Artist in African Societies, ed. Warren L. d'Azevedo (Bloomington, Ind., 1973), esp. pp. 37–42.

4 For which see E. H. Gombrich, "Art and Scholarship," in Meditations on a Hobby Horse and Other Essays on the Theory of Art (London, 1963), p. 108, coining the term, and also "On Physiognomic Perception," ibid., p. 51.

5 Particularly The Quattro Cento (London, 1932) and Stones of Rimini (London, 1934). The remarkable comparison between carving and modeling "conception" in the latter is included in the Pelican edition of The Image in Form: Selected Writings of Adrian Stokes, ed. Richard Wollheim (London, 1972), pp. 147–183. The kind of quality I have in mind is (from an account of Donatello's Dead Christ with Angels in the Victoria and Albert Museum [in Wollheim, The Image in Form, p. 168]): "To Donatello, changes of surface meant little more than light and shade, chiaroscuro, the instruments of plastic organization. The bottom of the angels' robes is gouged and undercut so as to provide a contrast to the open planes of Christ's nude torso. The layers of the stone are treated wholesale. Though some of the cutting is beautiful in itself, the relief betrays a wilful, preconceived, manner of approach. In brief the composition is not so much founded upon the interrelationship of adjoining surfaces, as upon the broader principles of chiaroscuro" (my italics).

6 There are translated excerpts – all I know of the author – in Osvald Siren, The Chinese on the Art of Painting (Peking, 1936), pp. 224–233, and Lin Yutang, The Chinese Theory of Art (London, 1967), pp. 169–219.

6

Baxandall and Goodman

CATHERINE LORD AND JOSÉ A. BENARDETE

I

Taking us behind the scenes into the inner sanctum of the art historian, Michael Baxandall confides to us an underlying anxiety concerning the rationale of his enterprise that many art historians may be supposed to share, if only subliminally.[1] The disquietude has to do with the propriety of responding with an outpouring of words, in the form of professional articles, to visual data supplied by the paintings and sculptures that engage his attention. Addressing this interplay of the verbal and the visual with great sensitivity, Baxandall's discussion will be seen positively to invite the philosophical reflections of the author of *Languages of Art*, Nelson Goodman, according to whom paintings (let them be as non-representational as you please) are constituted in no small measure by their verbal import.[2] Surprising? Yes, but let us approach this challenging thesis in easy stages. In the course of allaying the art historian's anxieties, the philosopher in his turn will be found to profit by his involvement in a wealth of recalcitrant data from which he is only too prone to abstract himself.

"In every group of travelers, every bunch of tourists," writes Baxandall in an essay of extraordinary charm, "there is at least one man who insists on pointing out to the others the beauty or interest of the things they encounter, even though," and it is precisely this that appears to render his words redundant, "the others can see the things, too," and Baxandall adds self-deprecatingly, "we [art historians] are that man, I am afraid, *au fond*," granted that "other roles have attached themselves to that basic one," such as "paid cicerone" and "antiquary collector." Pursuing this uneasy line of reflection, Baxandall confesses to a "worry" as to his "own nerve in verbalizing

76

at other people about objects they can already see." For if, platitudi-
nously enough, "the specific interest of the visual arts is visual" and
not verbal, that interest would appear to be, as a point of principle,
ineffable, or so we dare fill out the argument of Baxandall's subtext.

Suppose for a moment that the visual interest of a painting could be
translated without remainder in verbal terms, perhaps in the form of a
poem. Only the blind could benefit, for the sighted could hardly gain
from a translation that merely delivers anew the same aesthetic
content. No wonder that the "staple" of the art historian – "matching
language with the visual interest of works of art" – is felt by Baxandall
to be "pretty gratuitous" as far as their *specific* value is concerned,
though he can always "scuttle away and existentially measure a
plinth or reattribute a statue." By no means confined to Baxandall,
the "worry" here has long vexed the philosopher in the field of
aesthetics when it comes to the non-verbal arts of music as well as
painting. Inevitably, there has been the fear that (minor truths aside)
the aesthetician may have only one great truth to purvey in this area,
namely, that their specific interest is ineffable: the rest is silence.
Casting about for ways to resist the pull to defeatism, the philosopher
could do worse than sit at the feet of Baxandall when, after insisting
on "the basic absurdity of verbalizing about pictures" in what one in
retrospect is tempted to regard as a rhetorical exercise of overkill, he
proves to be eirenic enough as to remark on the "conspicuous
success" of "the best art critics" in meeting that basic absurdity "in
many different ways." And he proceeds to tell us, in detail, what
some of those ways are, thereby engaging in the kind of meta-
criticism that Monroe Beardsley proposed in 1958 (in his *Aesthetics*)
as defining the agenda of the aesthetician in an age of linguistic
philosophy. Just as the new philosopher surrenders any ambition to
construct a philosophy of nature à la Hegel, being content to replace it
with a philosophy of science that addresses itself above all to the
logic of scientific discourse, so too, in much the same manner, the
aesthetician is advised to replace traditional philosophy of art with
philosophy of art criticism: words about words. Here at any rate the
philosopher is very much at home, and his competence will not be
questioned.

Far from being merely rhetorical, the "basic absurdity" with which
Baxandall is grappling we take to involve a logical paradox in the
precise sense of the term, namely, how to talk about the ineffable.
That the practice of the best art critics might actually afford a solution
to the paradox, the philosopher will be very reluctant to believe if

only because the suggestion trenches on his own preserve. How then does Baxandall propose to resolve the paradox through recourse to critical practice? Well, one suggestion is this: the use of metaphor, as when we say in the presence of a painting (the example is his), "There is a flow of movement from the left to the center." Again the philosopher will be quick to balk. Metaphor smacks so much of poetry, being arguably a kind of quasi-poetry or proto-poetry in its own right, that one fears that one art is being betrayed to another, painting to poetry, in a transaction that caters to those lacking eyes to see. Much too premature, this adverse reaction fails to do justice to the subtlety of the suggestion, since in the use of metaphor "my purpose is not to describe" any part or feature of the painting, for that would involve a gratuitous use of language when it comes to the specifically visual. "A verbal sort of pointing" reminiscent of the man in the bus who insists on pointing out to others the beauty or interest of the things they encounter, this use of metaphor is instead to be taken as entirely "ostensive" where "my purpose is not to describe but rather to indicate (a) to someone who has not seen it, (b) such kinds of visual interest as I am finding in it just now." Relentlessly local, this visual interest must not be taken to involve any sort of extra-mural resemblance between movement and flow properly so called (as in the flow of water or the movement of swaying branches) and the relevant feature of the painting.

Honoring Baxandall's "purpose" which precludes any interplay of intra- and extra-mural considerations, one may yet protest that his metaphor commits him willy-nilly to just that sort of mimetic transaction. One understands well enough what he is after, a use of language that while being devoid of all predicative import functions purely referentially, as when one says "Look at that!" But if demonstratives like "that" are readily acknowledged to play that role, the difficulty is to understand how metaphor can be pressed into that service as well. Assume that it can be done, and the paradox will then be resolved as follows. Instead of talking about, that is, predicating something of, the ineffable, we are to be seen to be using talk merely to draw attention to it.

Can it be done using metaphor? Well, there is a certain sort of metaphor manqué or quasi-metaphor that offers Baxandall his best chance of success. Summed up in a single word – catachresis – this rhetorical device might even be said to be a "degenerate case" of metaphor in the mathematician's use of the expression, as when one speaks of the "foot" or "head" of a page. Someone who has never encountered that locution before might well despair on hearing it for the first time. Is the page in question whose foot one is being asked to examine supposed to resemble some exotic animal with a single foot? Amazingly enough, in the urgency of discourse where the context supplies various cues and clues people do often catch on to what their interlocutor is after. A certain part of the page is being referred to, but nothing whatever is being said, or predicated, *of* that item. In particular, no resemblance between that item and any animal or part of any animal has been seriously suggested, though the mimetic faculty has doubtlessly been called upon in some desperate, abortive fashion, as in the "hood" or "bonnet" of a car. Reference without predication: that is what we take to be the goal of catachresis, and it is certainly what Baxandall is after. Abstractly considered, there is no a priori reason why the characteristic metaphors of the art historian should not take that form. As a matter of empirical fact, however, we believe that such quasi- or anti-metaphors play only a marginal role in art historical discourse. Baxandall's own example of "flow" and "movement" strongly suggests that genuine predication has occurred, though we are quite as eager as Baxandall himself to block the proposal that something inside the painting is being said to resemble something outside it. But is that possible: genuine predication by way of metaphor that dispenses with the assertion of a resemblance? Traditionally, one has always supposed that it is impossible; and it is precisely at this point that Goodman poses his sharpest challenge.

II

According to Nelson Goodman, the painting, taken quite on its own as a work of visual art, really does refer outside itself to flow and movement! That is, real flow and real movement which can never be found within the painting. If any such external reference is felt to be of only secondary value when it comes to the primary mission of painting, Goodman has a further surprise to spring on us. Baxandall's painting proves to be *expressive* of flow and movement, and there is nothing more internal or intrinsic to a work of art than its expressiveness where expressiveness is taken as a property (in a sense to be clarified) possessed by the work itself. The painting at hand we may suppose to be entirely non-representational. Movement and flow fail then to be represented by it, and we must accordingly distinguish between representation and expression. Highly expressive of movement, the cavalcade of horsemen on the Parthenon frieze represents it as well. But the statuettes of Giovanni Bologna representing the muscular exertions of Hercules fail in our opinion to be expressive of them. That our opinion here is only too open to controversy merely highlights this difference between representation and expression. Very crudely put, the one is objective, the other subjective, though Goodman even while being a hard-nosed philosopher of science – some feel that he is hardly to be distinguished from a logical positivist – insists on the objectivity of expressive properties. Even he will agree, however, that aesthetic sensibility comes into play much more critically when it comes to the expressive as opposed to the representational features of works of art. Roughly, it can be said that the intention of the artist pretty much determines what is represented by his works, and it is here then that patient scholarly research is best rewarded.

So the *je ne sais quoi* of art is to be found in expressiveness above all? Yes, that is Goodman's thesis, and to this extent he agrees with the ineffabilists: no use of language that is entirely literal can succeed in adequately reporting the expressive features of works of art. With one exception! And here it will be found that the exception really does prove the rule. Take the predicate, "x is highly expressive of movement." That predicate does apply literally to the Parthenon cavalcade. But now we turn to Goodman's deepest insight, linking expressiveness to metaphor. What it is *for* that predicate literally to apply to the cavalcade reduces to this: inscriptions like "highly kinetic" apply to the cavalcade metaphorically.

What it is for a piece of music to be expressive of sadness lies in the fact that the word "sad" applies to it metaphorically. One must resist the notion that what renders the word "sad" metaphorically applicable to the music is some antecedent property, being expressive of sadness, that is possessed by the music. No. If we are to explain to ourselves the meaning of the jargon term "expressive of sadness' (for it hardly belongs to our mother-tongue), the only datum on which we can rely is our application of the word "sad" to certain pieces of music. And it is not a great discovery to find that our use of the word in these cases is non-literal and *a fortiori* metaphorical. We need not deny that a piece of music does possess the property of being expressive of sadness. It is just that the meaning of the inscription type, "expressive of F," cannot be thought available to us from the outset. Goodman is obviously not addressing artistic expressiveness in phenomenological or psychological terms.

On Goodman's account the property of being expressive of sadness (let's call it "E") just is identical with the property of being metaphorically sad. One must tread warily here lest one be charged with using the word "metaphorically" metaphorically, for metaphors are invariably affairs of language. As possessed by the music, the property of being metaphorically sad (namely "M") must then be identical with the property of being such that the *word* "sad" applies to it metaphorically (call that property "W"). The reference to words here cannot be eliminated. Expressiveness as such in a non-verbal or verbal work of art is found to be logically bound up with language, for E=M=W.

Words are no longer to be seen as merely heuristic or opportunistic devices instrumentally designed to draw our attention to certain purely visual features in a painting (although there is no reason to exclude them from this function). The metaphors of the art historian acquire a higher dignity when they describe – yes, describe is the right word – the expressive features of a work and in no merely extrinsic way, thanks to the *logical* connection that obtains between expressiveness and words. It is scarcely possible to exaggerate the importance of this result, let it be taken quite on its own or as providing a resolution to Baxandall's worry. Assume with Goodman that the aesthetic value of a work of art resides largely in its expressive and not its representational features. Assume, to go further, that those features are positively constituted by the applicability of certain words, for example "kinetic," in a metaphorical mode. We can now pose a further question. In what does that very applicability consist? And here the answer can only be this: in the readiness of our best critics – otherwise they would not be the best – to predicate words like "kinetic" in the metaphorical mode to works of art like the Parthenon cavalcade.

Someone must be prepared to apply the word "kinetic" if the cavalcade is to be expressive of movement! The word could hardly be supposed to apply metaphorically to a work if people declined so to apply it. The Goodmanian is committed to the denial of the thesis that "the specific interest of the visual arts" is entirely or exclusively "visual," as if people could be allowed to enjoy the expressive values of the cavalcade in an altogether language-independent fashion. Someone had better (be prepared to) speak up lest the cavalcade be deprived of its expressiveness. Far from being "gratuitous," Baxandall's verbalizing at other people about objects they can already see proves to be no small element in those objects being constituted as works of art. Were he to opt out others would have to take his place. Yes, there is a touch of Bishop Berkeley here with his slogan, "To be is to be perceived," but the only radical factor in the account is the insistence that the critic's words go quite as much into the making of a painting as do the brush strokes of the painter himself. For few philosophers have doubted (G. E. Moore is one) that in one way or another works of art are mind-dependent entities.

Once it is allowed that works of art are teleologically oriented towards the words or labels that critics apply to them, it may not be quite so difficult to accept Goodman's further thesis, namely that the Parthenon cavalcade serves in its own right as a semiotic device that refers to the word "kinetic." There is thus a two-way street. "Kinetic" applies (metaphorically) to the cavalcade, and the cavalcade in its turn refers (metaphorically) to the label "kinetic." There is also reference in the literal mode, for any red spot in a painting is taken by Goodman to refer literally to such labels as "red" and "red spot." In a more Platonic vein we are grudgingly allowed by Goodman to take the red spot to refer to redness itself or the property of being red, and it will be noticed that in the opening sentence of this section we availed ourselves of that license when a painting was said to refer to (the property of) flow and (the property of) movement rather than to the labels, "flow" and "movement." Invited by Goodman to choose whichever version of his theory, nominalist or Platonist,[3] that one finds especially congenial, aestheticians have been strongly moti- vated to go Platonic, contrary to Goodman's own personal preference. As a truculent nominalist long before he embarked on aesthetics, Goodman is inevitably suspected of *parti pris* when he plumps for the nominalist version of his theory of art. The awkwardness of his position is painfully evident to him. How can he expect to be credited when he urges the merits of the nominalist version simply on its own ground, quite apart from any metaphysical baggage one might other- wise have? That then is one factor. More specifically aesthetic can be seen to be the following consideration. Given a choice, no aesthetician today will be attracted to a theory of the non-verbal arts that insists on their being language-dependent. But that is precisely what the nomi- nalist version is committed to, in the most virulent form, as the very expressiveness of the Parthenon cavalcade was found to consist, in no merely extrinsic or accidental fashion, in a reference to words. Why not then replace its reference to the word "kinetic" by a reference to a Platonic object, namely, the property of being kinetic, particularly since it is nominalism not Platonism that has been on the defensive in metaphysics during the past generation? Instead of referring trivially to the mere word "serenity," a painting by Raphael will then be taken to refer to serenity itself where this word "itself" will be recalled in all its resonance from the pages of Plato.

In maintaining that it is the nominalistic version that is to be preferred Goodman turns out to be right. So much so that when it comes specifically to aesthetics even a Platonist might go that route! Notice how we proceed in establishing the equation $E=M=W$. Crucial here is the fact that metaphor is a matter of language, turning on the distinction between a literal and a non-literal use of words. On a Platonic version of the equation one would undertake to grasp the difference between the property of being literally sad and that of being only metaphorically sad in some language-independent way. Nominalistic scruples aside, let the property of being literally sad, namely sadness, be granted from the outset as a Platonic object. Can we be equally confident in the very different property, possessed by sad music, of being metaphorically sad where that is *not* understood to be the property of being such that the word "sad" applies to it metaphorically? (It is not as if the sadness of sad music *resembles* the sadness of a sad person by being a pale version of a person who is only slightly sad.) Our question will be probably answered differently depending on the Platonists' commitment, the more committed being more prone and the less committed being less prone to answer it in the affirmative. Prepared to "cut his losses," the moderate Platonist might well find it prudent to answer in the negative. He will then surprise himself by preferring the nominalistic version of Goodman's aesthetics of expressiveness to the Platonistic one. Goodman's approach is all the more attractive if one has rejected both the resemblance theory of expression, that is, sad music resembles sad people, and the causal theory of expression, that is sad music causes the listener to be sad. Once both these theories are rejected in their myriad versions, where else is there to turn, beyond, that is, to the fact of certain words applying to the music metaphorically? Nowhere is Goodman's reply. If metaphor in its own right can be said to be a kind of proto-poetry or quasi-poetry, the nominalistic account will be more "poetic" than the Platonistic account, and here we have every right to be surprised. Already in the pages of Aristotle there is the explicit charge against Plato that his Forms smack of poetic fictions. Over the centuries nominalism has always been supposed to be the more prosaic and Platonism the more poetic doctrine where the contrast has been felt sometimes to favor the one, other times the other doctrine. After Goodman the situation is reversed.

No unmixed blessing, the nominalistic version even as it succeeds in allaying Baxandall's worry as to the gratuitousness of his verbalizing may be expected to give rise to another worry that is even more disquieting. The age-old quarrel between painting and poetry in their fight for supremacy proves now to be decided in favor of poetry. Poetry is even seen to infect the art of painting at its very core, for the expressive features of a painting are found to be metaphor-dependent in an essential way. So we have embarked on the retrograde course of returning to the literary approach to painting against which Roger Fry and company inveighed so eloquently? Not quite, for they were protesting above all against an excessive emphasis on the representational content of paintings, and that remains far from our central concern. The fact remains that Goodman's is a literary approach, seeing that a painting is taken to be a semiotic device that refers to the labels, that is, predicates, that the best critics apply to it in the exercise of their competence. No longer autonomous, even the most non-representational painting refers outside itself to ... words. For a Jackson Pollock on this account refers to the word "action" quite as much as Gainsborough's *Blue Boy* refers to the word "blue," quite apart from the redundant title of the painting. Momentarily flattered to learn that his verbalizing actually constitutes (part of) the very meaning (recalling Gottlob Frege's use of *Bedeutung*) of a painting, Baxandall will certainly continue to "prefer to remain the augmented man on the bus" who is very far from being tempted "to strike untenably grandiose attitudes." In fact, no more grandiose role could be assigned the art critic than that of achieving the teleological fulfillment of a painting through the predicates he applies to it. Admittedly, the painting refers to those predicates before the critic applies them. If it may be possible along that line to keep the art critic's pretensions within some reasonable bounds, paintings remain essentially oriented towards words, and one may well feel (the words are hardly an exaggeration) that a sin has been committed against the art of painting.

Even a committed Goodmanian can respect these misgivings and undertake to allay them at any rate to some extent. Here is one way, prompted by our mention of Frege who is recognized in any case as the master figure presiding over the linguistic turn in contemporary philosophy. Prior to Frege one supposed naively that the meaning of an expression, for example, "the Morning Star," was its referent. One thus felt free to say that the meaning of "the Morning Star" was the same as that of "the Evening Star" (that is, the planet Venus). After Frege the locution strikes us as distinctly odd, though Frege's own idiom remains to the end pre-Fregean! *Bedeutung* is the ordinary German word for "meaning," and Frege never ceases to say that the *Bedeutung* of "the Morning Star" *is* the same as that of "the Evening Star." Equipped today with Frege's distinction between *Sinn* and *Bedeutung* which we can only understand as a contrast between the sense and reference of our expressions, we find ourselves saying that although "the Morning Star" and "the Evening Star" do have the same reference, they can surely be seen to differ in meaning, that is, sense.

In our post-Fregean wisdom we reject the naive view that takes the meaning of an expression to be its referent. Assume now with Goodman that a painting is a semiotic device, albeit a non-linguistic one like a traffic light. Grant further that the painting refers to the linguistic expressions that apply to it. So the meaning of the painting will indeed consist in those very words, but only on the assumption that the meaning of a symbol, that is to say semiotic device, is to be identified with its referent. But we have rejected that naive view which does, however, underlie the query of the ordinary visitor to a museum when he asks of a problematic painting old or new "What does it mean?" No longer content to shrug off the question as misguided, we *cognoscenti* can now accord it full respect. We will insist, however, that the term "meaning" needs to be disambiguated. Conceding that in one sense of the term the meaning of "the Morning Star" may be grudgingly allowed to be the same as that of "the Evening Star," for they have the same referent, we will insist that in another, much more suitable sense of the term their meanings differ sharply.

What then is the *Sinn* of a painting? Although a routine reading of Frege leaves one utterly at sea here, Michael Dummett provides us with the guidance we need.[4] Start with the routine reading, which takes the *Sinn* or sense of "the Morning Star" to be expressed by some such definite description as "the star in the heavens which is last to be seen when night gives way to day." If the referent of that definite description is none other than the planet Venus, its sense is rather to be identified with a certain "mode of presentation" whereby the planet is "given" to us. By parity of reasoning, the sense of the Parthenon cavalcade must be a mode of presentation whereby its referent, for example, the label "highly kinetic," is given to us. And if the routine reading of Frege is to be trusted, that mode of presentation will have to be expressible by some definite description. Such as? Here we draw a blank. Dummett reminds us, however, that Frege himself drew his original distinction between *Sinn* and *Bedeutung* in terms of the following episode. Travelling south, explorers come upon a mountain and name it "Afla." Later, after extensive wanderings, they come upon what they take to be another mountain and name it "Ateb," failing to realize that they are sighting Afla anew from a different angle. Different modes of presentation of one and the same mountain, the different senses of "Ateb" and "Afla" need not be supposed to be adequately expressed by any sort of standard definite description, and we are now free to take the sense or meaning of the Parthenon cavalcade to be irreducibly visual, even ineffable. To grasp the meaning of the cavalcade it will not indeed suffice merely to use one's eyes. The meaning of the cavalcade is a visual mode of presentation of the referent of the frieze. Presumably to grasp (Frege's word) any such mode of presentation one must understand it to be the way in which something external is being given to us. With his naive view of meaning, the gallery-goer is prepared to identify the meaning of the frieze with the label "highly kinetic," and he can be reproached with being satisfied with mere words. After Frege, however, he should be wise enough to realize that the label can only serve as the referent not the meaning of the frieze where the meaning is rather to be identified with an irreducibly visual mode of presentation of the label.

That Goodman does respect the irreducibly visual character of the visual arts comes through most clearly in his doctrine of exemplification. Slightly deviant, his use of the word "exemplify" needs to be contrasted with its standard use in metaphysics where we are content to say that any old red apple exemplifies (or instantiates) redness or the property of being red simply on the strength of being an example or instance of it. Goodman's use of the word "exemplify" can be explained most readily in terms of his paradigm, the tailor's swatch that serves as a sample of a bolt of cloth. More relevantly, it serves as a sample of a certain complex of properties, such as texture, weave, color, and pattern, to which it refers as a symbol or signifier thanks to its possession of those properties. Not every property of the swatch, for example, being rectangular or scallop-edged, will be signified by it. Those properties to which it does refer, in virtue of possessing them, are now said by Goodman to be *exemplified* by it. (It may be helpful to pronounce the word as "ex-samplified.") Only symbols exemplify, in this use of the word, and they exemplify (serve as samples of) only those properties to which they refer in virtue of possessing them.

The central thesis of Goodman's theory is that works of art are symbols, symbols that refer, and which exemplify what they refer to. Here, indeed, we abstract from the representational features of a work of art, for a picture of Churchill will refer to Churchill without exemplifying him. This is reference by denotation, not by exemplification. Paintings in particular, non-representational and representational alike, are over-all, replete symbols that refer to all the obvious (and not so obvious) visual properties of color and shape that are possessed by them. Any spot of color in a painting must then serve thematically as a sample of its precise hue, brightness, and saturation. Of course, on occasion any such spot could serve an interior decorator as a sample in his dealings with his clients. But such uses must be recognized as non-thematic when it comes to the work of art's functioning as a work of art. Otherwise, we might be forced to classify among works of art the tailor's swatch. Accordingly, Goodman's theory requires of us some antecedent sense of what the thematic uses of a work of art might be. But here one can only be disappointed by the absence of any full-scale account. With some trepidation, we offer the following suggestion that has at least the sanction of tradition. Because it is merely instrumental, the interior decorator's referential use of the spot of color may be ruled out as being insufficiently disinterested to count as a standard use of a painting. Some sort of disinterestedness may then be presumed when a painting is being thematically used as a sample. If one balks, quite naturally, at the thought of a painting being *used*, it is not to be denied that the referentiality of any symbol whatever lies in the use made of it by people. So if paintings are to count as symbols in their proper capacities as paintings, the disinterestedness we have come to demand of the spectator must be found to connect with his or her use of the painting as a signifying device. Beyond that, he must in fact himself be engaged in disinterested reference to what is exemplified by the painting. For if the word "red" refers to redness, that is only thanks to the fact that those who use the word use it to refer to redness.

Apart from disinterestedness, there is the criterion of "organic unity" that may be brought into play to help us specify the thematic use of a painting.[5] It will not be enough to use the painting to refer now to this spot of color and now to that one, as if one were free to use the work merely as a grab-bag of exemplified properties. Although the tailor's swatch may sometimes be used in this atomistic fashion, its principal role is much more holistic, as when the whole complex of relevant properties is called upon. (By "relevant" we refer to the fact that a rectangular swatch does not exemplify rectangularity.) No less holism can be asked of a painting even though the interior decorator has his revenge when he invites a client to hang a particular picture on a wall as but one element in his ensemble. Whether such a fairly holistic use of paintings is to count as thematic we take to be by no means as clear as we would wish. Viewed from the standpoint of Goodman's theory, the issue will turn on whether the purely decorative use of a painting suspends its referentiality. Décor aside, it is not as if the referentiality of a painting were perfectly obvious in the clinical light of the modern gallery where a uniform standard of illumination precludes the shifting play of shadows.

Non-representational paintings in the setting of the clinical gallery often appear to be positively insisting on their non-referentiality to anything outside (or even inside) themselves in an ostentatious affirmation of autonomy. The statement they make, loud and clear, over and over again is that, altogether autonomous, they are not referring to anything whatever. More than that, they say they are not making a statement of any kind. Infected with pragmatic inconsistency, these statements need not be laughed out of court. For although the predicate "x refers to nothing whatever, being altogether autonomous" can never apply literally to any work of art on Goodman's account, it can apply non-literally. Then the work will *express* both non-referentiality and autonomy. And there is no reason why that particular expressive value should not be prized by a Goodmanian. It is less obvious that the work will also refer to the predicate itself, albeit only in the metaphorical mode. This lack of obviousness is no great stumbling-block, for it is rather the mundane case of a spot of color in a traditional painting that may well occasion one's worry. Why should one credit the semiotic role ascribed to it by Goodman?

On Hilary Putnam's Twin Earth it is taken to be obvious that any spot of red in a painting refers to redness. That the word "refer" applies felicitously to cases of this sort, is also taken to be perfectly obvious on Twin Earth, which (as Hilary Putnam explains) is almost indistinguishable from our planet, at any rate on the macro-level. Speaking Twinglish, the inhabitants of Twin Earth one readily supposes to be speaking English, although subtle deviations can be detected in certain uses of words.[6] A case in point arises in connection with the Twinglish sentence "A pink spot in a painting refers to and signifies the precise hue, saturation, and brightness that are possessed by the spot." Taken to be obviously true on Twin Earth, the sentence by no means commands any such immediate assent on our planet, and one is tempted to suppose that the Twinglish word "refer" cannot be precisely synonymous with our own. When it comes, however, to the sentence "The word 'red' refers to redness" they seem to mean exactly what we mean by it. In Goodmanian terms the difference between us has to do with "projection." Starting from a common stock of uses of the word "refer" that Earth and Twin Earth share, they are moved to project the word onto cases where we hesitate to apply it. Despite our hesitation, we can fairly easily imagine ourselves falling in with their use of the word. These considerations lead us to believe that it may be pretty much up to us whether, in voluntaristic fashion, Goodman's theory is to count as true.

Viewed as involving a rational reconstruction of our use of the word "reference," Goodman's theory can only be evaluated in terms of the cash value of its payoffs. One may now be surprised to find that the whole issue of value, understood as involving the normative evaluation of works of art, which Goodman has made a point of studiously avoiding, can only serve to benefit his case. One instance of evaluation will suffice. Ever since Vasari, the Venetians have been congratulated on excelling in color, as the Florentines have been prized for excelling in line. Thanks, then, to being recognized as very fine *examples* of color, though in this regard they are scarcely to be distinguished from certain performances of the autumn season itself, Venetian paintings differ from those performances in being themselves used – qua works of art – as (fine) samples of color, where a sample of F-ness may be defined as an example of F-ness that semiotically refers to F-ness in virtue of being F. Less obvious, however, is the semiotic role of Venetian paintings when it comes to line, though it is no less a fact that in our *thematic* dealings with them (i.e., as works of art) they do serve us as (inferior) examples of line. A profound difference between the two cases lies in ostentatious reference to color being contrasted with what might well appear to be the absence of any reference to line whatsoever on the part of the painting itself or, if you prefer, on the part of the Venetian artist who is hypothesized as being engaged in the activity of signification. It is important to realize why Goodman is debarred from acquiescing in an absence of reference here. Paintings he takes to be *replete* as regards both color and design, which for him entails exemplification across the board, and it may even be the case that the property of being replete counts for him as itself an exemplified property of painting. That the chromatic features of Venetian paintings are indeed exemplified by them we take ourselves to have succeeded in rendering plausible even as we may pay the price of placing in some doubt the exemplification of their features of design.

Which properties a particular work of art exemplifies (as opposed to those it merely possesses) Goodman explicitly identifies as a major issue of interpretation, though he disappoints us by failing to flesh out his thesis in connection with some classic controversy in the history of art criticism. By no means hackneyed, the following instance we take to have a high cash value in its own right. In his negative evaluation of *Paradise Lost* F. R. Leavis convicts it of "tyrannical stylization" as regards the texture of the verse on a line-by-line basis. Although many devotees of the poem will be moved to protest that characterization, and here the quarrel has to do with possession, we are bold enough to regard it as a positive plus for the poem on the strength of which we take the Leavis label to be in fact exemplified by it.

No mere critical verdict issued from on high, our ruling can only be defended by showing how the poem functions in its internal work-ings as a sample of tyrannical stylization. How *we* have found ourselves using it as such a sample must serve as the primary datum of our argument, which others will be committed to accepting to the extent that they recognize themselves in our report. Assuming that the manifest theme of the poem has to do with liberty and bondage, we insist on the aesthetic relevance of its "neglect ... of Rime" that "is to be esteemed as an example set, the first in English, of ancient liberty recovered to Heroic Poem from the troublesome and modern bondage of Rimeing" (preface to *Paradise Lost*). By no means con-fined to the representational content of the poem, the theme of liberty and bondage infects its very texture, and looking ahead to (what we take to be) the great success of the rhyming couplet in Dryden's Virgil and Pope's Homer, we see Milton as being rightly anxious lest in the absence of the "jingling sound" afforded by "like endings" his work should lapse into mere prose. In order to redress the balance a new sort of "hindrance and constraint" will have to be imposed, no longer from without, however, in the fashion of rhyme but now dictated from within as a kind of moral self-discipline. Smacking of the tyranny that Satan at any rate attributes to God, the magisterial stylization of the verse can even be said to be expressive of tyranny seeing that Leavis's use of "tyrannical" is clearly metaphorical. If "Puritan poet" is an oxymoron, the contradiction in terms is vindicated by Milton when he demonstrates how the anarchic imagination can only achieve the perfection of poetry by subjecting itself to hindrance and constraint.

III

Although Baxandall takes metaphor to be one linguistic device available to the art historian, he is by no means tempted to exaggerate its importance. He writes in fact that "words inferential as to cause are the main vehicle of demonstrative precision in art criticism" (p. 461; compare p. 73 in the present volume), as when Adrian Stokes in the course of discussing Donatello's *Dead Christ with Angels* remarks that "the bottom of the angels' robes is gouged and under-cut." (See Baxandall's footnote 9; note 5 in the present volume.) No mere report of current observation, the word, 'gouged,' registers a causal hypothesis designed to explain certain visual features that one might despair of adequately identifying apart from some such hypo-thesis. Terms like "gouged" and "undercut" seem in fact to be largely prized by Baxandall in their *secondary* role as vehicles of demonstra-tive, that is, ostensive, precision rather in the way that metaphors were taken by him to rivet our attention onto certain manifest (but hard to specify) visual features of a picture.

We say "secondary" because the term "gouged" must be taken first and foremost as a word "inferential as to cause"; and the art historian cannot be indifferent to the purely factual hypothesis that gouging did occur precisely where Stokes says it did. Otherwise he would not be an historian. Suppose for a moment that gouging did not take place. Well, the word "gouged" will still succeed as a vehicle of demonstrative precision. Moreover, following Goodman, let the term "gouged" apply to the work but only non-literally, and the relevant visual feature will prove to be rewardingly expressive of gouging. In a more realistic vein we shall assume that gouging did take place, prompting now the following deep question: "Does the Donatello exemplify the label 'gouged'?" Alternatively we can formulate the query in the Platonic mode: "Does the Donatello exemplify the property of having been gouged?"

A test case for our entire approach, the question (call it "Q") challenges us to demonstrate our command of the concept of exemp-lification, though it must not be supposed that mere command of the concept should suffice by itself to supply a cogent answer to Q. We are sure in fact that equally competent Goodmanians will be found to divide on the issue, with most of them probably rejecting our own affirmative answer to Q. The case against us is very strong, and it can be summed up vividly enough in Baxandall's platitude, "the specific interest of the visual arts is visual," which is plausibly taken to rule out the merely historical property (call it "G") of having been gouged, as being aesthetically relevant to the Donatello. A good rule of thumb here to which both sides in the dispute can be expected to subscribe is this: only aesthetically relevant properties of a work of art can be exemplified by it. The property of looking gouged (call it "G*") will then be exemplified. But what about G itself, loaded as it is with inferentiality as to historical causation? Why not just be content with G*?

Why we are not content with G* but insist on G as well will emerge in easy stages as we break out of the straitjacket of western art, aided and abetted by Baxandall's extraordinary forays into the exotica of China and Nigeria. Two things should be clear at the outset. The main tradition of western art is powerfully disposed to answer Q in the negative thanks to its emphasis on perceptual surface. Accordingly, what goes on behind the scenes in the artist's studio, gouging or whatever, can only be of scholarly interest. Ergo the dignity of art history, taken seriously as history, proves to be greatly enhanced by our affirmative answer to Q. That answer can be defended, however, only if we have at hand some non-western model to which we can convincingly appeal.

It is no accident that Baxandall's use of Stokes is deposited almost entirely in a footnote, seeing that the label "gouged and undercut" does involve exposure to the backstage arcana of the studio. How, then, to break down the barrier between gallery and studio, thereby releasing "a mature inferential vocabulary in full play" with all its "formidable demonstrative precision and punch?" Baxandall's prize exhibit turns out to be "the resources classical Chinese criticism had for inferential characterization of the painter's brush marks." Witness the difference between wrist-dominant and finger-dominant strokes or dragged marks and slippery ones or splashed-ink ones and broken-ink ones, cutting strokes and led strokes and so forth. One sort of brush mark could even be identified by the "sousing" noise made by the stroke. Truly a mature inferential vocabulary, but what is of decisive importance here is the fact that an eighteenth-century critic like Shen Tsung-hsien could count on readers of the mandarin class who were themselves "active users of the calligraphic brush so that there was a firm background of reference in everyone's experience." Not that everyone need be supposed to have been a painter even of the amateur variety, but there was a bridge available between the art of painting proper and the practice of mandarin calligraphy.

By no means merely optical in emphasis, classical Chinese painting we take to be powerfully kinaesthetic in its appeal to the *cognoscenti* who are expected to relish the very draggedness of the dragged marks and the slipperiness of the slippery ones through a vicarious participation in the painter's activity in applying paint to a surface. Notice, however, that these kinaesthetic-cum-manual values figure not at all when it comes to "the demonstrative precision and punch" of Chinese criticism. "Demonstrative" here has to do solely with the critic's drawing our attention to currently available optical features that he can only identify by way of inference to causal antecedents. That at any rate is how Baxandall, himself a prisoner of the optical emphasis in western art, chooses to understand the relevance of Chinese to western criticism. What counts is the aesthetic surface in its visual immediacy, and any "words inferential as to cause" prove accordingly to be mere means, however roundabout, towards the recognition of otherwise ineffable features of the painted surface before us. In effect, process labels like "dragged" and "slippery" or "gouged" and "undercut" are taken to be at once possessed but unexemplified by visual works of art, according to this optical approach which insists on the thematic relevance of product labels alone. That Baxandall's sensibility is in fact keenly responsive to kinaesthetic values in their own right we have no doubt whatever, and it is largely under the spell of his rich sensibility that we protest against his reductive account of process labels in art criticism.

Our principal objection to the optical approach rests finally on a value judgment that, once it is brought out into the open, we expect to be widely shared. Contrast a purely visual response to the Donatello with one that has been enriched by a vicarious participation in the sculptor's kinaesthetic activity of gouging and undercutting. Although we freely acknowledge that there are indeed cases where less is more, we submit that the present instance is not one of them. We are not arguing from general principles, as if we were insisting in a Wagnerian mode that opera must be the supreme art thanks to integrating all or most of the others. Sticking to the art of sculpture, the issue turns on whether process labels are to be added to product ones when it comes to the overall evaluation of this or that piece of sculpture. Some process labels may be expected to function purely in the subservient mode of being "demonstrative"; others will operate rather in the intrinsic mode of exemplification. As to which is which in particular cases, fierce controversy may well erupt and a single critic may even find himself pulled in opposite directions. Listen to Stokes (as quoted by Baxandall):

To Donatello, changes of surface meant little more than light and shade, chiaroscuro, the instruments of plastic organization. The bottom of the angels' robes is gouged and undercut so as to provide a contrast to the open planes of Christ's nude torso.

The terms "light," "shade," and "chiaroscuro" we take to be painterly in emphasis while the term "changes of surface" we take to be specifically sculptural. Finally, the term "plastic organization" we take to be at once heavily sculptural and rich in tactile invitations, looking ahead to "open planes" as well as "gouged and undercut." The whole passage verges on incoherence. Initially, the sculptural "changes of surface" are taken to be subservient to the painterly value of chiaroscuro which, however, is taken in its turn to be subservient to the sculptural-cum-tactile values of plastic organization. Stokes is even prepared to say that "the composition is not so much founded upon the interrelationships of adjoining surfaces as upon the broader principles of chiaroscuro." Surely not. The sheer physicality of the adjoining surfaces cannot be allowed to yield to the airy interplay of light and shade. Talk about betraying one art to another, in this case sculpture to painting!

If these negative comments strike one as much too pejorative to be warranted, read on. Highly suggestive to the Goodmanian, with his insistence on a work of art being one sort of semiotic device, must be Stokes's use of the semantic term "meant." Changes of surface, which pretty much sum up the sculptor's art in any case, are said to mean little more than light and shade, in a Donatello. This is what they signify, and the Goodmanian will then ask whether the signifying function is to be taken here in the literal or in the non-literal mode. Well, the answer is easy. Literally speaking, a sculpture cannot fail to be founded on the interrelationships of its adjoining surfaces. Only a painting could be literally founded on the principles of chiaroscuro. It is only metaphorically speaking, then, that the Donatello could be so founded, in which case it will prove expressive of chiaroscuro. No betrayal to painting here, any more than the Parthenon cavalcade's being expressive of motion involves a betrayal to the art of cinema. Nor are we to suppose that in the two cases one art is aspiring to the condition of another. Any such suggestion betrays a failure to understand Goodman's theory of expression.

So maybe the process label "gouged," with its involvement in the sheer physicality of the Donatello, fails to be exemplified by it after all! Looking beyond the immediate dialectic to more general consideration, have we not contrasted Chinese with western art precisely on this one point, namely that the former exemplifies process as well as product labels whereas the latter is, at the very least, strongly inhibited from doing so? That, at any rate, has been our feeling about the two arts, but we do not pretend to speak with any authority as regards either of them. The only authority to which we do pretend, in all its fallibility, consists in our philosophical grasp of the relevance of Goodman's aesthetics to the verbalizing of the art historian.

As regards Stokes, in particular in his encounter with the Donatello, we do not doubt that there are two items, *a* and *b*, a *contrast* between which is taken to be exemplified by the composition. One of the items is easy enough to specify, namely the open planes of Christ's nude torso. The other is more difficult although even here we know that it consists in certain features (appertaining to the bottom of the angels' robes) that have been brought about through a process of gouging and undercutting. If Baxandall is to be believed, the ideal spectator need not recognize those features *as* involving any such historical process of gouging and undercutting. It is enough to recognize them in a purely optical mode; and it must be confessed that if the whole point of the contrast between the two items lies in an effect of chiaroscuro, as Stokes suggests, Baxandall must be allowed to be almost certainly right. The grounds of our own reluctance to accept their joint verdict we have made plain enough in our sheer relish of the kinaesthetic physicality packed into "gouged and undercut." Let the consensus of art historical opinion go against us, however, and we are only too ready to submit to the judgment of our betters. By way of compensation, we only ask that the concept of exemplification should be acknowledged and even appropriated as a useful analytical tool. If we have focused solely on the more formalistic features of the Donatello, we do not doubt that its representational content is also relevant to any effort to answer Q; and it is precisely in the interplay between the two sorts of consideration – representational and formalistic – that further discussion of the issue may be expected to proceed.

IV

Reaching far afield, what of the following outlandish suggestion? There are certain German wood carvings that exemplify – the whole issue turns on this word "exemplify" – the Yoruba term dídón even though *dídón* has hitherto only been applied locally to indigenous sculptures of Nigeria. Well, not quite. Maybe the term has been applied to those wood carvings, by Baxandall, when he writes,

I would very much like to have genuine access to the Nigerian Yoruba critical term *dídón* ... it would cover much of an interest I find important in some German wood carvings I study. But *dídón* is a fragment of Yoruba critical concepts and takes its rich meaning from just this set of relations. Even for my private exploratory purposes I cannot possess it except in a crude and shallow, a dissociated way ...

Let us suppose, then, that on being exposed to these German carvings the Nigerian *cognoscenti* applaud some of them as being very fine examples of *dídón*, so fine in fact as to be almost equal to the best specimens of their own country. Reminiscent of Stokes's concern with the light and shade of adjoining surfaces, "*dídón* ... indicates a degree of smooth but not glossy luminosity in the surfaces of sculpture, closely related to the contrast of these with sharp shadows and edges." Far from being content merely to acknowledge these German carvings as being some fine, others not so fine, examples of *dídón*, Nigerian connoisseurs may take the important, further step of using them as samples – good, bad, and indifferent – of *dídón*, and it is precisely here in the use of a work of art as a sample that Goodman's semiotics of art is centered. How dressmaker and client collaborate in their use of the tailor's swatch as a signifier provides us with our sole paradigm of exemplification, to which we are invited by Goodman to assimilate works of art, and not merely in the unthematic use of them that might be made by the interior decorator.

Puzzled by Goodman's invitation, his critics continue to doubt that works of art do in fact function characteristically, in their thematic role as works of art, as semiotic devices. Taking rapt contemplation to be the optimum response to a work of art, one may even protest that any thought of using a work of art in any capacity, for example, as propaganda in the case of *Guernica*, can only be justified as a kind of second-best. Notice, however, that rapt contemplation of a tailor's swatch, precisely in its capacity of signifying a subtle kind of weave which it instantiates, and quite apart from any sartorial considerations, has been known to occur on more than one occasion. Goodman's paradigm of exemplification can thereby be accommodated still more closely to the desiderata, for example, disinterested pleasure, of works of art.

Notice also how Goodman's paradigm connects in the most intimate fashion with Baxandall's preoccupation with "seen surface texture" as to which "the European languages discriminate ... very coarsely." (p. 456; p. 68 in the present volume) The swatch in fact is used expressly in order to remedy that defect of language from which Baxandall seeks to free himself by having recourse to the Yoruba term *dídón*, let it be only for his "private exploratory purposes." For he is keenly sensitive to the following difficulty. "Loanwords" like *dídón* are "cultural orphans, not properly part of the collective framework of our thinking," and it is that framework which might well be supposed to constitute the semiotic import (reverting to Goodman) of western works of art like Baxandall's German wood carvings. How then could they be taken seriously to exemplify the exotic label *dídón*? In order to do so these German carvings would have to refer trans-historically to a network of Yoruba labels lying altogether outside the frame of reference available to the German artists involved. It is very much as if one dared to argue that the predicate "x is evocative of the 1968 Mylai massacre committed by American troops in Vietnam" was actually exemplified, anachronistically enough, by the following lines in *The Waste Land*:

> There I saw one I knew, and stopped him crying: "Stetson!
> "You who were with me in the ships at Mylae!
> "That corpse you planted last year in your garden,
> "Has it begun to sprout? Will it bloom this year? ..."

Granted that the predicate does apply to these lines, albeit retrospectively, it is quite another matter to insist that they are semiotically engaged, timelessly, in referring to the predicate.

There are in fact two rules of thumb regarding exemplification that come into conflict here, one purely aesthetic, the other historical. The aesthetic or evaluative principle would have us count as exemplified any features of an art work whose recognition enhances our thematic, that is, aesthetic, response to the work. Let it be agreed (and one is always free of course to contest this point) that the interplay of Mylai and Mylae enriches the poem – compare the patina acquired by bronzes through weathering – and one will then be strongly motivated to count it as exemplified.

According to the historical principle, however, reference as such by any signifier, non-linguistic as well as linguistic, is largely determined by the intentions (and conventions) operative at the moment that the signifying act is performed. How then could the Mylai massacre figure proleptically among the "fragments I have shored against my ruins," even granting that "I Tiresias have foresuffered all?" Well, we may be forced to distinguish between two modes of exemplification, one primary or original, the other secondary or acquired, where it is only the former that is determined by the artist's intentions. Thus even the label "classic," which is ostentatiously attached to the Parthenon frieze, may be exemplified by it only in the secondary mode. Did the Greek sculptors know that they were engaged in producing classic art? Or is the very concept of the classic rather to be viewed as at once Hellenistic and post-classical, as alien to the Parthenon as *dídón* is to the German wood carvings? That we do in fact conjure with the Parthenon as a supreme sample of classical art in our thematic dealings with it, goes to show that we at any rate use it, sometimes perhaps pejoratively, to refer to the classical. If even a tailor's swatch – for example, a slightly abraded piece of denim – may come in time, as fashions in bluejeans change, to exemplify a property, abradedness, that was absent from its original repertoire, much the same process can be expected with works of art. We dare hypothesize in fact that a mature response to art consists in the recognition of an interplay between these two modes of exemplification, primary and secondary, as when one takes the Parthenon to exemplify the label "classical" in the latter but not in the former mode.

In the first instance a piece of philosophical jargon, Goodman's term, "exemplification," can succeed in fully paying its way only in the rough-and-tumble of art historical controversy. If Baxandall's allusion to *dídón* poses one sort of challenge, another puzzle case may be implicit in Richard Wollheim's recent discussion of Cézanne where he takes an earlier painting, *View of Auvers*, to be a case of "pre-style" or a "non-stylistic" work as contrasted with the later fully stylistic work *View of Médan*.[7] Although both works possess the property of being a Cézanne, Wollheim may be urging in effect that only the latter, later work exemplifies the property. Fully realized Cézannes will certainly be used by us as exemplary samples of this stylistic property, and we take such use to be as much intra-personal as inter-personal. Furthermore, encouraged by Goodman's theory, we are led to view such inter- as well as intra-personal uses as being fully thematic when it comes to appreciating a work of art as a work of art.

Less obviously thematic we take to be the floral arrangements that commercial florists have been known to read off from paintings of Fantin-Latour, particularly since, as sold on the market, these arrangements were not designed to allude to the paintings. Allusion to Beethoven's Fifth Symphony was ostentatiously evident in the opening notes, signifying V for victory in Morse code, that introduced

BBC broadcasts into Nazi-occupied Europe, and we are accordingly prepared to regard such public quotations as being at least as thematic as any private humming to oneself. Quoting from a work, publicly or privately, can now be seen to be one of those acts in the performance of which thematic appreciation of a work of art might be supposed to consist. Semiotic in their very nature, these acts of quotation and allusion particularly invite a Goodmanian approach; and in that vein one can hardly refrain from asking whether reproductions of the *Mona Lisa*, in whole or in part, are not properly to be viewed as (more or less accurate) quotations of the original that inevitably refer back to it.

Geoffrey Grigson having said that the best critics are those who quote best, criticism itself can be recognized to be another of those acts in which the thematic appreciation of works of art consist. Granted further that criticism can be expected to be largely verbal in character, one will no longer demur at the thesis that linguistic activity can enter deeply into the thematic appreciation of non-verbal works of art. Even so, one may well wonder at how precisely this interplay of verbal and non-verbal considerations can be understood to proceed on a level of detail. Two sorts of words above all (*dídón* is a third case) Baxandall has superbly emphasized, namely words metaphorical and words inferential as to cause, in regard to both of which the semiotic aesthetics of Nelson Goodman has proved to be especially rewarding.

NOTES

1 Michael Baxandall, "The Language of Art History," *New Literary History*, 10 (Spring, 1979), pp. 453–464. (Michael Baxandall's revised version of this article appears as chapter 5 in this volume.)

2 Nelson Goodman, *Languages of Art: An Approach to a Theory of Symbols* (Indianapolis, 1976), chapter 2.

3 Platonists insist that all red things have something in common, namely redness, in virtue of which they are called "red." Being an abstract entity, redness, that is the property of being red, lies outside space and time. Denouncing these items as the merest fictions, the nominalist refuses to look beyond the simple fact that the word or label or *nomen* "red" applies to all red things.

4 Michael Dummett, *Frege: Philosophy of Language* (London, 1973; Cambridge, Mass., 1981), chapter 5, especially pp. 97–98.

5 But see Catherine Lord, "Organic Unity Reconsidered," *Journal of Aesthetics and Art Criticism*, 22 (Spring 1964).

6 Putnam's prize exhibit has to do with the stuff on Twin Earth that to all appearances we would suppose to be water, and which they call "water," drinking it, bathing in it, etc. The trouble is that on the micro-level the stuff is found to be chemically composed of XYZ and not H_2O. Does our word "water" (as it is used by the plain man not the scientist) apply to that stuff? According to the traditional theory of meaning, which goes by the manifest qualities of things and which is traced back to John Locke, the answer is "yes." Answering "no," Putnam's revolutionary proposal insists that our word "water" means rather something like "stuff that has the nature, i.e., micro-structure, of this stuff here" where a pointing gesture comes into play. Putnam's seminal discussion "The Meaning of 'Meaning' " appears in vol. II of his *Philosophical Papers* (Cambridge, 1975), pp. 215–21.
7 Richard Wollheim, *Painting as an Art* (Bollingen Series, 15: 3, Princeton, N.J. and London 1987), pp. 28–29.

Figurative language in art history

CARL R. HAUSMAN

Art historians sometimes devise ways of using verbal language to focus attention on the intrinsic qualities of works of art.[1] They do so when their purpose is to put us in direct contact with created works of art insofar as they are regarded in abstraction from cultural contexts. This endeavor faces a special difficulty when it concerns works of art that are outcomes of creative acts. The discourse used for interpreting the new created meanings exhibited in these outcomes must be stretched beyond the resources of language available up to the time of the creation. Language needs to articulate new meanings that are appropriate to the new meanings of the outcome.

In what follows, I shall consider how figurative language – specifically, metaphor – may be creative and thus integral to this stretching of language. After first sketching the main ingredients of my suggestions, I shall turn to some of the uses of interpretive discourse found in the work of Svetlana Alpers and Michael Baxandall.[2] This application is intended both to indicate a way of using metaphor in art criticism and to offer a partial justification or confirmation of my suggestions.

THE NEED FOR FIGURATIVE LANGUAGE

Radical creativity

The point that language sometimes is stretched and constitutive of new meanings presupposes that there is radical creativity in the world. Let me then begin by reviewing rather quickly some of the reasons I have offered elsewhere in support of this presupposition.[3]

The meaning of "radical creativity"

The term "creativity" applies to a condition for bringing something into being. Since Kant wrote in his *Critique of Judgment* that genius in fine art is the capacity to produce an outcome that exhibits originality and exemplarity and that cannot be taught, the idea of creativity, through the tradition of Romanticism in the nineteenth century, has been given a radical sense according to which to create is to bring into being something new that may be cognitively significant and irreducible. According to this conception of creativity, the term "created outcome" refers to a product of an activity that is new in the sense that it exhibits a form or type of articulation that is intelligible, although it is not fully traceable to antecedent conditions and meanings. I have called this kind of newness "Novelty Proper" to distinguish it from newness of particularity, which is found in any individual thing insofar as it is different from all other individuals. Let me briefly develop this idea of radical newness.

I suggest three expectations or criteria for creativity: newness, newness of intelligibility, and valuable new intelligibility.[4] With respect to the third expectation, it should be said that the value expected is both inherent and instrumental. The latter function of the created value is the condition for its advancing the style, school, or tradition into which the creation is introduced. In the context of the present discussion, I shall put questions about this and inherent value aside.

Of particular importance are the first and second criteria, both of which concern the kind of newness attributable to a created outcome. Such newness must be more and other than numerical newness, because every distinguishable thing we experience, including each individual experience itself, is numerically new. But a creation is new in the more extreme, radical sense; otherwise, a work of an artistic genius would be no different with respect to its newness than a piece of hackwork, a duplicated photograph, or even a stone. The more radical kind of newness (Novelty Proper) required is newness of type, that is, newness of intelligibility. Thus, the newness expected is attributed to an unpredicted and unpredictable integration of components that appears to have an identity sufficient to differentiate it from the identities of past integrations and syntheses. It is with respect to this differentiation that there is a resistance on the part of the creation to being reduced to, or derived from, what was intelligible before the advent of the creation.

There are many issues surrounding this brief account of what we expect of a creation. However, I must bypass these in order to return to the point that instances of radical creation do sometimes occur in the world.

Reasons for acknowledging radical creativity
That there is Novelty Proper exemplified in some products of activities – activities that we call "creative" in part because they seem to have led to results that exemplify Novelty Proper – is, I submit, at least phenomenologically incontrovertible. If one denies that such products are "really" instances of Novelty Proper, but insists that they are instead unfamiliar or merely surprising occurrences that can be understood in familiar terms, given time and sufficient information about data and laws or regularities, then one presupposes some form of metaphysical determinism. By "determinism" I refer, among other things, to any view that supposes that every thing and event is in principle predictable. Arguments against this have been offered not only in my own work but also, and probably more convincingly, by Charles Peirce (as well as others).[5] In short, these arguments turn on the point that the deterministic position requires that the phenomenological presentation or the observations of occurrences of newly intelligible outcomes be regarded as appearances hiding implicit, pre-determined necessities. What is observed as radically new is only something surprising that will be understood when more knowledge about antecedent circumstances and laws is gained. Yet the determinism that proposes this is faced with issues that are as puzzling as – indeed, more challenging to intelligibility than – the acknowledged appearances of spontaneity affirmed by anti-determinism, which insists that there is irreducible irregularity or spontaneity in the world. The determinist presupposes that all the regularities that supposedly would make phenomena exhibiting spontaneity intelligible are generated all at once in some prior state of the universe. The anti-determinist takes irregularity and what appears as spontaneous, new intelligibility to be real and incremental in the evolution of the universe.

The puzzle of unfamiliarity and intelligibility
Before turning to the relevance of the view that creativity is real to the topic of metaphor, let me pause for a moment to address an issue raised by this view. The issue concerns a puzzle that is unavoidable for both determinism and anti-determinism. How is it possible to grasp cognitively something that is unintelligible in terms of our

established expectations of intelligibility? The determinist faces this because even if the initial unintelligibility given in something unfamiliar is to be rendered intelligible in terms of familiar data and regularities, there must be an initial recognition of the possibility of subsequent connection between the unfamiliar and the familiar. Unless the determinist denies even the appearance of spontaneity and newness of intelligibility, this appearance must somehow be cognized, or recognized as potentially intelligible, before it is rendered familiar.

What I must appeal to here is a willingness on the part of the reader to agree that sometimes human beings have pre-cognitive experiences that exhibit the possibility of being cognized or rendered intelligible. Thus, in order to understand created outcomes with reference to their Novelty Proper, it is necessary to engage in some degree of transformation of our ways of intelligent response. In making this claim, I must emphasize that by "understanding," in the context of initially apprehending created outcomes, I refer not to the development of an inferential process by which what is said to be understood is derived deductively or inductively from prior thinking. Rather, I refer to an incipient inferential process by which one who understands recognizes that the thing to be understood is an integration that shows signs, as a logical or real possibility, of being related to future thoughts.[6] Thus, it is appropriate to regard this kind of understanding as "immediate apprehension of an intelligible identity," or what R. G. Collingwood calls "primary thought," which is pre-relational or pre-conceptual. In any case, whatever the mode of apprehension be called, we face the problem of how such immediate apprehension can concern intelligible identity when that identity is as yet not wholly familiar – that is, it is unconnected with available, familiar ways of identifying things. This is a problem faced by all epistemologies that are concerned with the origin of relational thinking – which is to be caught in a hermeneutical circle of accounting for how we can know relations without first knowing relata, which poses the problem of accounting for how we can know relata unless they are recognized for what they are in some relation.

My answer to this question as it is applied to our topic of apprehending new intelligibility consists of two points. First, it should be emphasized that the initial, pre-cognitive apprehension of new intelligibility is an apprehension of something attended to that is unique, and that is recognized as unique. Such recognition of what is new is not an understanding of the relationships the new object of attention may have to previously and subsequently known works; consequently, it is not yet knowledge that what is confronted is not merely something surprising, perhaps bizarre, rather than an instance of Novelty Proper. A second stage of attention is required for this further recognition, a stage in which awareness of actual and potential relations is adumbrated. Context, then, must come into play as attention develops from the initial pre-cognitive experience into a cognitive experience.[7] Thus, the second point to be mentioned in responding to the problem of the origin of relational thinking is that we must acknowledge some fundamental transforming act by which what was new and initially unrelated becomes related to relata, some of which themselves depend on the new thing. Cognizing something manifesting novelty requires recognizing that what is new in that thing has sufficient structure to be identified by relations to be discovered and to be relevant to relations that may function in its future.

Metaphors as created outcomes

Let me next propose that metaphors are at least sometimes instances of radical creativity. This claim is made in light of the interactionist view that some metaphors create meanings that result from mutual influences of the clusters of meanings or connotations implied by the key terms of the metaphor. This view may be supported by contrasting metaphors with another candidate for achieving linguistic change, namely, analogy. If analogies enhance our ways of using language, they do not do so by generating significance that is radically new. Analogies as traditionally understood are paraphrasable or translatable into literal meanings – relations and relata – to which they can be reduced without remainder. In contrast, metaphors, according to the interactionist view, are irreducible. Thus, the creative achievement of metaphors can be highlighted by comparison with analogies.

Three reasons support the conclusion that creative metaphors are distinct from analogies. The first depends on an appeal to our ways of interpreting metaphors. This point can be made by the hypothetical proposal that there must have been a first utterance of verbal significance. This suggests that there must have been at least one radically new achievement, the original utterance of verbal linguistic meaning having no established system of meanings to which to be traced and reduced. It will not do to attempt to trace such meaning to non-verbal modes of communication, because there would still be the need to leap from the meanings of physical gesture or other modes to the verbal medium. It should be observed, however, that we no longer need to utter the first word before there are words. Nevertheless, we sometimes need to utter new meanings within established language – new meanings that not only add quantitatively to the meanings already available within the system of meanings articulated in the evolving language, but that also may enhance the language qualitatively in the sense of giving it new possibilities as distinct from simply giving it determinate associations and references, or simply different ways of saying the same thing. In this limited way, we still do need to utter the first word. Can analogies meet this need? I think not, at least given the way they are traditionally conceived, namely, as equivalent to expressions referring to familiar although sometimes unnoticed relations. As such, they do not offer radically new meaning, but seem to be the creatures of a determinism which construes everything as traceable to antecedent meaning. Yet if some changes in language are not at bottom pre-formed in some deterministic scheme according to which such changes are inherent or implicit in thought and language, or are in principle predictable, then there must be some instances of linguistic change that are irreducible. What other use of language, then, can perform the function of articulating new meaning that is not reducible? The interactionist view proposes that this function of language is found in metaphors, for some metaphors cannot be identical with analogies – which is to say that, unlike analogies, at least some metaphors are irreducible.

It should be mentioned that contrasting metaphors with analogies depends on an appeal to our recognition that if creative metaphors were elliptical similes or translatable as analogies, they would be impoverished, at least to the degree that they lose the force or impact granted them insofar as they take us beyond the familiar and the antecedent. This appeal to our responses is reinforced by the second reason for distinguishing metaphors from analogies.

The second reason for the distinction has been suggested by Nelson Goodman and Mary Hesse, as well as others. It consists of the point that when we try to understand and explain analogies, we fall back on using metaphors, that is, on other figures of speech that are untranslatable by literal language. For instance, to make use of Goodman's argument, if one treats the metaphorical expression "the painting is sad" as a simile, we should see that "What the simile says in effect is that person and picture are alike in being sad, the one literally and the

other metaphorically."[8] Or, to take another example, an atom, understood in terms of Bohr's theory, is a miniature solar system metaphorically, because the idea of "solar system" applies differently to it
than to that within which our earth orbits. There are clusters of
differences that give force to the figure of speech and that help it work
in generating new meaning assigned to the concept of the atom as it
was available before Bohr's metaphor. This is not to say that the
conception of a miniature solar system cannot, and does not, also
function as a model and as a metaphor that is restricted so that it
serves as an analogy for purposes of explanation. Such paraphrases
may help to explain creative metaphors even though they are not
therefore equivalent expressions.

The third reason overlaps the second, and consists of the observation that when we try to paraphrase a creative metaphor, we
inevitably encounter the need to continue filling out the paraphrase.
No finite set of statements is sufficient to exhaust the meaning of the
metaphor. Thus Stanley Cavell points out that if we try to paraphrase
Shakespeare's "Juliet is the sun," said by Romeo, we need to add
"and-so-on" to whatever number of paraphrases we offer.[9] The
conception of sound as waves works against a background of comparisons – pulsating, rhythmic changes noticed in both sounds and
visible waves. Yet these comparisons serve to approximate rather
than capture the significance of the figure. Similarly, comparisons
between the properties of waves and the propagation of light do not
exhaust the significance of the metaphor "light is waves." Otherwise,
the conception of waves could be dispensed with as a model for light.

Such experiences promise what Max Black called "resonance,"
which he attributed to creative metaphors. We expect unfamiliar
appearances that are not at the moment intelligible to resonate with
future intelligibility. Further, this resonance is made possible by the
new appearance with which the process started. Thus, as Max Black,
Paul Henle, and others (including myself) have suggested, new
similarities or relations may be created by the creative event that
advances language and has resonance.[10]

Metaphors as appropriate for art criticism

The point that metaphors offer irreducible, unparaphrasable, and
created meanings may now be applied to art criticism. It seems to me
that if a critic, or art historian acting as critic, in order to approach the
intrinsic meaning of created works of art, searches for the most apt

way to apply verbal expressions to these, then metaphor is at least one of the appropriate ways, if not the most appropriate way, to do this. When instances of creativity occur in art, our concepts and our language expressing these must undergo evolution. As already suggested, familiar ways of speaking and expressing interpretations of these works are challenged. New ways of using language are needed to "catch up" to the new outcome. The critic George Heard Hamilton makes this point nicely in discussing Cézanne. He explains that critics during Cézanne's time "had to find verbal equivalents for what seemed to them unorthodox pictorial situations for which few of the customary words were adequate or relevant. Until new terms could be found the old ones necessarily imparted a negative, derogatory tone to such criticism." Hamilton then points out that the new terms that served more adequate expressions in interpretation emerged only after Cézanne's death. They include "architectonic," "plasticity," and "spatial tension," which became almost standard parts of the Cézanne criticism lexicon.[11] It should be noted that the new terms Hamilton identifies are not neologisms. Instead, they are familiar terms moved to an unfamiliar context. The application of terms such as these to works of art constitutes metaphors – just as is the more stereotyped expression, "This is a sad painting," cited by Nelson Goodman as one of his key examples of metaphor.[12] Metaphors, then, are necessary not only when criticism faces new creation, but also each time an art historian returns to a former advance and finds – and tries to help us see – something or some aspect about a created outcome that had not yet been recognized. They are necessary each time formerly interpreted works are seen in a new light and discovered to have created significance not formerly recognized. This is illustrated well by Svetlana Alpers's account of seventeenth-century Dutch art, which will be treated at greater length later. Alpers works from a frame of reference that is temporally distant from the styles that are subjects of her study. Thus, she deals with examples that already have been subjected to attempts to find adequate discourse for whatever new or created character they manifest. But within her framework, she must find discourse that brings out unnoticed aspects that, presumably, flow from the newness of style already addressed by those critics who have tried to show their audience what merits attention in the paintings. In short, there is a uniqueness to be dealt with in created outcomes that places limits on, and also is a source for, new interpretation.[13] Metaphor is appropriate for this evolving task. However, that it is so is particularly evident from the perspective of the interaction view. Let me then return to this way of understanding metaphor.

The appropriateness of the interaction view of metaphor

According to interactionism, some metaphors are creative by virtue of the interacting of two or more key terms or meaning units. The terms that interact are sufficiently different in domains of connotations and reference to exhibit at least a minimal degree of tension or incongruence in context. The more radical way of making this point is to say that the terms are in tension because either they belong to different, conflicting categories or the contexts of the metaphors in which they appear show that a literal reading is inappropriate. Without deciding whether the domains of connotations and references constitute different categories, it should be said that these constitute domains of significance that show some incongruity with themselves or with the context of the metaphor when understood literally, that is, as these significances have been accepted according to established conventions before they were linked in the metaphor. For instance, to take the overworked "Man is a wolf," the literal or standard significance of "man" – including upright posture, tool-making and using, rationality, and so on – conflicts with the literal or standard significance of "wolf" – including being four-legged, hairy, territorial, and so on. However, the connotations (including logical intention and psychological associations) of these terms interact with and influence one another. The significance of "man" and the significance of "wolf" both change sufficiently so that after the introduction of the expression into the language, conceptions of man and wolf are not what they once were. Men are beastly and wolves are less beastly – perhaps more human. Or to take an example from a situation in the history of art that has already been mentioned, the statement, "Cézanne's painting in his middle period builds form out of plasticity of color," brings together the terms "painting," "plasticity," and "color," so that "plasticity" and "color" contribute to a tension between one another. The connotations and references of these terms, understood apart from and prior to the occurrence of the expression, affect one another, and when applied to Cézanne's work, they generate a new way of seeing Cézanne's style. For instance, his paintings, or some of them, can be seen as architectonic and, by virtue of their newness, as Cubistic seeds of the future. Their colors are malleable yet resistant; their forms are color-planes that construct solid objects; their patches of brush strokes build interlocking spaces. At the same time, what it is to be architectonic – say, to be a mountain – is now affected by seeing in a Cézannish way. It is examples such as this, of course, that will be the main concern of this study.

Interactive metaphors, then, serve well as the ingredients of art historians' language when it is aimed at the uniqueness of the new intelligibility of a particular work of art. They are appropriate – or, more accurately, the least inappropriate – ways of speaking or writing for this purpose, because they exemplify the structure of created outcomes. Their structure is an integration of dissonant meanings that exhibits a *Gestalt*-like new meaning that is not reducible to the integration – this new meaning is referred to by I. A. Richards as "the resultant meaning," by Paul Henle as "induced content," and by Max Black as a "created similarity."[14] Metaphors integrate familiar meanings and their established references with other familiar meanings that are appropriate for different domains or categories. In generating such dissonance of meanings, they break with what was established and familiar, and new insight emerges. This structure, common to creative verbal metaphors and non-verbal created outcomes, can perhaps better be regarded as a family resemblance, where the members of the family exhibit tensions as well as intersecting strands of meanings. In any case, they are ready to serve as models of the things to which they are applied. And, given this their structure, they are capable of leading us beyond established ways of speaking about, and seeing, works of art. In having the fundamental kinship of exhibiting a created structure of the sort exhibited in instances of creation in the visual arts, they are not restricted to the past ways of matching language with prior creations. They can then spawn new ways of speaking about, and seeing, the created works with which they are concerned.

For example, suppose that we try to describe one of Cézanne's paintings with the language established for Impressionism. The idea of the evanescence of color-atmosphere itself would be inadequate to the Cézanne. But if the fragility and purity of light and color were mentioned in connection with still older ideas drawn from pre-Impressionist landscape painting such as linear continuity and breadth of color areas, then we have an interaction that might well have prompted the term "plasticity" and later "architectonic" as apt avenues of access to Cézanne's middle period.

Interactive metaphors, then, are capable of stretching language to accommodate the critic's verbal responses to created outcomes to the extent that metaphors are themselves creations and thus exemplify that at which they aim. In being creative, they generate new significance. Of course, this point applies to the possible use of metaphor in expressing verbal response to works in any medium. Literary criticism is profuse with such use of metaphor, as is music criticism. Thus it should be obvious that I do not want to suggest that metaphors are appropriate only in the visual arts.

Before developing further the issue of how metaphors may work in art criticism, let me pause to acknowledge an interesting but problem-generating consequence of the point about the created character of metaphor as it relates to art works that have created character. There is a difficulty in seeing how creations can be applied to other creations. Both the applied and what it is applied to are irreducible. Consequently, must not the art critic who uses the best metaphors be a verbal artist in his or her own right? The critical statement seems to be its own unique work of art. How can it offer access to another unique work of art? My response to this question must take the form of expanding briefly on the kind of interactionism to which I am committed. And although I do not claim to solve the puzzle posed by the question, I do think some suggestions can be made about the relation of verbal creations to visual creations.

The new significance generated by metaphors is both connotative and denotative; that is, a metaphor has meaning or sense and reference. In having reference, it has a relation to a referent that is new. What I mean by "referent" is a condition of constraint on the interpretation that yields an articulation of the connotations, or visual qualities as seen. Thus the referent need not be some object or state of affairs in the world that is represented by a work being interpreted. It may be some constraining condition in human nature, or even, sometimes, in psychological factors in the interpreter and in what is expected to be psychological responses in the audience. I would resist such a relativistic consequence, because I think we should answer the question of what in the work, and thus in its constraining conditions as an object of attention, grounds such psychological factors. The issue raised is not easily settled. However, for my present purposes, the issue can, I think, be side-stepped, because the main point here is that there is something, no matter what its locus, that is the pole in a referential relation – a pole that serves the function of keeping interpretation from falling into the relativistic trap that now seems so attractive to those caught up in what I believe is a narcissistic trend in some theories of criticism, narcissistic

111

because the trend aims at a self-indulgence inspired by the rejection of any kind of objective base for interpretation.[15] To return to the specific point about how referents of visual works and verbal interpretation are related, it should be said that the referent of the new meanings of a metaphor or a work of art that exhibits Novelty Proper is new in the minimal sense that it is not one of the referents to which the antecedent meanings of the terms of the metaphor apply. The antecedent meanings of the subject and modifier of a metaphor have their own antecedent referents. But when integrated within the metaphor as a whole, the resultant meaning has its own unique referent. For instance, the referent of "a sharp tongue" considered as a whole, in its metaphorical significance, is neither sharpness as found in a knife nor a tongue as found in a mouth, but it is rather a non-spatial-temporal object that serves as the relatum in the metaphorical reference relation. The metaphorical referent, then, is new in the sense that it is what uniquely satisfies the new meaning(s) that follow from the interacting ingredients of the metaphor. If the new referent, although itself unique, is somehow an approximation – recognized through the interacting meanings – to the work being interpreted, then it should share a family resemblance with the focus of visual meanings that function as the referent of the work of art to which the metaphors are supposed to point us. And if it does share such a resemblance, then it approaches an adequate matching of intrinsic discourse with a work of art. It should be emphasized, however, that the place of objectivity in this approximation to a matching of verbal metaphor with new creation is not wholly dependent on antecedent, fixed referents or meaning clusters that have these referents. The objectivity is one that must itself evolve through traditions and schools. Thus new objective controlling conditions emerge just as do new interacting meanings that constitute metaphors in the evolution of art history and criticism.

Another way in which metaphorical language approximates the new significance of a visual work is effected through the interaction of meanings exhibited by the verbal metaphor, not only among themselves, but also with the visual meanings of the visual properties of paintings. This "external" interaction between verbal expression and visual work is the basis for recognizing a family resemblance between the significance of the work and the significance of the verbal metaphor. The external interaction not only occurs between verbal metaphor and something in a non-verbal medium, but it also exemplifies a fundamental relation between language and the world, or between cognition and the object of cognition insofar as this object is not itself still another cognition. In the case at hand, this relation between language and the world is reflected in the relation between the two media of articulated meaning, the verbal and the visual.

The relation between verbal metaphors and referents that depend on visual qualities is not a simple one-to-one correspondence. Nor is the relation between metaphors used in interpreting works of art and those works always direct and linear. There are what may be called "levels" of metaphorical discourse correlated with the generality of the referents at which the discourse is aimed. This is not to say that any individual metaphor is itself more or less general, but it is to say that the target of a metaphor in the context of what is being said may include the uniqueness of a single work or of a multiplicity of works. A multiplicity of works may exemplify a style of an artist (such as that of Picasso in his so-called "blue period"), a style of a group of artists (the Barbizons), a whole school (Impressionism or Expressionism), or a tradition (Post-Impressionism or seventeenth-century Dutch art). The distinctions among styles, schools, and traditions are not crucial. The distinctions are as much a matter of degree as of clearly demarcated kinds. More crucial is the broader distinction between the appropriateness of a metaphor for a single work and the appropriateness of a metaphor mobilized for more than one work. In order to sharpen the distinctions I have in mind, it will be helpful to elaborate briefly on what I should like to call "levels of metaphorical discourse."

Levels of metaphorical discourse

The purpose of the kind of discourse that points towards the uniqueness of single created works cannot be dissociated from the purposes of pointing toward styles, schools, and traditions. This interdependence of purposes is particularly relevant to art historians, because their interests are not restricted to interpreting single works, as those of the critic may be. In fact, focusing on single works is often, if not always, a means to a larger purpose for the art historian, who looks for a larger picture, a context of conditions that at least link groups of individual works. Consequently, figurative language may be expected to frame a context such as a style or school, while additional metaphorical discourse is required to exemplify the new significance encountered in individual works. This is the appropriate place to point out that I do not intend to propose that art historians such as Alpers or Baxandall must be consciously looking for newness or for new ways of regarding the works they discuss. What they attend to, I assume, are the intrinsic qualities of the work for their own sakes as well as for their connections with contexts. However, in doing this, they find the appropriate tropes and literal terms (frozen metaphors as well as so-called literal expressions), and sometimes – perhaps often – these expressions are called on in order to get at something in the context of the work with whatever newness it may have.[16] In any case, the main distinction between levels of discourse, then, must be made between what I suggest calling "framing figures" of speech or "framing figurative discourse," and "specifying" or "individuating" metaphors that are essential to focusing intrinsic discourse on its objects. It should be noticed also that, on the one hand, figurative discourse might include figures of speech other than metaphors, analogies, or similes while, on the other hand, individuating discourse must eventually include metaphors when it comes to focus on a single work. This point follows from the character of created products, which are initially individual and which demand uniqueness of focus in order to be interpreted by discourse. Once we turn to various works that share a style that has been initiated by the earliest members of the group, we can speak in terms of resemblances among the members, and sometimes these resemblances are common to two or more members or examples of the style. Framing figures, then, delineate the distinctive character of groups of works, indicating what sets them off as exhibiting a family of features distinctive of more than one individual work, yet each of which exemplifies Novelty Proper. The newness of the collection of works as a whole first must have been exemplified in the earliest member of the group. But it more than likely was not clearly exemplified exclusively in any one member, but should be regarded as a created character that gradually becomes recognized as one or more marks by virtue of which a style is attributed to the group. In contrast, an individuating metaphor targets an instance of Novelty Proper that is distinctive to an individual work. In individual cases, what is new is a specification of the generic intelligibility or character that emerges like a family resemblance and that comprehends intrinsic features functioning as members each of which contributes to a singular, unique created character. Further consideration of the two levels of figurative discourse will be offered through their application to the art historians I have selected for illustration.

114

APPLICATION: FIGURATIVE LANGUAGE IN THE WORK OF
TWO ART HISTORIANS

Michael Baxandall's language for art

As an entry into the task of seeing how figurative language can be
applied to works of art, it will be helpful to draw on some remarks of
the art historian Michael Baxandall concerning the problem of
speaking about the visual arts. Baxandall proposes that a way to
match verbal attempts to speak appropriately concerning visual
interests in art can be described in terms of three classes of words:
causal, comparison, and effect words. It is important that he believes
that these serve as indirect ways in which the historian or critic uses
words in order to speak about pictures. They are indirect because
they contribute to our thinking about, rather than directly seeing, a
picture, but more specifically they are indirect because they concern
effects of the picture, of things *compared* with the picture, or of
causes of the picture. However, Baxandall slides over – perhaps
"eludes" is a more accurate expression – a distinction in his account
of what is indirect about the three kinds of words, and this point is of
particular importance in what he says about the function of comparison words. Thus, on the one hand, he explains his point about
indirection with respect to comparison words by saying that the
comparison words refer to the effects of "other things." Yet, on the
other hand, he says that "other things" are compared with the
picture, or that comparison words refer to "other things" that have an
effect comparable to that of the picture on which the historian is
trying to bring the audience or prospective appreciators into contact:
"many of the more powerful terms in the description will be a little
indirect, in that they refer first not to the physical picture itself but to
... other things that would have a comparable effect on us ... as the
picture does."[17] And interestingly in another, although earlier, book
on fifteenth-century Italian art, he says that the fifteenth-century
critic, Landino, has an *advantage* over Bernard Berenson, who wrote
of Masaccio by referring to his own reaction to Masaccio's pictures,
because he, Landino, talks of pictures in painter's terms and not by
speaking about himself.[18] In neither way of making his point,
however, does Baxandall deny that some reference to the picture or
other things compared with it must be made directly. In order to call
attention to the effects, the cause of the effects – the picture itself or
the other things – must be described. If this is not his intention, then

he would be suggesting that the effects of the other things are compared with the effects of paintings. But his discussion of examples belies this, and, indeed, late in his book when he refers to the authority of the pictorial order, he does not refer to the authority of the effects of the pictorial order. My purpose in mentioning this turn from effects to the picture that produces effects is to suggest how important metaphor must be for the sort of discourse Baxandall discusses. As he says, most of the comparison words are metaphorical, and my point is that it is the metaphorical function of comparison words rather than their possible reference to effects that makes them indirect. The historian's language need not be directly psychological in order to be indirectly relevant to the objects of visual interest. But in attempting to speak relevantly concerning these objects, the metaphorical discourse required to stretch and transform verbal accounts of acts of appreciating, which themselves require stretching and transforming our schemata of seeing, must, if the discourse is creatively metaphorical, aim at circumscribing rather than striking the target directly. A creative metaphor creates new significance that, because of its own newness, can only parallel – as closely as possible – the visual significance that is new. Let us next turn to some of Baxandall's uses of metaphorical discourse.

If we confine attention to his *Patterns of Intention*, there is a problem in finding the metaphorical discourse of the kind of comparison words Baxandall mentions. The book is developed in terms of the overall purpose of offering a meta-discourse, a discourse about discourse; consequently, Baxandall is more concerned with explaining the content and direction of what art historians can say than he is about focusing on works of art for the specific purpose of reconstructing them for appreciation. In other words, his use of comparison and effect words occurs chiefly for purposes of brief illustration. Perhaps this is the main reason why the figurative discourse he uses is most often designed for framing rather than individuating. However, there are moments when figures of speech come into play in helping focus styles and individual paintings. I shall comment on four examples: his discussion of some of the works of Picasso, Chardin, and Piero della Francesca, and, in an earlier book, his own illustration of some of the commentary offered by the Renaissance critic Landino with reference to Masaccio.

Baxandall enters into his discussion of Picasso with a general consideration of the problems inherent in explaining pictures. Accordingly, he formulates what is at least a step toward offering what I have called a "framing figure" for representational painting in general: "representational painters like Picasso represent a three-dimensional reality on a two-dimensional surface."[19] If we are accustomed to using or reading statements of this kind, the figurative force of the quotation might be overlooked. But the origin of such expressions, I think, is figurative – indeed, specifically, metaphorical. Here the use of the term "reality," which carries with it an indeterminate range of meanings, effects an interaction with "two-dimensional surface." Thus a frame is established – to be sure, for anyone who has reflected on the matter, an obvious one – for interpreting a bounded range of referents, namely all representational rather than non-representational paintings. The frame is a reminder that what is to be seen in any example of this class exhibits an interaction of surface and represented depth. The term "reality," as well as "represent," focuses the interpretation of two-dimensionality and three-dimensionality, for we are reminded that the flat surface itself must come to life while the represented referent is thrown back onto the two-dimensional presentation. That is to say, the eye attends to the surface and the represented in one visual act rather than attending to the represented while neglecting the function of the surface. This reminder calls attention to the special tasks of painters.

However, it is more helpful in citing examples of the use of figurative language to note Baxandall's next move toward an initial individuating use of figurative language, a move in which he offers a smaller frame, or a frame established within the larger frame for representational painting in general. The smaller frame is Impressionism: "Impressionism had offered canvases that played on a tension between an openly dabbed-on plane surface and a rendering of sense-impressions of seen objects that put emphasis on their hues."[20] Passing over the extent to which "sense-impressions" as something "rendered," and as something being rendered into "seen objects," are terms used figuratively, the expression "dabbed-on plane surface" relies on the interactions of the meanings of "dabbed-on" and "surface" along with the meanings of "hues" that serve as the substance of the dabbed surface. And here we have a more specific frame for the general boundary surrounding representational painting in general. We are brought closer to one style – or group of partially common styles – within the history of (representational) painting.

Another example of a move toward the use of a specifying figure is found in Baxandall's account of Picasso's *Demoiselles d'Avignon*, an account which prepares the way for a closer analysis of Picasso's *Portrait of Daniel-Henry Kahnweiler*. After some casual observations about Picasso's studies of African masks and about the appearance of forms in Picasso's work that apparently reflect these studies, Baxandall says, "the picture offers little sense of represented three-dimensional space; nor is phenomenal perspective observed in the forms of the figures."[21] Like the quotation concerning representational painting in general, this description might seem straightforwardly literal insofar as it includes already recognized, now conventional, expressions, yet ones which may well have been innovative at one time. However, it also seems clear that "three-dimensional," qualifying "space," merges coordinate meanings implied by the idea of measurement with significance that must come from wider systems of meanings than one confined to geometrical space; otherwise, the coupling would be redundant. A more manifest figurative way of framing Picasso's work follows in the next paragraph, in which a framing figure for Cézanne is transferred to Picasso's painting in 1908: his (and Braque's) pictures

show, among other things, a preoccupation with absorbing and using in new ways the advanced style of Cézanne, and particularly Cézanne's reduction of the local plane-structure of objects to a limited number of, so to speak, super-planes registering not so much the seen surface of things as a perceived underlying structure. The term *passage* is sometimes used in relation to this.[22]

And moving forward a step toward the use of individuating metaphors, he continues: "The perceived structure, however, is not Cézanne's kind of perceived structure but a kind that appears to evolve from the re-arranged element of the right-hand side of the *Demoiselles*." What is significant here is the use of the terms "local plane-structure," "super-planes registering," and a structure that exhibits "passage." The individuating of these figures when the focus is moved from figures common to both Cézanne and Picasso to Picasso's *Demoiselles* in particular presents us with the idea of visual structure constituted by pictorial planes that work together so that the structure as a whole is in evolution within the individual painting. It is also significant that when Baxandall shifts sights from Cézanne to Picasso, the frame is modified. And this move gives the second, Picasso, frame an individuating function that enables the critic to use words approximating adequacy to the creative advance that Picasso achieved after (not over) Cézanne's own creative achievement.

When Baxandall turns to Chardin, he seems more alert to some of his own reflections on the need for the art historian to turn critical sights on particular paintings. He opens the chapter that makes use of Chardin's *A Lady Taking Tea* with the notice that "In what follows now I want to do several things which will lead to a different texture, a closer and smaller grain." He proposes to "address a piece of detail," in contrast to the "very schematic and general" account of Picasso in 1910. And he reflects that "art criticism, quite apart from trying to go beyond current accounts, typically works close to particulars."[23] Five pages later, when he fulfills his promise to offer smaller grain, he refers to certain puzzling aspects of the painting. These include "something strange" about "the perspective here and there." This is illustrated with reference to the chair-back, which is "odd: if the lady were sitting comfortably on the chair, surely the chair-back would not be turned to face us and the picture-plane as much as it does."

Thus far, the discourse is relatively literal, except for the suggestion that the chair-back faces the picture-plane, the latter being by now a standard term. It should be observed that "picture-plane" is not a live metaphor, if it ever was, but is a framing figure because it emphasizes the formal aspects of paintings, colors, lines, images, and so on, in relation to the surfaces of paintings regarded in terms of a geometrical conception, the plane. In any case, discourse of this kind gives paintings framing figures and in this case is individualized through being related to the "facing" – another frozen metaphor in this context – on the part of the chair-back, which, we should keep in mind, is not a chair-back but rather a pictorial chair-back. The introduction of figurative – I believe that here it is metaphorical – discourse is extended in the next part of the account: "The tea-pot also is rather 1910: spout and perhaps also handle are *flattened out on the canvas*" – italics added to highlight the introduction of figures, which, in this instance, are words commonly used with reference to paintings. Further, we are told that there is a range of striking color devices – "The most obvious is the red-lacquered table assertive, but *almost unstable*" (emphasis added).[24] More general figures are proposed a few lines later, when Baxandall uses a framing expression that applies not only to Chardin's work in general but also to both visual and scientific interests (especially in optics) in his own culture – thus we have a use of language that bridges intrinsic and extrinsic or external discourse. The discourse used here refers to a feature of Chardin's work; it is "differential distinctness and brightness."[25] The element of tension and figurative character in this expression may seem relatively weak, if one understands it primarily as having quantitative reference to differences of sharp and contrasting blurred outline coupled with differences of lightness and darkness. But consideration of the meaning systems of "differential" and "distinctness," interacting with "brightness," is more suggestive of the figurative function of the expression. Just focusing on "differential" mobilizes the idea of multiplicity and opposition, while "distinctness" gives prominence to singularity and autonomy. "Brightness" and "distinctness" seem harmonious, if for no other reason than that distinctness requires sufficient brightness to be seen. But the differentiation between these qualities brought together reinvokes the figurative tension. However, if this tension appears minimal in terms of considering the words without attention to the referent that invites the expression, when the referent of the whole expression is given its proper function, the figurative character and tension of the expression carries greater weight. For here there are, in this painting, no sharp contrasts between light and dark, and only subtle contrasts of sharpness and blurring of line and shape. The individuation of the framing figure makes this increase of figurative tension more obvious. This individuation occurs in the discussion of *A Lady Taking Tea* in the words "there seems something extraordinarily deliberate and determining about the differential distinctness and lighting of the picture. There is a determinate plane of distinctness on the line of teapot, hand and arm ... "[26] Not only is specifying focus on the referent forced on our attention but additional ideas are called on to interact with the framing figure. Distinctness and lighting are now deliberate and they are said to function as agents, for they determine something in or about the painting.

Baxandall's discussion of Piero della Francesca's *Baptism of Christ* follows from consideration of a historical-critical approach to the tasks of painters in periods "remote from our own." Thus, a large part of the discussion includes an account of framing figures, the chief one springing from but not restricted to Piero's own acknowledged *commensurazione*, which, Baxandall says, comes from numerical analysis.[27] It has to do with proportioning "contours by perspective method."[28] But what most explicitly exemplifies metaphor, and a step toward individuation, of the *Baptism of Christ* are expressions that appear in Baxandall's discussion of "The authority of the pictorial order." Writing of Piero's specifying of his *commensurazione*, he says, "The effect of this [systematic perspective] is to give further weight to the representation of space in the picture," and, "In modern terms the problem is that the picture *plane* was losing its weight, or that the relation between picture surface and picture space was losing its balance." Further, he says, "It is as if he were counterbalancing, on a sub-representational level, the energy of his representation of spatial depth," and "Another means by which he addressed the problem was through what I shall call accommodation paradoxes ... A single and minor example is offered by some incongruously sharp and bright blooms he has chosen to paint on the bushes." Finally, "The effect is both to soften, in the picture-plane register, the violence of the spatial distancing in the picture-space and, by acting on our attention, to compensate on a straight narrative level for their diminution."[29] It seems that the language here, compared with the frame, *commensurazione*, has reached a quite sharply focused reference through the complex metaphors within metaphors of "softening," "violence of ... spatial distancing," integrated with the systems of meanings of the "picture-plane register."

Another, direct, and obvious illustration of the use of figurative, specifically metaphorical, discourse in Baxandall's practice is to be found in his earlier work on fifteenth-century Italian painting. And it is significant that here, functioning as the historian, when he turns to discussing the style of Quattrocento pictures themselves, rather than giving more emphasis to their social and economic context, he refers the reader to what fifteenth-century critics said. Thus he lists a series of terms in what he calls "a tradition of metaphor" that were used by Landino. "Like Pliny he used metaphors, whether of his own coinage or of his own culture ... 'prompt,' 'devout,' and 'ornate,' for instance."[30] Let us consider still another word Baxandall finds in fifteenth-century criticism, "pure," used to contribute to a framing figure for circumscribing Masaccio's style:

Puro sanza ornato is almost pleonastic, since *puro* nearly means *sanza ornato*. *Puro* is one of Landino's latinisms and copies the literary critical sense of an unadorned, laconic style ... It turns a negative idea – "without ornament" – into a positive one – "plain and clear" – with an element of moral overtone ... *Puro*.[31]

Baxandall does not say what it is that turns the negative idea into a positive one, but presumably it is its interaction with *sanza ornato*. However, given my proposal about the function of figurative discourse as a way of access to the uniqueness of the new character of styles of paintings, it follows that the transforming of the negative idea is not only an outcome of the interaction with other ideas in the larger expression, but it is also an outcome of interaction of both these

121

and the whole expression with the properties of what it applies to, the painting itself – in this case, the interaction of the critic's expressions with the properties of the style of the paintings of Masaccio. The reference of the expression *puro sanza ornato*, as it functions in a discussion of Masaccio's work, is to Masaccio's work, and it is this additional condition that yields a reverberation in the expression so that the meanings of individual terms are modified.

Svetlana Alpers's framing figures

In turning to Svetlana Alpers's *The Art of Describing*, we encounter immediately the most comprehensive framing figure that guides her account of Dutch art in the seventeenth century. The title itself forms this frame – a frame drawn carefully from commentary found in the seventeenth century – for the group of paintings to which the title refers, namely, "seventeenth century Dutch art is descriptive." But this largest frame is only the highest – or lowest, if we think in terms of generality rather than specificity as more fundamental – of a hierarchical nesting of framing figures. There are many layers. The next is one that is implied rather than formulated directly as a figure of speech: "Seventeenth century Dutch art is the eye of the camera obscura," or "Art is the record of the image in the lens." Variations on the descriptive-camera frames are numerous. But, before elaborating, we should notice how the figure of the art of describing applied to Dutch art articulates an advance, or a transformation, of the schema that had been used to approach both Dutch and Italian work – an advance over the frame that served (and still does serve) as a model for criticism concerned with Italian Renaissance art: "The art of the narrative."

The advance in question, then, need not be thought of as indicating an improvement within the way painting is achieved but rather as a new and valuable way of putting the viewer in touch with something that distinguishes Dutch painting from earlier Italian painting. The advantage of recognizing this distinction within the framework of the overall figure Alpers formulates is that it alerts us in definitive terms to the purely presentational function of forms within seventeenth-century Dutch painting. These works do not depend on a story knowledge of which enhances what we see in the paintings. As Alpers explains,

In referring to the notion of art in the Italian Renaissance, I have in mind the Albertian definition of the picture: a framed surface or pane situated at a certain distance from a viewer who looks through it at a second or substitute world. In the Renaissance this world was a stage on which human figures performed significant actions based on the texts of the poets. It is a narrative art.[32]

This conception of art served as a model that blinded interpretations of Dutch art before the advent of Post-Impressionist painting. To see Dutch art as designed to fit a frame construed in terms of seeing in the way a camera obscura displays images is to see it in a way that frees the viewer from expectations appropriate to different pictorial schemata. It should be noted in this connection, however, that even though the idea of Dutch art as descriptive is not itself new with Alpers, her framing figure is a striking way to alert us to the force of the idea of descriptive art when this idea is applied to seventeenth-century Dutch art. Thus the nesting or cradling principle applies here, namely that the relativity of what functions as a frame and what at the same time may also function as a specifying or individuating figure depends on which direction we look. "Seventeenth century Dutch painting is the eye of the camera obscura" individuates the framing figure of "the art of describing" while it frames the range of Dutch art in the period with which Alpers is concerned. What additional individuators does Alpers suggest?

One of the most striking individuating figures – in this case, it is a metaphor – is Alpers's image of the magic-lantern show which, she points out, was a device produced by Drebbel, and which she applies to Rembrandt: "If we follow Rembrandt from his early, etched self-portrait as the beggar seated on a mound ... to the royal demeanor that he takes on in the Frick *Self-Portrait* ... we are surely witnessing Drebbel's magic lantern ... " It should be acknowledged that as she explains the significance of this image, its function is perhaps sufficiently different from the camera obscura figure to warrant the suggestion that it is more an alternative for seeing a different uniqueness than it is an individuation of the camera obscura figure. Yet it does overlap the language by which she approaches painting through reference to devices designed to serve as eyes for visual interests. And it is an articulation of a basic metaphor: "Rembrandt's painting" – that to which she refers us – "is the eye of a magic lantern."

Another figure that moves toward individuation is found in Alpers's explanation of how multiple perspectives introduced within a single painting differentiate the eye of the Dutch painter from the eye of the Italian Renaissance painter, as the latter's perspective system is explained by Alberti – and applied and further explained by Leonardo. In the latter, there is a vanishing-point that is central to all pictorial objects and, in particular, to the assumed eye of the viewer, which is located outside the picture frame. In Dutch art, there are multiple vanishing-points, and the consequence is that the viewer is drawn into the picture, inside the frame. The figure, then, is "Seventeenth-century Dutch painting is painting that exhibits through the eyes of multiple perspectives." It should be noted that this assertion is a specification of the camera obscura figure; it follows from one of the uses to which a variation on the camera obscura was put. A long cylinder with a convex glass at one end and a concave glass at the other, one end placed at a small hole in a darkened tent, projected a series of images on the wall. Artists could then trace these images on paper. Different, discrete images could be drawn in succession, each being a partial aspect, with its own perspective system. Further, apart from the specific use of the instrument here, individuation can be seen in the figures themselves, because the idea of a camera obscura implies that there is a definite perspective necessary to each image formed by each position of the camera. Discreteness of visual field, then, opens up the possibility of moving from one image to another, as if there were a series of frames, within a single outer frame. One of the individuators for this multiple-perspective figure appears in Alpers's discussion of a painting by Jan Vredeman de Vries:

The effect is that adding-on of view of the moving eye ... When figures enter they are captives of the world seen, entangled Gulliver-like in the lines of sight that situate them ... The many eyes and many things viewed that make up such surfaces produce a syncopated effect. There is no way that we can stand back and take in a homogeneous space.[33]

The metaphorical tensions and sharpness with which these and other such figures can help us participate in an approximation to the unique visual qualities of creative achievements in painting are, I think, obvious. In the tensions here that emerge from the interactions of the meanings of being "captives of the world seen" with the Gulliver image and, in turn, the ideas of multiple eyes and a syncopated effect, all in interaction with the paintings seen with the appreciator's eyes yield a dynamic and vivid approximation to the created character of the examples of works with reference to which Alpers uses her own discourse of the art historian.

Alpers's book is rich in both framing and individuating figures, and it is fascinating to identify them and see how effectively she uses them. However, I must conclude these remarks on the figures of speech of the art historian.

CONCLUSION

It is tempting to return to the suggestion that one of the reasons, and perhaps the main reason, that figurative discourse may be used appropriately to direct appreciation to what I have said cannot be avoided in the proper practice of art history – attention to the individual work – is that works of art themselves exhibit a structure or set of dynamic relationships that have a family resemblance to verbal figures of speech. However, the main point of this suggestion was the theme of my *Metaphor and Art*, and pursuit of it here would not only move this discussion beyond its proper length, but would also take us into a philosophy of art and metaphysics extended beyond the boundaries of the question of the language of art history. Yet the point does deserve mentioning again, because it brings us back to one of the main issues with which we began and which was central to Baxandall's concern about how verbal language can be used to serve interests that are intrinsically visual in nature. If some verbal discourse can take the form of interaction, as indicated for metaphor, and if such interaction is present in the inner dynamics of the direct objects of visual interest, then there is hope for appropriate speech designed to direct us to those objects. Suggestions about some of the ways in which art historians design speech, and thereby lead us to styles and individual works, have been the final aim of this discussion. I have tried to show that there are framing figures of speech that set boundaries within which narrower boundaries can be constructed. The narrowing of frames brings increasingly specific or individuating visual focus on styles and works. The frames, larger and smaller, must, in origin, be figurative, because language needs to be stretched and innovative in order to approximate the newness of interactive structures encountered in created achievements.

NOTES

1 The following discussion is based on my extended discussion of metaphor and its relation to the arts in general in *Metaphor and Art: Interactionism and Reference in the Verbal and Nonverbal Arts* (Cambridge, 1989). Also, I must acknowledge the careful and well-conceived

commentary offered by Gregg M. Horowitz in response to a portion of this paper presented at a session of the American Society for Aesthetics, Eastern Division, meetings at The Pennsylvania State University, in March 1990. I take these comments into account at several points in the discussion.

It should be noted that my topic raises an issue that concerns how to use discourse that is adequate to what is intelligible visually rather than verbally. Michael Baxandall's understanding of the art historian's task brings out this point succinctly. He says that he most worries about issues "connected with the pretty gratuitous act of matching language with the visual interest of works of art." And, in emphasizing his point, he refers to John Passmore's comment that it is difficult to say anything about a painting "except by talking about its relationships to something else ... " ("The Language of Art History," New Literary History, 10 [1979], p. 456; Michael Baxandall's revised version of this article appears as chapter 5 in this volume). Baxandall is concerned with determining the appropriate things with which relations can be made and talked about. As already indicated earlier in the book, there must be two kinds of things most closely related to works of art regarded in their own right – to things of "visual interest," as Baxandall expresses it, or, as I would prefer to say, things with respect to their visual qualities. These two kinds of things are (1) other works, which are necessary to comparison words, and (2) responses of appreciators, which are necessary to effect words. But how can using words to refer to relationships to other works and to appreciators bring into focus any particular work or style of a painter regarded for its intrinsic (as well as external) features? I assume that it is this question that lies behind Baxandall's "worry."

A ready answer might be that the issue I am raising is no more difficult than that facing any descriptive task for which what is described is in a non-verbal medium of expression. In fact, the very idea of description seems proper to the idea of using the medium of words to refer to visual or audible qualities, and even tactile and odorous qualities. Why should Baxandall, then, "worry" about matching language with visual interest in works of the visual arts? I shall not propose to answer this question for Baxandall. That is not my purpose.

2 I shall rely primarily on Svetlana Alpers's The Art of Describing: Dutch Art in the Seventeenth Century (Chicago, 1983) and Michael Baxandall's Patterns of Intention On the Historical Explanation of Pictures (New Haven and London, 1985).

3 Carl R. Hausman, A Discourse on Novelty and Creation (Albany, 1984.)

4 In Discourse on Novelty and Creation and "Criteria of Creativity," Philosophy and Phenomenological Research, 40 (1979), pp. 237–249 (also published in The Concept of Creativity in Science and in Art, ed. Denis Dutton and Michael Krausz [The Hague, Boston, London, 1981], pp. 75–89).

5 Charles S. Peirce, "The Doctrine of Necessity Examined," in Collected Papers of Charles Sanders Peirce, ed. Charles Hartshorne and Paul Weiss (Cambridge, Mass., 1934), vol. V, paragraphs 35–65.

6 What I am describing is the initiating of something like C. S. Peirce's abduction or hypothetical inference.

7 What I have said about the first point in my response was prompted by a question posed by Gregg Horowitz, at the American Society for Aesthetics meetings mentioned in note 1.

8 Nelson Goodman, *Languages of Art: An Approach to a Theory of Symbols* (Indianapolis and New York, 1968), p. 77.

9 Stanley Cavell, "Aesthetic Problems of Modern Philosophy", in *Philosophy in America*, ed. Max Black, (Ithaca, N.Y., 1967), pp. 74–97.

10 Max Black, "More About Metaphor," in *Metaphor and Thought* (Cambridge, 1979), pp. 26–27; Paul Henle, ed., *Language, Thought and Culture* (Ann Arbor, 1958), see especially pp. 186–195; Hausman, *Metaphor and Art*, chapters 1 and 2, in particular.

11 "Cézanne and His Critics," in *Cézanne: The Late Work*, ed. William Rubin (New York, 1977), p. 139.

12 Nelson Goodman, *Languages of Art*, p. 68.

13 Let me add that I shall not engage the issue of analyzing the concept of uniqueness, but I shall rely on my discussion, which follows in a moment, of what it means to be a created outcome as a basis for at least claiming that what is created is necessarily recognized as being unique in some respects.

I should also point out that I do not mean to deny that created outcomes have relations to their pasts or to the contexts in which they are generated. The point is that some intelligible aspect or feature of a created outcome (as distinct from a routinely constructed product) is introduced so that there is at least the possibility that the school or tradition in which the creation is generated will be advanced, which is to have a character not present before the introduction of the creator's achievement. Consequently, even past influences and contexts that were contemporaneous with the work are reinterpreted by virtue of the new features introduced in that work. As Bergson says, Neoclassicism must be understood differently once Romanticism has evolved. And we can add that, after the turn of the century, Cézanne's work is understood differently in terms of the Cubism to which Cézanne's work helped give rise.

My insistence on the subtle interplay of newness with the past is a point that some commentators on my writings about creativity have missed. I have in mind in particular David Perkins and Sharon Bailin. In "The Possibility of Invention" (in *The Nature of Creativity: Contemporary Psychological Perspectives*, ed. Robert J. Steinberg [Cambridge, 1988], pp. 362–385), Perkins cites one of my discussions of creativity as an example of what he wants to refute for his own purposes. The result is that he sets up a "straw man." If he had read the more substantive treatment of the issues in which I build up a basis for my position – a treatment in fact referred to in the piece he uses to illustrate his straw man – he might have recognized that I do not say that created outcomes are completely unpredictable and that they therefore cannot be explained in any sense at all. Such an extreme view would, of course imply that creations would be severed from all antecedent and contemporaneous contexts. I do not say that creations are unpredictable and unattached in every respect. They do not completely elude familiar categories and old ways of discoursing; such radical leaps must be left to divinity. The point is that certain *aspects* of creations are unpredictable or indescribable by familiar language, and it is these aspects that pose problems for explanation and description. If there were not such aspects, the advancement of a school or tradition, would be illusory with respect to its being a "real" advancement. For everything, and every detail that makes things intelligible, would be prefigured or pre-determined. The same point applies to Sharon Bailin's comments about my view (*Achieving Extraordinary Ends: An Essay on Creativity* [Dordrect, Boston and Lancaster, 1988]). If one wishes to use another's view as a foil, it seems reasonable to expect that specific points in that view should not be taken out of context so that the main point, which is built on the specific points, is thereby ignored.

14 I. A. Richards, *Philosophy of Rhetoric* (New York, 1936), p. 100; Black, "More About Metaphor," p. 37; Henle, *Language, Thought, and Culture,* p. 191.

15 The conception of reference and some of the issues raised concerning whether or to what extent criticism can have an objective base is discussed in my *Metaphor and Art*. The question of finding a way to bring verbal metaphor and the creative aspect of visual significance together without losing objectivity was raised by Horowitz in his commentary on part of this paper at the American Society for Aesthetics meetings referred to earlier.

16 The point that art historians have various reasons for discussing works of art, some of which may not be to try to bring into focus the intrinsic and new qualities of the work, is made in response to Horowitz, as indicated earlier.

17 *Patterns of Intention*, p. 11.

18 Michael Baxandall, *Painting and Experience in Fifteenth-Century Italy: A Primer in the Social History of Pictorial Style* (Oxford and New York, 1972), p. 122.

19 *Patterns of Intention*, p. 44.

20 *Ibid.*, p. 45.

21 *Ibid.*, p. 37.

22 *Ibid.*

23 *Ibid.*, p. 74.

24 *Ibid.*, p. 80.

25 *Ibid.*, p. 81.

26 *Ibid.*, p. 80.

27 *Ibid.*, pp. 111–113.

28 *Ibid.*, p. 113.

29 *Ibid.*, p. 134.

30 *Painting and Experience*, p. 117.

31 *Ibid.*, p. 122.

32 Alpers, *The Art of Describing*, p. xix.

33 *Ibid.*, p. 58.

8

Cézanne's physicality: the politics of touch

RICHARD SHIFF

"TWO AND A HALF APPLES"

When preparing the standard catalogue of Paul Cézanne's works, Lionello Venturi decided to title an unusually small canvas "Deux pommes et demie" (see Plate 8.1). His choice seems born of a stubborn literalness, nevertheless resulting in ambivalence. The picture is of three apples, but apparently a fragment, so that one apple is truncated by the framing edge. This leaves "two and a half apples." It also leaves a question: is a painting properly described in terms of pre-existing physical objects that fall within its view (in this case, three apples)? Or is it described by the material marks that fall within its immediate physical borders (here constituting only two and a half apples)?[1]

The choice parallels a distinction often used to define modernism in painting in relation to an antecedent classicism. Modernist critics privilege proximity, even when commenting on representations of things, such as apples, that have presumably been viewed from a distance. They stress whatever meaning can be derived from painted surfaces when considered as delimited objects themselves, direct products of artistic craft and individualized expressive action. For the modernist, how things impress an artist (as if coming to exist within a particular eye or mind) counts more than how external objects look "in reality," with their physical distance preserved (as if such distance allowed things to retain their very own properties, unaffected by an individual's point of view). A work of modernist art will seem to be authored, personalized, its image so closely identified with the mind and body of its maker that its market value may simply correspond to that accorded the artist. A minor work by a major artist – Cézanne's Deux pommes et demie – can be expensive.

129

Plate 8.1 Paul Cézanne, *Three Apples* (*Deux pommes et demie*), no signature, oil on canvas, 10.2 × 16.6 cm., photograph © 1990 by The Barnes Foundation.

Modernist standards have so dominated the twentieth-century understanding of what art is and what artists do that the classical alternative has usually been defined in simple opposition. The classical mode of artistic representation appears to set things off for detached inspection. An interpreter in the classical spirit is more likely to locate the meaning of a work in its represented scene, allegory, or narrative than in the psychology or genius of the particular maker. For this reason, classicists could imitate their predecessors' masterful renderings of favored subjects without experiencing anxiety. The value of a classical work was to be associated with the nobility of its theme or the skill required to produce the rendering in a convincing and legible manner.[2]

Any strict differentiation between classical and modernist modes of representation is no doubt reductive and designed to articulate a specifically modernist conception: that the configuration of an artwork should express a self and/or whatever social, ideological, or environmental conditions bear upon a given artist.[3] The fundamental opposition has often been stated in terms of transparency, which is classical, and opacity, which is modernist. The figure of transparency converts a picture surface into an immaterial plane – according to the usual metaphor, a window – that renders visible what lies beyond it, the world of traditional pictorial representation.[4] Pictures become transparent when normalized through standardization of technical procedure. Such pictures have the potential to look "real" (even when rendering the fantastic) because they exhibit a prevailing style, one so expected – and hence "transparent" – that it can depict objects without seeming to distort them. Simply put, a standardized style is empowered, that is, socially authorized, to represent the "real." In contrast, the figure of opacity suggests that a picture surface retains an undeniable materiality, displaying it in all its unique and deviant particularity. For the modernist, self-expression becomes most evident when the normative look of represented objects is transformed by the material substance of paint applied to a surface. We are led to a broad conclusion: whatever physical "reality" a *transparent* picture possesses must belong to the external objects it represents, since the picture itself has become an immaterial plane; whereas an *opaque* picture holds "reality" within its own surface, which never ceases to manifest its physicality.

Just as neither "reality" can be absolute, so every picture may seem to possess both transparent and opaque features. Obviously, transparency facilitates vision, while opacity impedes vision's course, its materiality seeming to invite the touch. The figures of transparency and opacity thus evoke the two senses directly and simultaneously involved in the practice of painting – the eye's vision, the hand's touch. Vision corresponds to transparency and distance, touch to opacity and proximity. Typical descriptions of Cézanne's paintings entangle metaphors of vision and touch. Such complex metaphors have been repeated so often they tend to go uninvestigated and unchallenged.[5] This chapter questions and reorients their critical significance.

PANORAMIC VISION AND PARONYMOUS TOUCH

The initial pattern of response to Cézanne's paintings crystalized rather suddenly in 1895 in the wake of an exhibition of about 150 works arranged by the dealer Ambroise Vollard. Cézanne had been painting since the 1850s, yet this was the first time his mature art could be seen in sufficient quantity for a general effect to register. Until that moment the artist remained a shadow without substance. Rumored to be shy and of violent temper, alienated even from the few who admired him, he fitted the type of the mysterious genius, providing occasional good copy for writers attracted more to odd personalities than odd paintings. He lived apart: there is no indication that he ever attended his exhibition in Paris, even though he frequently visited the city; privacy seems to have been of greater concern to him than either commercial success or fame.[6]

Before Vollard converted Cézanne into a public presence, knowledgeable accounts are few and sketchy. Evaluations based on interviews and extended observation came only later when a variety of enthusiasts visited the artist, usually on his own terms, at Aix-en-Provence. One can read detailed recorded "conversations" with Cézanne, most of them published only after his death in 1906; those of the painter Emile Bernard (1904, 1907), the poet Joachim Gasquet (written 1912–1913, published 1921), and Vollard himself (1914) have been the most often cited. All accounts seem to take liberties, whether for the sake of enhancing emerging reputations, promoting an artistic and ideological program, or merely telling a good story. These textual sources have been so widely disseminated and influential that it may now be impossible to "see" Cézanne independent of them.

Among the storytellers Vollard, perhaps the least scrupulous, proves the most entertaining. He published a set of reminiscences in which he featured his own role in securing for Cézanne a place in history. He spoke also of the activity of his predecessor, the paint merchant Julien Tanguy, whose modest shop served as a gallery for those outside the normal commercial channels. There a limited number of paintings by the "unknown" Cézanne could be purchased or simply studied (Vollard himself obtained four Cézannes at the auction of Tanguy's estate in 1894).[7] According to Vollard, Tanguy held a key to Cézanne's studio where the painter had prepared

some canvases [containing] several little studies of various subjects. [Cézanne] left it to Tanguy to cut them up. These little sketches were intended for collectors who could afford neither one hundred nor forty francs [the prices for larger works]. So one might have seen Tanguy, scissors in hand, disposing of tiny "motifs," while some poor Mycaenas paid him a louis and marched off with three *Apples* ...![8]

This anecdote amuses because it plays on our sense that the works of a "master" should always be preserved whole – thoroughly "original" creations should have no retrievable component parts (whether elements of a preconceived system, or borrowings from anterior sources) and hence should not submit themselves to subdivision.[9] What Vollard describes is a set of unorganized sketches, independent of one another. Yet it is disconcerting to think that Cézanne the master did not instinctively respond to the proportions of his chosen pictorial field. Could even such sketches lack this aspect of composition? In making the cuts himself, how could Tanguy preserve the master's touch? It runs counter to our mythology to imagine the master delegating to the whim of dealer or collector the authority to determine a work's final dimensions.[10] And there is an additional irony: if anyone cut and trimmed Cézanne's works in order to facilitate sales, the practice may have been Vollard's more than Tanguy's; for he received the master's paintings in varying states of finish, condition, and presentability. Perhaps Vollard recognized the provocativeness of his story, but projected a practice of his own onto Tanguy.

We can go further: Vollard's account is particularly striking because Cézanne is the artist most likely to survive repeated decimation. He has always been known for the significance of his mark and touch, even if detached from the context of an identifiable image. A canvas of a mere four inches could be reduced still more without ceasing to attract admiration. Cézanne's contemporary Auguste Renoir said that this painter "had only to put a single stroke [*touche*] of color on a canvas for it to merit interest"; and our own contemporary Jasper Johns comments that this art "makes looking equivalent to touching."[11] Touching is performed piecemeal, touch by touch, just as a canvas surface is painted; whereas vision is more readily (but not exclusively) conceived as a totalizing mode of instantaneous survey. Touch is particularizing; vision is panoramic.[12] Given the prevailing interpretive pattern, Cézanne's works might be reduced to mere patches of brush strokes and still convey meaning. Collectors could value such fragments, individual touches, as viable "pictures."

Pictures of what? – one might ask. This abrupt question challenges the viewer who approaches Cézanne's paintings having already experienced a history of abstract art and having become familiar with a critical rhetoric that dispenses with conventional representation. Harold Rosenberg, among many others, employed such a rhetoric. Witness his account of Abstract Expressionist works, which he characterized as necessarily fragmentary: "This fragment, this sketch, is a succession of wholes in that each gesture [or touch] of the brush that goes into the composition is a totality in itself."[13] For Rosenberg, every touch becomes the equivalent of a completed picture. This entails a certain cutting, not of the picture itself, but of its chain of signification. Like a fragment of handwriting under the graphologist's eye, each gestural mark simply refers a viewer back to the originating artist as an independent actor with an identifiable character. The meaning of a work need not depend on perceiving a higher order of integrated forms. Within this interpretive context, the question of what Cézanne's touch "represents" – a question that persists because his paintings patently depict objects such as apples, all the while referring to sensations and exhibiting gestures – can never yield an unequivocal answer.

When we allude to pictures as if consisting of touches, we enter a dense field of metaphoric exchange between vision and touch, eye and hand. The painter's touch is a heavily figured notion that refers to at least three aspects of a painting and its process. First, touch is the gesture that deposits the painter's mark as an imprint or impression; we regard this mark as the indexical sign of the gesture. Second, touch is the applied paint mark itself in its capacity as a visible form; discernible features of a touch (or a group of touches) relate it iconically to things of similar form seen both outside and inside paintings – both apples and pictures of apples. Third, touch is the tactile sensation the painter actually experiences or the viewer imagines to be associated with making such a mark. Each of these aspects of the experience of painting (both painter's and viewer's) are "touch."

In a straightforward way, touches, not vision, make a picture. Yet even this statement carries a double signification. Do we mean that a painting is created by touching? Or, rather, that it is composed of touches? The ambiguity of pictorial touch arises from a common metonymy: the name of an action, touching a surface to leave a mark, is transferred to the mark itself as the effect of this cause; touching (usually with the aid of a brush) makes a paint mark, so a paint mark becomes a touch.

Two modes of touching are the most familiar: running the hand along a continuous surface; extending the hand forward to make simple contact with the resistance of a surface. The latter mode corresponds to the discrete and potentially repetitious action that produces the simplest kind of paint mark, the dab or "touch." But most paint marks result from the combination of contact and lateral movement – pushing, dragging, "drawing." (Note that the forms of touch that relate most familiarly with painting practice are active rather than passive; to paint is to enter the world rather than suffer it).[14]

During the nineteenth century, the problem of pictorial touch was complicated by increasing cultural investment in touch as the immediate mark and the marking (production) of authorial identity.[15] To make a painting was to assert oneself as an independent author (with connotations of social liberation and political independence), and purchasing a painting was to participate in, by buying into, a social system of transferable identities and fashionability. Authorial idiosyncrasy enjoyed collective recognition and followed conventions of its own – including, in painting, the accentuation of signs of the hand. The distinctively handled brush stroke connoted genuineness and immediacy and thus functioned as a *mediated* reference to the authorial identity of its maker; it was a member of a class of marks recognized as authored, and an instance of the particular mark by which its artist-author was known.

The wave of commentary Cézanne received around 1895 capitalized on his own exaggeration of touch and carried the interpretive complexities along with it. The writings of Gustave Geffroy, friend and eventual biographer of Claude Monet, provide a distinguished example. Monet had already found a receptive audience for his own pronounced paint surfaces and encouraged Geffroy to address Cézanne's art. Geffroy could not be as secure in writing about Cézanne as he was with Monet. His various statements convey an apologetic tone, as if he knew that his readership would have to overcome resistance to the extreme oddity of Cézanne's style. Yet his statements become all the more valuable because they indicate what must have seemed disturbing about the paintings as well as what seemed remarkably right.

Two things in particular were right, both related to Cézanne's touch. First, when Geffroy reviewed the Vollard exhibition, he stressed the prominence of the mark – that is, the marking, the activity itself as indicated by the marked surface of the paintings. Alluding to the fact that most of the exhibited works lacked signatures as well as other signs of professional finish, Geffroy advised his reader: "Have no fear, the works are [indeed] signed, better marked than by a signature."[16] Geffroy's word was "marqué," which, like the English "marked," connotes identification as well as visual, or sensible, articulation. The surface details of each of Cézanne's paintings bespoke the same character at work throughout a long career (Vollard's exhibition was retrospective). Cézanne was in each and every mark and the mark could only be his.

Second, in a later review, Geffroy converted a fault – the possibility that the marks failed to form a single coherent image – into a virtue: "They say Cézanne's canvases are not finished. It doesn't matter, so long as they express the beauty [and] harmony he has felt so deeply. Who will say at what precise moment a canvas is finished? Art does not proceed without a certain incompleteness, because the life it reproduces is in perpetual transformation."[17] Each mark could be regarded as the representation of a moment of sensation and experience, of a continuing encounter with the world. Since, according to Geffroy's characterization, life's experience is unbounded and unpredictable, its appropriate image would lack the completeness of the conventionally well-composed picture. Geffroy's association of Cézanne's mark or touch with immediate experience establishes it as a quality that cannot be affected by quantification. One mark is as valid a statement – identifying, authentic, expressive – as ten or ten thousand. It is not in the nature of such touches to total up, forming a panoramic view already fully comprehended in an independent vision or in the images of "the mind's eye." Instead, each mark retains a certain isolation, representing a personal "signature" as well as the artist's living experience of something beyond him yet having become part of him through the touch of painting. (But, still, what precisely is this "something" that is "represented"? Perhaps it need be no more than the resistance of an encounter of hand and canvas.)

Subsequent commentary on Cézanne reiterates Geffroy's interpretive themes while it exhibits some nagging confusion concerning what the painter represents. One of the most sustained attempts at characterizing Cézanne's art can be found in an essay by Meyer Schapiro, written for a sophisticated but general audience. Schapiro's study was published in 1952, when he was very aware of the issues of Abstract Expressionism. At about the same time, Harold Rosenberg defined such non-representational art as "action painting" and wittily suggested that it brought Cézanne's kind of modernist representation to an end: "The apples weren't brushed off the table in order to make room for perfect relations of space and color. They had to go so that nothing would get in the way of the act of painting."[18] In effect Rosenberg assigned only one function to visualized touch in the new American painting – to refer back to the act of an artist. This same sense of historical evolution allowed Schapiro to assign Cézanne's art to a mediate position, "between the old kind of picture, faithful to a striking or beautiful object [that is, the "classical" mode], and the modern 'abstract' kind of painting, a moving harmony of colored touches representing nothing."[19] Schapiro (like Rosenberg) indicated elsewhere that although abstract art did not "represent," it could still signify. Namely, it referred to "the occasion of spontaneity or intense feeling. The painting symbolizes an individual who realizes freedom and deep engagement of the self within his work."[20] Such meaning, as it establishes an ideal social type, becomes sociopolitical; perceived as the product of an action, the painting – or rather its description – allegorizes a particular relationship between self and world or self and other(s). Despite the fact that Cézanne painted objects as well as gestures, Schapiro extended to his art the same meaning pure abstraction would convey: "the conception of a personal art [such as Cézanne's] rested upon a more general ideal of individual liberty in the social body and drew from the latter its ultimate confidence that an art of personal expression has a universal sense."[21] The ideal social being must assert his or her independent subjectivity, make a mark.

How can the broad political allegory of Cézanne's style – of, actually, his touch – be correlated with observable pictorial features? For critics like Rosenberg or Schapiro, one of the most "visible" qualities shared by the politics of modernity and by modernist art is spontaneity (recall Schapiro's reference to "the occasion of spontaneity or intense feeling"). Spontaneity can be seen in Cézanne's vigorously marked surfaces, which display unconventional texture as well as irregularity in degree of finish. But beyond the general manner of handling paint (characteristic of both Cézanne and later abstractionists), what allegorical role might be played by the very act of reaching out to represent objects? Would a different type of social being have a different strategy for picturing objects?[22] It is not clear that the modernist critical discourse can generate detailed answers to such a question, for its preferred political allegory is so broad that it applies to any painting described as original and distinctive, regardless of its mode of representation. Both the description and the allegory view the modernist's hand as a favored organ of free choice, free even of its own physical limitation of movement within a certain range or reach. (I will argue eventually that painting by touch can evoke a political allegory less tied to notions of individual distinction and expressive spontaneity.)

Schapiro, like Geffroy before him, seems to privilege "piecemeal" touch over panoramic vision in his description of the making process (although the writer himself seeks to integrate his observations): "[Cézanne] loosened the perspective system of traditional art and gave to the space of the image the aspect of a world created free-hand and put together piecemeal from successive perceptions, rather than offered complete to the eye in one coordinating glance ..." Schapiro argues, moreover, that Cézanne's stroke also establishes the touch or tactile sensation of the depicted model: "The apple looks solid, weighty, and round as it would feel to a blind man."[23] Indeed, Cézanne has always been known as a painter of solidity in this double sense: his pictures are said to have a dense surface construction of interlocking parts and simultaneously to capture the volume and material substance of objects (and in this double capacity he is often compared to Renaissance and "classical" masters).[24] If this is so, if Cézanne's mark makes his painted apple look like a real apple would feel to blind touch, while this mark also functions as the self-referential touch of the artist, what kind of touch, in sum, does a painting by Cézanne represent?

Schapiro and other interpreters offer no straightforward answer. To obviate the question, we commonly conclude that paintings consist of marks that perform a double function. Such doubleness – and duplicity – characterizes the general class of cultural objects to which paintings belong, communicative signs. Signs have the potential to develop normative (conventional, "literal") as well as deviant (figured) reference. We cannot assume that direct pictorial reference to objects (apples, for instance) must always be the normative or ruling function, despite our having defined the classical mode of representation in terms of such reference. The interpreter of a painting must decide which function of the mark is best regarded as the normative one, or which of the two functions appears to dominate the other.

In narrating a history from Cézanne to Abstract Expressionism, modernist critics have stressed two related matters. First, the artist's individual mark – as opposed to larger units of signification, such as represented objects or compositional motifs – has assumed great significance (recall Geffroy's account of Cézanne). Second, the self-referential or gestural function has become dominant, even to the point of seeming more literal than figured (Schapiro's remarks on Cézanne are consistent with such a history). In other words, within the modernist tradition the indexical function has been privileged over the iconic: a mark refers to its maker (or cause) more emphatically than it refers to some detached object which may happen to exhibit formal qualities consistent with the configuration of one or more marks. (It could be said that marks, for the modernist, are "naturally" expressive, but only conventionally mimetic; hence the dominance of theories of expression over theories of imitation.) Deviance in representation may be tolerated for the sake of a certain normative self-expression, a style recognizably odd but "natural" to its author.[25] Emphasis on the mark as index of a maker-author correlates readily with an ideological concern for originality, spontaneity, and self-expression.

In the case of Cézanne the relationship of the self-referential and representational functions is especially difficult to determine. Recall that Schapiro assigned a mediate historical position to this artist and marveled at the persistent strength of his representational function: the painted apple appears "as it would feel to a blind man." Checking this description of powerful illusionism against an actual painting, we note a discrepancy for which the critical response of 1895 already prepared us. Geffroy and other early critics saw that Cézanne gave to background areas the same tactile materiality and visual intensity that defined foreground areas, causing backgrounds to project forward.[26] This often rendered his pictorial illusionism, his capacity to represent the volume and weightiness of objects, incoherent. Consider the background of *Wine Glass and Apples* (c. 1879–1880, see Plate 8.2), which contains a pattern of marks recognizable as leaves. Illusionistically, the leaves seem "real" (note how they hover above the glass). Yet we know from documentary evidence, as well as accumulated pictorial indications, that this is a painting of painted – that is, stenciled or printed – leaves; these leaves derive from the patterned wallpaper in the artist's studio.[27] Because of the pronounced marking of this part of the canvas, Schapiro's "blind man" would most likely discover rounded, or perhaps faceted, volume rather than flat planarity. Cézanne's painting exhibits a feature that conventionally allows a viewer to coordinate touch with vision – namely, a repetitive pattern of marks that, when varied in color, can be perceived as facets of a turning surface (comprehended ultimately by touch). But the artist has failed to coordinate this feature with the spatial properties of the objects represented. A flat thing, a papered wall, has been rendered aggressively volumetric. A related problem arises from the fact that Cézanne's surface asserts itself ubiquitously, even in the recessive spaces immediately surrounding objects of attention such as apples. As a result Cézanne's apples might actually be perceived as half-apples – not in Venturi's sense, because they may be cut by a framing edge – but because they exhibit fronts without strong indications of backs. If the proof of represented volume comes from the viewer's imaginative application of "touch," such touch will pass along the marked surface rather than turning, illusionistically, behind it.

Cézanne's paintings can be characterized in general. His surfaces consist of abruptly juxtaposed strokes, each distinguished from its neighbors but linking up to establish planar continuity, with passages of color often extended across the proper boundaries of depicted objects. The net effect of Cézanne's touch is to render background areas more volumetric and foreground areas flatter than one would expect. The distinction between flatness and volume becomes rather confused and perhaps irrelevant. Cézanne represents "real" things, but, contrary to what we have been in the habit of believing, their pictorial look does not correspond to how they would feel to the touch; nor does the artist's touch imitate the look of things, at least not in familiar ways.[28]

The situation of *Wine Glass and Apples* amounts to a kind of paradox thematized in many of Cézanne's works, a visual pun created by touch.[29] Either by his choice of problematic motif – a still life suited to naturalistic rendering, set off by wallpaper already containing a naturalistic image – or through the equalizing effect of his technical procedure, Cézanne has accentuated the inherent duplicitousness of visual signs: like words, they are forever caught up in conditions of partial resemblance (paronymy) and thereby elicit contradictory interpretations. The potential to resemble sometimes depends on properties of the sign itself (the curves of a depiction of a

Plate 8.2 Paul Cézanne, *Wine Glass and Apples*, no signature, oil on canvas (mounted on board?), 31 × 40 cm.

schematic leaf-pattern recalling the curves of a depiction of "real" leaves) and sometimes on the context of presentation (as when wallpaper leaves appear near still-life objects of a class to which leafy plants might actually belong). Who can say how to render a pre-existing image of printed leaves? Should the painter aim to reveal the material flatness of the wallpaper, or the *pictorial* volume of the leaves? Cézanne, I believe, chose the latter, but his sensitivity to the implications – as well as our own sensitivity – must depend on prevailing attitudes toward interpreting pictures.

In *Wine Glass and Apples* (and similar works that have more than one level of pictorial "reality") Cézanne has exaggerated a notorious feature of western representation – the play between literal surface and figured depth, or between signifier and signified. Somewhat less obviously, all his works force this issue since they render it more explicit than is to be expected in images belonging to the traditional genres, such as still life or landscape. What matters is not the presence of the problem (which may be ubiquitous), but the degree of entanglement. Hence the sense viewers have always had of Cézanne's fundamental strangeness.

The general principle at work in his art is analogy: one thing is made to look like, or somehow be like, another, despite the differences and dissimilarities that otherwise obtain. The analogies seem obsessive and always at hand. There are more of them than the demands of coherent composition would require, so many more, in fact, that conventional compositional hierarchies – including the "foregrounding" of figures by less articulated "background" areas – fail to emerge. As the analogies pile up, the paintings appear fragmented and even incomplete because of an abundance of compositional relationships seemingly only half pursued (not resolved into higher orders). Accordingly, Cézanne's early enthusiasts directed viewers to watch the pictures unfolding. As Roger Fry wrote, "to the inquiring eye new relations, unsuspected harmonies continually reveal themselves"; indeed, he also noted that the presence of fixed hierarchical structure in some of Cézanne's paintings diminished their effect.[30]

Fry's reservation pertained especially to the *Grandes Baigneuses* of 1906 (see Plate 8.3) with its predominant triangular motif formed by a horizontal screen of figures below arching trees. Yet in its details this painting contains a characteristic abundance of overdetermined analogies. Pictorial analogies "distort" normative images by subordinating any one part of the representation to some other, giving it, as it

Plate 8.3 Paul Cézanne, *Les Grandes Baigneuses*, no signature, oil on canvas, 212.5 × 250.9 cm.

were, an unnatural motivation. Once analogy is established as a principle, the particular appearance of one thing can always be attributed to the presence of some other (which exhibits a comparative property) rather than to its own "true," unfigured look. The relationship of subordination is reciprocal, with each term of the analogy conceivably a dependent one.[31] Analogy draws its component parts into a self-sufficient network detached from the world of "neutral" observation.

A striking example from the *Grandes Baigneuses* is the disproportionately tiny head of the large crouching bather belonging to the left-hand group. We can regard this head and its hair as if terminating a localized motif formed primarily by the upper part of the standing bather at the extreme left – note the right-angled arm and the comparably right-angled configuration of torso and thigh. The head and hair of the crouching figure also direct attention to the similar hair and elongated torso of the standing figure. The severity of the distortion, which surpasses that of neighboring bathers, has its consequences. Such a bizarre feature calls attention to itself as if a bump on an otherwise smooth surface, something that breaks the surface and interrupts, even shocks, the eye as it performs its visual scanning. It may be that the painting hand's piecemeal operation – its search for analogies of shape, size, and direction, its concentration on the immediate moment, but not the immediate totality – liberates it from the accumulated tradition of "correct" proportion and perspective (which are devices of totalization). At any rate, the smaller elements of Cézanne's great composition retain a sense of fragmented touch because they fail to blend into the order of panoramic vision.[32]

Once we recognize analogy as the issue, some of Cézanne's drawings become blatant illustrations of the technique; they exhibit a single dominating analogy, expressed with an intensity that excludes other pictorial considerations. In *Camille Pissarro Seen from the Back* (c. 1874–77; see Plate 8.4) a chair joint and a shoulder joint have been drawn in accord with each other. It would be misleading to attribute such an analogy to observation of the visual effects of objects. The image represents instead a skillful act of drawing in which the hand supplements the eye's distanced scanning by its own scanning at very close range. The hand moves along the surface of the paper, repeating or imitating gestures already once made, with such gestures including the rhythmic spacing of elements of the chosen, repeated motif. (Significantly, the concept of motif relates to motive, motivation, and movement.)

In the paintings – especially in images of landscape or foliage – Cézanne's gestures often consist of individual strokes; so too in many of the drawings. In the case of *Camille Pissarro*, however, a relatively large area of surface constitutes the unit of repetition; the drawn lines of the back imitate those of the chair and vice versa. The resultant exchangeability of parts is a property of picture surfaces, not of the objects under survey. Cézanne's analogy exists only in his pictorial configuration since the medium of linear drawing produces it. The hand establishes what the interpreter retrospectively attributes to the eye, presumed to be the motivating cause and guide of the hand's actions. But since the hand has habits of its own we wonder which sense really dominates and assumes priority. One thing is certain: the hand crafts the picture. So common language, employing metonymy, calls the elements of a painting or drawing touches rather than looks.

Cézanne's "touch," then, belongs to his canvas or paper surface,

Plate 8.4 Paul Cézanne, *Camille Pissarro Seen from the Back*, signature not in Cézanne's hand, pencil on paper, 125 × 150 mm.

145

not to his sense of the objects depicted. His tactile gesture was never a matter of comprehending real objects by imaginatively tracing their contours, allowing a primitive application of touch (running the hand along a surface) to substitute for a more nuanced understanding. Thus the artist denied that (tactile) line could capture nature, which was instead to be realized through (optical) color.[33] Yet that color, for the painter, existed as touches – in French, both *touches* and *taches* (the terms are related metonymically).

Cézanne's interpreters confirmed this conversion when they gave his brush strokes the capacity to represent vision metaphorically so that a look might become a touch on the canvas. A stroke of pigment coordinated with neighboring touches of related but varying hue (the device of "modeling" discussed in treatises written by the painter's contemporaries) could evoke the look of a volumetric object under illumination.[34] Painting thereby transferred or converted vision into touches of paint, performing both iconic and symbolic functions. Neither the iconic, a "naturally" motivated relationship, nor the symbolic, an arbitrary or conventional association, is found in isolation.[35] To some extent the artist's paint imitated iconic aspects of the represented object, usually its color or quality of illumination. But since Cézanne's manner of "modeling" significantly departs from prevailing standards of iconic resemblance applicable to painting, it needs to be considered as a (mere) sign or symbol of the visual effect depicted.[36] A double irony is evident: the recognition of "natural" iconic resemblance depends on the application of conventional standards for determining such resemblance; and, while critics evoke Cézanne's "realism," he yet departs from iconic norms. We might claim, then, that Cézanne's modeling – and ultimately all modeling – merely *refers* (contextually, historically) to its associated "natural" effect rather than definitively creating that visual effect through incontrovertible resemblance. The attitude of the interpreter will determine whether the iconic or symbolic function dominates.

Beyond the iconic, the transference of vision into touch brings forth other functions of touch, which are indexical: first, an indication of authorship; second, a drama of force and resistance acted out in the physical contact between hand (with brush) and canvas or paper surface. All this is inherent in traditional painting and its conventional interpretation, much being caught in the often repeated thought, "Touch is the [expressive] handwriting of the painter."[37] But many of Cézanne's critics went further, as if reversing the usual direction of the metaphoric transference: they argued that his remarkably naive realism captured even unseen details of an external object's physicality (weight, for instance), rendering such qualities accessible to the eye. For the interpreter, then, the artist's touch produced a visual effect which in turn elicited a tactile response.

This becomes especially curious when we consider the difference between Cézanne's surfaces and those of paradigmatically "realistic" pictures such as photographs. The one is coarse-grained and relatively discontinuous – bumpy to the imagined touch – whereas the other is sufficiently smoothly gradated so as to inhibit the viewer's attending to tactile qualities.[38] With "touch" (brush stroke or any other discernible element of marking) minimized, all becomes a matter of vision. In the photograph, as well as in paintings having comparable surface gradients or other factors of refinement, visual passage from one depicted object to another is facilitated by the perceived continuity of the "real" space represented. It is as if nothing has been either selected or eliminated; all appears before the scanning eye. For modern viewers, the appearance of such inclusiveness connotes an objective realism; rhetorically, photography constructs an "effect of the real."[39]

In contrast to photographic seamlessness, Cézanne's device of analogy draws out features for specific comparison, further fragmenting a surface already broken by individual touches.[40] Yet analogy is itself a figure that establishes continuity by creating pictorial relationships (we see, for example, that a shoulder belongs to the same visual order as a chair, and we can even note that one accentuated brush stroke belongs to the same system as neighboring strokes of the same type). It was analogy that Henri Matisse responded to in the small picture of bathers he purchased from Vollard: "Everything there was in order [hiérarchisé], hands and trees counted in the same manner as the sky."[41] Indeed Cézanne gave features of anatomy the same scale and directional paint application as adjacent patches of "background" foliage. Such blatantly configured continuity arrests the eye and must seem less natural than the unobtrusive (but still configured) "real" continuity of a photographic image or any panoramic totality. For this reason Geffroy – who lacked the ease of a Matisse or a Schapiro in accepting assertive surfaces – wrote that certain effects were by-products of an intensive study pursued with inadequate technical expertise. The critic enumerated the most apparent flaws in Cézanne's rendering as if technical procedure were their cause. With an obvious logic he implied that the situation was not to be seen in nature but had been created by hand, by an active touch disjoined from familiar vision. Several of the problems Geffroy noted – "forms sometimes become awkward, objects blend together, proportions are not always established with sufficient precision"[42] – are conceivable as aspects of the painter's mode of pictorial analogy.

Cézanne's surface lacks the transparent wholeness of the photograph, yet his analogies suggest that his *depicted* world, like that of the photograph, has coherence – it coheres – and thus succeeds in evoking the physical integrity of real objects and their surrounding spaces. By metonymic exchange, the viewer attributes the peculiar physicality of Cézanne's painted surface to the objects represented. Hence the innumerable references to the "solidity" of Cézanne's surface constructions as well as to the perceived "solidity" of his depicted apples, mountains, and human figures. Although the two instances of the descriptive term play off and even depend on each other, neither can be said to be applied "literally."[43]

In sum, the surface of a photograph – and of any comparable kind of painting – becomes panoramic (or "illusionistic") because its appearance inhibits the interpreter from applying a descriptive discourse of touch, despite the fact that the picture is a product of manufacture and/or handicraft. Such an image will seem a natural product of common vision, or perhaps of the equally natural point of view of an individual, or, in the case of the photograph, of the given, "natural" properties of the apparatus. In all three cases, vision seems to retain its "natural" immediacy and wholeness. Whereas a painting by Cézanne, however many qualities of visible objects it may seem to capture, requires touch for its explication; it never attains the visual integrity, distance, and completion of the panorama.

To be sure, the distinctions I have just made are complex and evasive. A more economical account of the physicality of Cézanne's art will follow.

AN ALTERNATIVE TOUCH

I see. By strokes of color [*taches*].
One touch [*touche*] after the other, one touch after the other ...
　(Cézanne's statements, imaginatively reconstructed by Joachim Gasquet)[44]

The usual way of ordering the confusion Cézanne creates is to invoke the irresolvable dualism of touch – touch signifies the artist's gesture and aesthetic choice (references to subjectivity) while simultaneously depicting "solidity" (a reference to objectivity and the "real").[45] Schapiro's elegant phrasing succeeds as well as any in capturing this commonplace dualism; he writes of Cézanne's "tangible touches of color each of which, while rendering a visual sensation [objectivity], makes us aware of a decision of the mind [aesthetic choice] and an operation of the hand [an identifying gesture or habit]." Schapiro adds immediately: "In this complex process . . . the self is always present . . . mastering its inner world by mastering something beyond itself [presumably, 'reality']."[46] Here touch ultimately serves the subjective self in its mastery of objective things, including itself conceived as a thing one seeks pre-eminently to know through self-reflection.

Process and mastery are guiding principles for the development of Schapiro's account of how touch represents vision metaphorically. As the sense capable of panoramic totalization, vision connotes mastery; the eye looks outward or from above to survey objects at its disposition. I have already noted that touch, in contrast to vision, is commonly conceived as procedural; the artist employs "one touch after the other" in order to grasp in paint what vision possesses all at once. Tactile experience is thus inherently subdivided (touch by touch), whereas vision comes whole. The distinction derives from temporality, vision seeming rather like immediate revelation, touch more of a probing investigation. We habitually extend this presumed difference in temporal mode to the spatial dimension so that vision appears all-encompassing while touch is limited to a local or proximate area. This understanding supports Schapiro's conclusion (recall also Geffroy) that "each stroke carries something of the freshness of a new sensation of nature."[47] In effect, touch acts as the figuring agent for vision. It converts vision's totality into personalized, fragmented experience identified with the time and place of the artist, experience that can be resumed from day to day (just as Cézanne returned to his canvases while, according to critics, remaining faithful to initial viewings). The notion that paintings reflect mastery derives not only from the presumption that artists possess creative genius and technical skill; it is also supported by the fact that touch offers the artist procedural access to the encompassing mastery associated with vision.

No doubt, to recognize both subjective and objective aspects of the painter's touch improves over insisting on one alone. Yet we do no more than repeat modernism's received wisdom, applicable to works far less problematic than Cézanne's. As one turn-of-the-century critic put it, speaking of a Romantic landscape by J. M. W. Turner, "every line of the pines . . . is a picture-line ['subjective'], but also a tree-line ['objective']."[48] And to control both aspects of a line – that is, to gesture toward nature while yet transforming her imprint into a distinctive and reflexive picture of one's own gesture – constitutes a form of artistic self-expression familiar at least since the Romanticism of the early nineteenth century.[49]

A few writers on painting have suggested something otherwise, sometimes only in passing, by invoking an insistent *reciprocity* as an alternative to dualism and opposition. To speak of reciprocity is to eliminate the possibility of setting subjective (or deviant) metaphorical elements against objective (or normative) literal ones. Within the flux of reciprocity either everything becomes metaphorically figured or everything has the reality effect of the literal. The rhetorical figure that mediates and conflates the metaphoric and the literal is catachresis, which is sometimes called false or improper metaphor. A catachretic term is used when no proper, or literal, term is available. It borrows from another field of discourse as if without recognizing the distance, seeming to convert a metaphor into the literal name for something; yet a sense of metaphor remains.[50] The reciprocity or shifting produced by catachresis undermines any polarization of subject and object, self and other, deviation and norm, touch and vision. Among Cézanne's commentators, the "catachretic" alternative is clearest in statements by Maurice Merleau-Ponty, where it served his broad philosophical critique of self-reflection and self-constituting subjectivity.[51]

Merleau-Ponty analyzed touch as an incessantly reversible experience; he then used it as the model for a radical conception of vision, evidence for which was to be found in Cézanne's painting. As Merleau-Ponty explains it, touch preserves an essential ambiguity of chiasm, or reversibility, the touching and the touched never settling into a fixed relationship of subject to object, consciousness to brute matter. We readily discover the ambiguity of touch by referring to the most ordinary experiences, whereas substantial effort may be required to grasp an analogous ambiguity in vision (mutual exchange of seer and seen). Touch, however, can be an effective guide to such an understanding of vision. Merleau-Ponty writes: "When I touch my right hand with my left ... it is not a matter of two sensations felt together ... but of an ambiguous set-up in which both hands can alternate the roles of 'touching' and being 'touched' ... I can identify the hand touched as the same one which will in a moment be touching."[52] Some later remarks recapitulate as well as extend the thought: "To touch" – even when touching an object – "is to touch oneself . . . things are the prolongation of my body and my body is the prolongation of the world . . . [There is] indivision of this sensible Being that I am and all the rest which feels itself [*se sent*] in me."[53] Merleau-Ponty argues that this chiasmic feeling can be visual as well as tactile, and capable of appearing externally in the form of a painting: "Thus there appears a 'visible' of the second power . . . It is more accurate to say that I see according to it, or with it, than that I see it."[54] Why? Because the "visible" picture retains a physical – or, in Merleau-Ponty's precise neologisms, "carnal" or "fleshly" – engagement with the very functioning of the eye; the visible (seen) is not to be separated from the eye (seer), just as what is touched is never distanced from the hand that touches.

In this vein Merleau-Ponty described Cézanne's project – "to make *visible* how the world *touches* us," to create a picture of undeniable physicality.[55] He was attracted to what he knew of how the painter worked, reflections of the mythologized accounts offered by Bernard, Gasquet, and Vollard.[56] The famous essay "Cézanne's Doubt" begins: "He needed one hundred working sessions for a still life, one hundred and fifty sittings for a portrait. What we call his work was, for him, only an essay, an approach to painting."[57] Immediately the image is of intense involvement, a struggle for a resolution that does not come, and may not even be desirable. Merleau-Ponty wished to counter interpretations that derived the meaning of a work from an artist's pre-existing and fixed psychological state – from, simply, a life regarded as if formed independent of perception. He argued instead that although a life made its works possible, the works gave life's inherited conditions "a figurative sense" they would otherwise not possess.[58] Artistic form was never prefigured by a context, nor would it ever appear whole.

Beyond the anecdotes about Cézanne's quirks, doubts, and hesitations, there were, of course, technical features that attracted Merleau-Ponty's attention. He knew that critics had always regarded Cézanne's paintings as formally dense, packed with signifying touches and sensations even when unfinished. The surface of such painting, like that of a fleshly body, possesses physicality at all points; it is a mobile sensory field having neither fixed privileged locations nor dead spots, and engaged everywhere in reciprocal touching (Cézanne's technique puts all elements of the picture in touch through an ever-expanding network of analogies). Under this metaphor of carnality, Cézanne's surface of touches corresponds to Merleau-Ponty's description of the person who sees: "Our glances are not 'acts of consciousness,' each of which claims an invariable priority, but openings of our flesh which are immediately filled by the universal flesh of the world."[59] Again, touching becomes the metaphor for a conception of seeing that challenges a subject-oriented, distancing vision. Cézanne's seeing has a closeness comparable to his density of touch as well as to the odd order of proximities among the objects he renders (recall that his figures and grounds merge and that his analogies cause disparate things to assume the same painterly, or fleshly, form).

Following Merleau-Ponty's hints, we might say that Cézanne's paintings do not represent physicality but share in it, *possess* it, so that the painting as an index of the artist's subjectivity converges upon its observed model and partakes of its reality. Yet such a statement remains within the realm of prevailing critical description. Using familiar but mystifying metaphors, Schapiro, for example, allowed painted surfaces to become amazingly apple-like – "[Cézanne's] constructed form ... *possesses* in a remarkable way the object-traits of the thing represented: its local color, weight, solidity, and extension."[60] It takes only a small effort to reformulate this comment within a discourse of reciprocity; we simply accept the painting's metaphoric possession of physical qualities that normally cannot apply to thin, flat surfaces. This allows the near painting surface and the distant model-object to share and exchange visual and tactile properties.

The still evasive alternative – if it is to be articulated – can be pursued only by regarding the physicality of Cézanne's art in an uncompromisingly literal way. To the extent that he was a critic of Cézanne, this was not Merleau-Ponty's intention. Nevertheless, he suggests how to do this when he describes spaces or gaps as if they possessed material substance. In order to restore physicality to the perceived distance of an object, Merleau-Ponty defines that object "in relation to our power of grasping it."[61] If we judge it to be very far away, this is because it is remote to the touch. In terms of touch, literally, painters do not paint things that lie at a distance, the panorama; they paint only what is within reach, at arm's length, and what is (already) on the canvas, its surface. We must regard a painting as a surface available to touch in the way that distant objects cannot be. In a straightforward way, a painting is always subject to the painter's grasp, at least while being crafted.

"The painting is an analogue or likeness only according to the body," writes Merleau-Ponty.[62] It is a way of saying that painting provides a view of objects having the closeness of touch, a view that cannot be distanced from the body or occupy a space defined by abstracted mathematical description. Painting preserves the particularity of an encounter or engagement of two physicalities, what paints and what is painted (traditionally, the artist-subject and the model-object), each playing both active and passive roles in the process.[63] If we choose to ask what – literally – "is painted," our answer is this: the material surface that the painter touches.[64] In consequence, the painter's vision is always close, *never farther than an arm's length*, the space traversed by the hand as it metaphorically traces out the eye's directed seeing by means of its own capacity to touch. Thus painting literalizes the physicality of seeing. It participates in the give and take of physical force and resistance, the antithesis of the panoramic view that encounters no resistance and likewise has no reciprocal effect on the viewer.

Merleau-Ponty's sense of touch and vision lends itself to political allegorization, just as Schapiro's does. His, however, is a politics leading neither to mastery of a situation nor to self-mastery, but one that remains inconclusively engaged in the physicality of historical events. Like an artist's life, the objective conditions of history seem, retrospectively, to have predetermined whatever acts have been committed; yet people's actions have given history its configuration. Such reciprocal engagement with history translates into an ideal of community and collective thought and practice. No person has the perspective to view history as a panorama set out for the understanding. At one point, Merleau-Ponty provides an image appropriate both to his political allegory and to an account of touch (it involves, coincidentally, the touching of right and left hands): "[Social and political] exchange, in which no one commands and no one obeys, is symbolized by the old custom which dictates that, in a meeting, speakers join in when the audience applauds. What they applaud is the fact that they do not intervene as persons, that in their relationship with those who listen to them a truth appears which does not come from them and which the speakers can and must applaud."[65] Merleau-Ponty found such collective, unmasterable "truth" in Cézanne's paintings. Neither preconceived nor definitively executed, this truth achieved its figuration on the painting surface as the result of collaboration between forces and resistances, one physicality and another.

There is no need to find the cause of Cézanne's pictorial idiosyncrasy in aspects of a model or an artistic temperament or even an imperfect technique; the physicality that forms a picture can be contained within the movements of a hand in response to the material substance and the scale of brush, paint, and receptive but also resistant surface. If what we locate at arm's length is the "medium," a locus of tactile creation situated between the artist-subject and the model-object, the proper metaphoric reference to this medium must now be recognition, not mastery. Cézanne's picture recognizes the properties of the medium rather than using the mastered medium as an instrument to reach beyond itself (to, say, apples or a mountain). As in the case of one hand grasping the other (and in analogous cases of interpersonal "social touch"[66]), the analysis of Cézanne's mode of painting requires a notion of mutual figuration: the painted surface affects the painter as much as he affects it; neither force dominates. Indeed, it is not uncommon for modernist artists to rely on this critical device for grasping what they experience.[67] Matisse, for instance, explains that a drawing is motivated by an idea understood "only as it develops through the course of the picture."[68] And Barnett Newman states: "It is as I work that the work itself begins to have an effect on me. Just as I affect the canvas, so does the canvas affect me."[69] Both imply that the distance and perhaps the very distinction between artist-subject and model-object may be lost for the painter.

Such productive loss may also be experienced by the viewer. Walter Benjamin, who shared Merleau-Ponty's concern for collectivity, noted that vision could acquire the force of touch, including its reciprocity. One of his many statements to this effect derived from his engagement with Cézanne. Seeing the artist's works led Benjamin to conclude that great paintings do not induce passage into the represented space, "rather, this space [*Raum*] thrusts itself forward."[70] It was Benjamin's way of recognizing that Cézanne's painting was insistently particular; its surface was opaque, its physicality acting to bar or disrupt comprehensive panoramic vision. Having acquired material identity (or never having lost it to the force of prevailing interpretive fictions), the "space" of a painting could impose itself on the viewer. Benjamin's commentary accepts materiality in a more literal way than does Schapiro's, yet still returns to the metaphorical realm: in his account of Cézanne's painting, a dematerialized visual "space" configured by the hand regains the immediate physicality and resistance that belongs to touch.

AN ALTERNATIVE "VISION"

I have alluded to Cézanne's pictorial analogies and paronymous resemblances, that is, his imperfect likenesses that appear within the immediate pictorial context. The interpreter recognizes such relationships only to realize that they violate or contradict others that the conventional practice of painting seeks to establish. Cézanne's touch combines or associates pictorial elements so that description in terms of familiar visual effects, including spatial illusion, becomes remarkably difficult.

As a rhetorical convenience, I will refer to the artist's actions as causal origin of what we now see in his art, describing the effect of Cézanne's problematic style as if he intended to achieve it. But there is little evidence that would establish motivation for the more extreme stylistic features. Nor should we assume that the present effect of Cézanne's art necessarily has its source in his own concerns. What we need – what the paintings and our continuing interest in them seem to require – is a principle and a corresponding mode of description that will produce the unsettled effect of Cézanne's art "naturally." Mode of painting and mode of description *together* will then expand the field of meaning (just as Merleau-Ponty capitalized on a particular mode of description to establish a political analogy and evoke an alternative sense of social action).

Still Life with Plaster Cupid (c. 1892–94; see Plate 8.5) is one of the most striking of Cézanne's paintings with regard to our concerns. Here and in similar works (for instance, *Wine Glass and Apples* [Plate 8.2]), the artist removed from contiguous elements of the composition their figurative sense as spatially distinct objects. Deprived of consistently transparent figuration, the viewer can no longer be assured of identifying represented objects – or the juxtaposed marks that collect to form them – as if they were situated at discrete spatial levels.[71]

The issue can be generalized: painting's traditional principle is figuration; conventional pictorial viewing necessitates the acceptance of figuration; when we regard a picture, the figured or metaphoric sense becomes the normative one. This is another way of saying that traditional paintings are illusionistic rather than ideographic or symbolic, even when the subject matter is allegorical. In illusionistic renderings, every minor variation has the potential to make an interpretive difference since it may well represent a shift in the spatial dimension of the image. By undermining and perhaps negating normative pictorialism – its metaphoric conversion of a tactile, material realm into a visual, fictive one – Cézanne did something other than create or reconstruct a reliable "literal" alternative, a picture with an obvious "surface" meaning. Indeed, it would be wrong to compare his art to those twentieth-century abstractions that avoid the look of things outside themselves, seeking to eliminate the

Plate 8.5 Paul Cézanne, *Still Life with Plaster Cupid*, not signed, oil on paper, laid on board, 70.6 × 57.3 cm.

duplicitousness of illusion. Instead, Cézanne's pictures retain represented objects, but reorient their, and the artist's own, physicality. They may well also change the viewer – a "subject" who is formed experientially and socially.

What specifically did Cézanne do, and how should we describe the process and its effect? In *Still Life with Plaster Cupid* the central depicted object is a cast of a sculpture, placed on a table to form part of a still-life arrangement. The background shows canvases propped against the studio wall: at the upper right, a painting of a sculptural cast of a flayed man, a common study piece for artists; at the middle left, an unfinished still life with a patterned cloth corresponding to Cézanne's *Still Life with Peppermint Bottle* (National Gallery, Washington); and, in the center, directly "behind" the Cupid, a stretched canvas that appears to be blank, prepared but unarticulated (although it, too, consists of touches).[72]

There is no obvious description for what one sees in *Still Life with Plaster Cupid* because the picture diverges from a normative view of the recognizable objects within it. In the preceding paragraph, I placed the word *behind* within quotation marks to indicate a necessary shift or split in the level of reference in my own attempt at description. Cézanne's configuration of a depicted blank canvas "behind" a depicted sculpture subverts the pictorial fiction that a measure of "space" must separate the foreground Cupid from its pictorial background. Instead, the composition suggests that the sculpture – which is, after all, a piece of painting and looks so – has become "literally" a painting.[73] This interpretation follows in part from an analogy established between the Cupid and the flayed man, the latter being a painted image of a painting of a sculpture. The depicted canvas "behind" the Cupid is itself without specific figuration, as if becoming the neutral background for the very image that both masks and occupies its center, the figure of the Cupid. The Cupid covers the background canvas not only by lying in front of it, but by lying upon it, touching it.

As in the case of the word "behind," I have also put quotation marks around the word "literally." This is because the image of the sculpted Cupid has been converted – by the figurality of Cézanne's picture – into the image of a painting, not a simple picture, but a picture of a picture. The represented cast becomes "literally" a painting, being both painted and set into a pictorial context that indicates its nature as a painting – after all, this image covers the surface of a depicted canvas (which, of course, covers an actual painting surface).[74]

157

Placing the word "literally" within quotation marks creates a lexical curiosity, an awkward construction indicating that critical description is reaching its limits. One could refer instead to a figurative literalness; this would eliminate the need for quotation marks, which do no more or less than counter the normalizing force of literality by adding a level of distance or figuration. What kind of representation or linguistic construction conflates the literal and figural in such a manner? Clearly, we are dealing here with catachresis, not metaphor; for catachresis accomplishes precisely this: it applies a figurative sense as a literal one, while yet retaining the look or feel of figurality.

In *Still Life with Plaster Cupid* not only identifiable parts of the representation shift between figurality and literalness, but also sensory modes. For touch and vision are caught in reciprocal figuration: it is touch that is figuring vision, and vision that is figuring touch. As we view Cézanne's painting, the fictive sculptural quality of the plaster Cupid converts (back) into a "literal" surface of paint. A visual illusion becomes (or returns to) tactile reality, material surface.

We can choose to retain a visual mode of interpretive description, allowing the painting to become metaphorical and reflect its painter-subject's distanced view of objects. But if we instead opt for a tactile mode, the image becomes catachretic; it literalizes its metaphors, rendering them impersonal, anonymous, and collective. The tactile image belongs to the medium and materials as much or more than it does to either the look of the model-object or the vision of the painter-subject. The painter's touch, which creates the picture, mediates the visuality of subject-seer and object-seen. By custom, art criticism allows visuality to infect the material realm of touch; but we can just as well allow relationships of touch to transform what is usually understood as visual.

I have been attending to Cézanne's visual peculiarities while pursuing a tactile descriptive mode; accordingly, I have claimed that the painter's depicted plaster cast shares an identity with a depicted painting "behind" it. It might be objected that since the Cupid extends beyond the boundaries of its background canvas, it can hardly be contained within it. One of the artist's pictorial analogies counters this objection by indicating that the descriptive metaphors "within" and "without" as well as "front" and "back" can no longer be applied coherently (despite the fact that we continue to discern represented objects). Note that, at the lower left, the "real" patterned cloth forming part of the still-life arrangement on the foreground table extends into or merges with its "painted" counterpart in the still-life canvas "behind" it. To which field does the cloth belong – foreground or background? Perhaps to neither field exclusively, and if to neither, Cézanne's painted surface has somehow been "literalized" as a plane across which a hand can move; it ceases to be a figurative space through which an eye projects itself. The same kind of effect is achieved when the artist allows the stem of the "real" foreground onion (bottom, left of center) to merge with the "painted" table leg "behind" it.[75]

Seen in this manner, Cézanne's painting represents only one surface and one distance, the surface the artist touched and the distance laid out by his hand. The onion and the table leg, for example, occupy the same location, not in fictive space but in the material space of the canvas surface. There are no doubt many ways to interpret this effect of equivalence and uniformity.[76] Perhaps the simplest interpretation is to attribute Cézanne's results to a physical orientation. *Still Life with Plaster Cupid* indicates that the artist – whether intending it or not – concentrated on the movement and rhythms of his hand across the painted surface rather than projecting the passage of his eye from one level of depth to another. This allowed him to combine the forms of disparate objects positioned in his studio at different distances from him, lending these forms a "literal" physicality. They are, first of all, what they appear to be, painted figures covering a canvas surface (just as the artist's characteristic repetitive brush strokes also map out a surface). If, standing at arm's length from the canvas, the viewer assumes a tactile orientation and imagines a condition of reciprocal touch, of hand and pictorial surface acting one upon the other, then Cézanne's formal structures cease to be distorted or paradoxical. Foreground and background become one because the hand can respond only to what it can touch, the "literal" painted surface. It grasps that surface by moving across it, linking elements together and shaping them analogously (recall the case of the *Grandes Baigneuses* [Plate 8.3]).[77] We detect the artist's "natural" involvement with this responsive movement, yet we also perceive a certain self-consciousness and distancing: in *Still Life with Plaster Cupid* Cézanne created a set of visual puns (paronymies) that exaggerate the conflict between what is expected of vision and what of touch – think again of the painted sculptural Cupid that, within its pictorial context, becomes a painted painting.

Most of Cézanne's paintings are less immediately problematic. Nevertheless, many works offer evidence that the artist became conscious of the seductive habits of his hand and resisted them, despite the ultimate predominance of touch over vision in his act of representation. In a view of the valley of the Arc with a distant Mont Sainte-Victoire (c. 1883–1885; see Plate 8.6), Cézanne allowed paint handling to obscure spatial illusion in ways that are now familar to us. For example, as the low branch of the central tree extends out into the fields of the valley, it appears not so much "in front of" and above the valley, but embedded in it. Since the paint strokes articulating this branch are actually overlaid by those defining the fields, we observe that, as in *Still Life with Plaster Cupid*, "foreground" and "background" (or middle-ground) seem to occupy one and the same position. The "foreground" tuft of foliage at the end of the branch can even be mistaken for a "background" mass of vegetation in the valley.

The telling sign of Cézanne's resistance to such "literal" touches – his worry over catachretic marks, and his consequent reversion to metaphoric ones (which are, I have argued, normative in painting) – appears not here but just below this branch where the tree passes "in front of" the line of the river in the valley. The painter represented the river and its banks at a scale consistent with and with a form analogous to the branch above, subjecting the river to being mistaken for another branch. As if recognizing the potential loss of visual illusion, Cézanne added dark blue strokes at the juncture of tree and river, along either edge of the trunk. These strokes counteract the tactile or surface analogy and reassert "spatial" differentiation between "foreground" tree and "background" river, a distinction to be associated not with touch but with vision. The dark blue marks are so thin as to be barely noticeable; yet, once seen, they appear entirely deliberate. They violate the tactile integrity of the general system of analogical forms and gestures. It is as if the eye were holding in check the natural inclinations of the hand. Under visual description the thin blue lines represent a necessary corrective. But under tactile description they are anomalies, marks that break the prevailing rhythm; they work to establish a visual effect while denying their own touch.[78]

By focusing on tactile qualities, we reinforce certain historical connections, but in somewhat unconventional ways. Traditionally, Cézanne has been regarded as a precursor of or even a formative factor for Picasso's (and Braque's) Cubist practice around 1908–1914, a style often described as anonymous or collective precisely because of the depersonalized nature of its touch.[79] While Cézanne may have been ambivalent concerning the physicality of his own represen-

Plate 8.6 Paul Cézanne, Mont Sainte-Victoire, not signed, oil on canvas, 65.5 × 81.7 cm.

tations, Picasso exploited such effects, making touch and its multi-valent connotations an inescapable feature of his pictorialism. He consciously explored the role of touch not only through sculpture and assemblage, but through radical forms of two-dimensional imagery, especially collage. How does collage relate to the touch of Cézanne's painting?

Collage features the hand so as to divorce the artist's touch from its traditional references to vision. In collage, touch sometimes leaves its mark in the form of brush stroke and linear accent, just as it does in modernist painting; but its effect is decidedly more pronounced in the cutting, tearing, folding, and binding of papers and other materials. Such gestures never entered the discourse of "expressive" pictorialism; it would seem odd for a connoisseur to speak of Picasso's "style" of cutting, nor have we ever developed a discriminating vocabulary for the use of knife, scissors, and straight-edge. As mundane actions of which anyone is capable, such "touches" neither index a personalized authorial moment nor elicit the kind of visual metaphor associated with artistic mastery. Cuts, tears, and the like, which characterize materials by altering them, define and retain localized physicality (the character of a cut indicates qualities of the given material). Returning to the figural scheme of transparency and opacity, we see that cuts can be even more opaque than heavy strokes of paint. They call attention to themselves, the action that generated them, and the physicality of the material they transform.

Picasso often configured "literal" cuts (marks or contours made by cutting) so that the distinction between visual illusion and tactile physicality becomes a necessary part of any attentive description of the picture. His viewer is led to discover what is metaphorical and what is otherwise. Consider a *papier collé* of 1913, *Bowl with Fruit, Violin, and Wine Glass* (see Plate 8.7).[80] Depicted at the upper left are five pieces of fruit in a bowl. These illusionistic fragments have been cut from a pre-existing set of chromolithographic botanical illustrations, then combined with other pieces of paper to form part of an elaborate still-life composition. Picasso arranged the five pieces of paper so that three pieces (of fruit) seem to be "in front" and two "behind." This is how it looks initially. But when the cuts themselves are inspected – under a tactile mode of description – it becomes apparent that all five pieces of paper abut on the surface with no overlap. In fact, Picasso left narrow, but decidedly visible gaps between the three "front" papers; this causes the viewer to reflect on

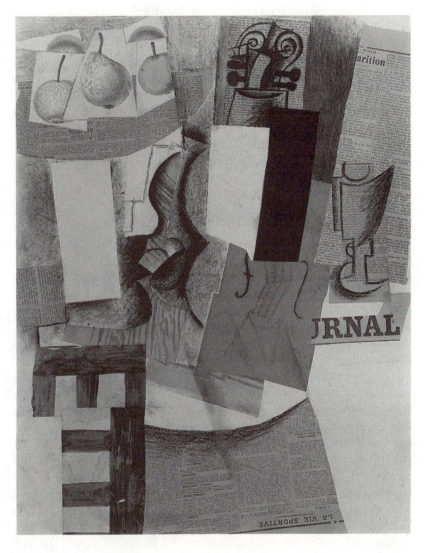

Plate 8.7 Pablo Picasso, *Bowl with Fruit, Violin, and Wine Glass*, not signed, charcoal, mixed media, colored papers, 65.3 × 49.9 cm.

the tactile maneuver, here imperfected, of aligning separate pieces of material along a common edge. Furthermore, the two pieces "behind" prove to be nothing other than the cut-away remains of two of the "front" pieces. Thus, the material foundation of Picasso's total image is less "substantial" than what the eye might initially imagine – only three collaged lithographs have been used, not five.

As a result, Picasso's representation becomes "literal," that is to say, catachretic – but only after the particular physicality of this collage has been noted. At first we perceive two whole fruits partially blocked from direct vision by three others (two of which are themselves partially obstructed). This is a case of normative figurational order; within the representational context of "bowl of fruit," fragments will be interpreted as the visible parts of larger "real" entities. Recall the case of Lionello Venturi and Cézanne's "two and a half apples" (see Plate 8.1). Venturi may have ignored the conventional assumption (that the part of an identifiable object cut by a picture frame still exists, merely being blocked from view) because he suspected that in this instance part of Cézanne's painting had been cut away sometime after its completion. The viewer was then left with half of *Cézanne's* apple. Picasso's collage creates analogous conditions of interpretive ambiguity, but as a factor of its initial construction.

By attending to the physicality of this collage, we observe that the fragmentary images of fruits are particularly closely identified with their paper supports. We are, after all, looking at pictures from a preexisting printed page; when Picasso cut his paper, he simultaneously cut his image of fruit. We also discover that the material support of each piece of fruit extends no further than what is visible on the surface of the image – this despite a configuration of cut papers that initially gives the (false) impression of layering as opposed to juxtaposition. For these reasons we conclude that the two "back" fragments are *"literally"* fragmented: they may have looked fragmentary from the start according to pictorial metaphor; but inspection reveals this physical state is actual, as opposed to mere visual appearance. And because we recognize the actual material limits of these fragments, the extended visual metaphor that allows us to see them as "in back of" others cannot be sustained. It is as if Picasso has truncated this pictorial metaphor, along with his fruits and the cut papers themselves. Having lost its "literal" support, the pictorial metaphor becomes false, a case of catachresis. Materially, the pieces of fruit may be fragments cut from something larger; but, strangely, they do not become fragments within a visual, panoramic order.

To put it simply, the viewer of *Bowl with Fruit, Violin, and Wine Glass* experiences the difficulty perceived also in *Still Life with Plaster Cupid*: visual difference between "front" and "back" cannot be secured. Picasso's collage creates something other than a coherent "scene"; it has pockets of illusion, but no unified illusionistic order. The artist has selected or prepared pieces of material, most of which either *exemplify* those features of objects that facilitate conventional visual representation (recognizable contour, color, "texture") or already present an illusionistic visual image. These materials have been arranged so as to convert any implied or residual sense of "front" and "back" to the terms of the physicality of the support surface, which allows a shifting up or down, to left or right. Within this tactile order an object in "back" is constituted just as one in "front" – by juxtaposing one piece of paper to another across the surface.

The hand acquires the habit of moving from side to side or up and down through its experience with surfaces, which are everywhere accessible to glancing touches but resistant to penetrating ones.[81] The actions of "glancing" and "penetrating" connote antithetical modes of vision as well as of touch. Metaphorically, vision can "penetrate" the "depth" of a picture (both its "outer" pictorial illusion and its "inner" expressive content), whereas touch is confined to the surface. But once visual metaphors and the language of subjective expression have been abandoned, we understand that the "space" of a painted surface is neither infinite panorama nor pathway to the self; it extends only so far as does the arm, remaining always at hand, and limited by the artist's physicality, which corresponds to our own.

Consider again the opinions of Cézanne's early viewers: he "had only to put a single stroke [or touch, *touche*] of color on a canvas for it to merit interest" (Renoir); and despite incompletion his "works are signed, better marked than by a signature" (Geffroy).[82] Such evaluations signal the artist's paintings as individualized and expressive. The various comments refer to Cézanne's touches as if they might be mistaken for ordinary marks that anyone would make, yet they become markers of self-centered personal vision. One is less inclined to transform touch into vision in the case of the more emphatically tactile art of Picasso's collage. Picasso's touch implies dispersal of interest and energy, and an even greater sense of fragmentation than one finds in pictures by Cézanne (after all, Picasso engages in cutting and tearing). Yet traditional criticism of Cézanne's art, with its awkward mix of metaphors of touch and vision, indicates that his paintings never accommodated a straightforward "visual" interpretation. Cézanne's art resembles Picasso's Cubism not because, as the familiar metaphor goes, objects are seen from multiple perspectives, but because the general "perspective" of both bodies of work might best be described as tactile.

CÉZANNE'S RESISTANCE

"A painting is an explicit trace of a certain cultural relationship to the world," wrote Merleau-Ponty; "when one perceives the painting, one also perceives a certain civilizational type."[83] More needs to be said: opposing "civilizational types" can coexist in a single representation in the way that such types and their conflicting ideologies can coexist in a society, acting to shape a single conflicted subject, the viewer-consumer of the image. The interpreter's perception of a painting's civilizational type, political allegory, or ideological formation is not predetermined by the work's "objective" appearance, which must be multiform (that is, it will vary according to the momentary constitution of the observer as well as the conditions of and motivations for observing). Interpretation is produced when the viewer "contacts" the work through some discursive mode, which sets priorities and delimits conclusions. The viewer – as both "subject" for the work and its interpreter – either is passively induced (psychophysically? ideologically?) to inhabit a particular discursive mode, or actively chooses to adopt one. (And deciding this question – as to whether viewing takes its form passively or actively – will depend on the discursive mode through which this matter is addressed. It is not that such questions are undecidable – they can be decided quite arbitrarily – but that each decision produces yet another problem, each more remote from initial concerns. Here we approach an infinite regress from which it is best to retreat; we are concerned with the pragmatics of what can be "seen" in front of a painting, not questions of the origin or basis of artistic communication.)

My argument has assumed that any historical moment affords certain options with regard to interpretive discourses (or at least the illusion of such options). I have addressed a tension related to this condition of ambiguity and opportunity, an overdetermined tension. It appears in viewing Cézanne's pictures whenever we sense that metaphors of vision reduce to catachretic assertions of tactile physicality. Such tension likewise appears within the tradition of critical commentary, in the many conflicted figurations of vision and touch. And it is generated also between the prevailing mode of descriptive analysis oriented to vision, and an alternative discourse of touch elicited by the accentuated physicality of Cézanne's paintings. I have suggested that the choice of a tactile mode of description obviates many of the conflicts and contradictions that characterize the tradition of Cézanne commentary. But we can also assume that the tactile mode produces conflicts and resistances of its own.

Viewed through touch, Cézanne's paintings remain close at hand like a person we engage in intimate conversation. The paintings address the interpreter as a collaborator and an equal, as if viewer and artwork possessed complementary physicalities. We tacitly recognize a natural affinity between the bodily actions implied by the appearance of Cézanne's paintings and actions our own bodies could perform. We require only arm and hand of our own to identify with the "vision" of the artist; we need not seek the idealized position – were it to exist – from which a given representation might unfold as a unique coherent panorama.

There is nothing fundamentally peculiar about Cézanne's gestures and touch, even though his resultant visual representations deviate from canonical ones (much of the critical tradition discusses these images as if they were designed to *demonstrate* such deviation). Anyone can respond to the paintings' tactile relationships of contiguity and their traces of movement across a surface. From the position of touch, the artist's brush stroke becomes accessible to all, virtually anonymous (despite what the "visual" connoisseur might detect, for whom no mark is without its author). Ironically, when viewed as the product of an action, Cézanne's mark loses the authorial specificity associated with the indexicality of *artistic* touch; while the visual form of his characteristic mark, its generic iconicity, retains a sense of the specific. If this is confusing, consider once again that Cézanne's mark differs, iconically, from that of a painter who displays conventional technique and skill. Yet, indexically, this mark does not seem especially difficult to make; it lacks distinction, connoting no hidden talents, rarefied skills, or physiological refinements.

We conclude that the choice of mode of description, visual or tactile, determines which sense is empowered to represent the generalities that all interpreters can recognize as their own. Under a visual mode of description, vision affords access to whatever the painting communicates; we identify with what the artist saw and how it looked, even when the touch that performs the rendering makes an odd appearance. Whereas under a tactile mode of description, touch – the sense that particularizes – acquires vision's potential to generalize; we identify with the artist's touch as if our own hand could possess it. The opposing connotations of vision and touch are subject to reversal whenever we switch our attention from one sensory discourse to the other.

When I see Cézanne's paintings, I do not know that the artist thought things looked as he represented them, but rather that this is how surfaces and other things can be "seen," articulated, and understood through a certain mode of touching. The paintings elicit a tactile mode of description not only by their accentuated physical marking, but also by creating a system of visual resemblances that undermines the usual kinds of pictorial order. The paintings do not look "normal" enough for the conventional mode of description to apply. They direct attention away from prevailing visual metaphors related to individual expressive style, point of view, and artistic mastery. As a result, Cézanne's touch returns vision to the primordial experience of immediate physical contact, and perhaps even to a time before the body is distanced from objects, before it requires language or a symbolic order to negotiate a constructed reality.[84]

Yet it may be that we comprehend such "meaning" in Cézanne's art only because we begin, even today, by viewing his images within the context of a tradition of painting and criticism that most often privileged the visual mode. Our realizations are comparative, analogical, diacritical. We know the difference between touching something and looking at a painter's touch, a difference more readily conceptualized than that between visual "reality" and visual "illusion." We recognize that Cézanne's physicality as well as our own cannot be "present" in his art when we view it as a completed picture, but only when we engage our hands in his, or in his painting. This is experience we cannot have through the mere act of viewing. Physicality cannot be in a hand or a painting we do not touch, only physicality's representation. Representations, like visions, are inadequate to the closeness of touch.

Cézanne's painting thus distances its viewers despite its implicit political allegory of collaboration, reciprocity, and social bonding. The peculiar nature of Cézanne's pictorial distancing – its tensions and passive-aggressive quality (recall Benjamin's commentary or even Geffroy's) – induces interpretive insecurity and resistance to critical doctrine. It leaves the viewer uncomfortable with the explanations political allegories provide as to how artistic (or any other) representations connect to ideologies and forms of life. The insistent "literalness" of Cézanne's art incapacitates the interpreter who would apply allegorical and analogical modes of understanding. This art distances, yet resists the distancing act of interpretation.

Perhaps Cézanne's pictures continue to provoke because they display a discourse of the senses that fails to correspond to, and cannot be satisfied by, any of our preferred modes of critical evaluation. We take a certain satisfaction in our confusion, our failure to master the art of another, Cézanne's art. But there is no evidence that confounding the viewer was the artist's intention. It may be useful to assume that the pictures in question – consistent in their technical oddity over a period of several decades – were as natural to this painter as the habits of his hand. It follows that the patterning of Cézanne's touch, as opposed to his visual order, becomes the basis for evaluating his pictures. Even works as complicated and self-conscious as *Still Life with Plaster Cupid* cease to be metaphors in need of deciphering; instead they become catachretic, an artist's standard deviations that must be taken "literally."

Conceiving Cézanne as a painter who interacted with paint surfaces rather than seeing through them, we make of him the very figure of resistance to a social and intellectual order he may never have actively, or even consciously, opposed. Whatever the "true" case of Cézanne's personality and politics may be, his pictures and their associated allegories cannot determine its resolution; for we cannot conclude that these artistic gestures were integrated with other social acts. Yet Cézanne's paintings will continue to articulate sensory and social positions for any interpreter who needs or cares to take a position. While some viewers do not allow themselves to be touched, some do.

NOTES

1 See Lionello Venturi, *Cézanne, son art, son œuvre*, 2 vols. (Paris, 1936), vol. I, p. 110 (cat. no. 202). It seems that Venturi's curious reference to half an apple followed from his judgment that the canvas had been cut down; the "half" thus refers to half of a *painted* apple, presumably once complete. In contrast, Albert C. Barnes, owner of the painting in question, titled it "Three Apples"; see Albert C. Barnes and Violette de Mazia, *The*

Art of Cézanne (Merion, Pa., 1939), p. 329. This work has an unpainted (but gray-primed) area at the upper left; the fact that no unpainted areas can be observed at the right tends to confirm that the picture was cut down.

2 The two values, as well as their possible conflict, are evident in Lessing's claim that the majority of ancient painters "represented nothing that was not [already] beautiful"; but some made "a display with mere manual dexterity, ennobled by no worth in the subject" (Gotthold Ephraim Lessing, *Laocoon*, trans. Ellen Frothingham (New York, 1969 [1766]), pp. 8–9; (dates in square brackets here and below generally indicate dates of first publication).

3 It should be evident that the term "classical" is being used here as it was understood within a modernist discourse, to the modernists' advantage; this usage does not necessarily conform to an understanding of the "classical" that might be gathered from an historical study of documents of pre-modern periods. On classicism and modernism, cf. Richard Shiff, "On Criticism Handling History," *History of the Human Sciences*, 2 (February 1989), pp. 65–87. Modernist critics typically conceive of the artist as an expressive self or subject already formed by any number of forces, some perhaps of only temporary effect – historical, genetic, environmental, ideological, or otherwise. Accordingly, an artistic image reveals its author's formation at a certain moment, instead of contributing to or transforming that subject's constitution. (The latter possibility is also a "modernist" one, but not so common as the former; it is relevant to the discussion to follow in 'An alternative touch', below.) From the perspective of modernist art production, the subject-author remains independent even when seeming to express no more than a prevailing ideology, because each subject has a unique manner of expression. On the critical tradition that established Cézanne's art as both modernist and classical, see Richard Shiff, *Cézanne and the End of Impressionism* (Chicago, 1984), pp. 125–140, 175–184, 219.

4 "Plane" is the abstract, geometrical analogue for material surface and hence the appropriate term for a picture surface regarded as if having no inherent visible or tactile properties. Cf. James J. Gibson, *The Ecological Approach to Visual Perception* (Boston, 1979), p. 33: "Planes are color-less; surfaces are colored. Planes are transparent ghosts; surfaces are generally opaque and substantial. The intersection of two planes, a line, is not the same as the junction of two flat surfaces, an edge or corner."

5 This holds not only for painting but for other forms of signification: "Sight and touch, linked by the act of handling an object, define the basic metaphor of 'knowledge' " (D. O. Edge, "Technological Metaphor," in D. O. Edge and J. N. Wolfe, *Meaning and Control: Essays in Social Aspects of Science and Technology* [London, 1973], p. 44).

6 Cf. John Rewald, *Cézanne, Geffroy et Gasquet suivi de Souvenirs sur Cézanne de Louis Aurenche et de lettres inédites* (Paris, 1959), p. 17.

7 On Vollard's purchase, see Merete Bodelsen, "Early Impressionist Sales 1874–94 in the light of some unpublished 'procès verbaux'," *Burlington Magazine*, 110 (June 1968), p. 346.

8 Ambroise Vollard, *Cézanne*, trans. Harold L. Van Doren (New York, 1984), p. 48. For examples of the type of painting to which Vollard refers, see Venturi, *Cézanne*, cat. nos. 202, 508. No. 202, *Deux pommes et demie* (described above), measures only 6½" by 4". No. 508, *Quelques pommes*, appears to be two separate studies of groups of apples on one fragment of canvas. Some of the details of Vollard's account of Tanguy's practices may derive from Théodore Duret, *Histoire des peintres impressionnistes* (Paris, 1906), p. 188.

9 On the issue of originality in relation to parts and wholes, see Richard Shiff, "The Original, the Imitation, the Copy, and the Spontaneous Classic: Theory and Painting in Nineteenth-Century France," *Yale French Studies*, 66 (1984), pp. 27–54.

10 This is not to say that Vollard's anecdote lacks all plausibility. Many of Cézanne's existing small canvases appear to be studies painted over fragments of what were initially larger compositions (cf. Venturi, no. 353, *L'Assiette bleue*). By all accounts the artist had little concern for the future state and condition of his own works. Yet it remains possible that paintings with fragmentary images were reduced to that state by Cézanne himself; John Rewald describes a painting that includes two whole fruits but less than half a plate as "part of a larger still life from which the artist salvaged this as the only satisfactory detail" ("Some Entries for a New Catalogue Raisonné of Cézanne's Paintings," *Gazette des beaux-arts*, 86 [November 1975], p. 168).

11 Auguste Renoir, cited in Georges Rivière, *Cézanne, le peintre solitaire* (Paris, 1936), p. 19; Jasper Johns, quoted in Grace Glueck, "The 20th-Century Artists Most Admired by Other Artists," *Art News*, 76 (November 1977), p. 87. Johns was referring to Cézanne's *Bather* in the Museum of Modern Art, New York. His statement is cryptic, but I believe that he (like Meyer Schapiro, as discussed below) is claiming that Cézanne's touch captures the look of an object in such a way that the depiction conveys the object's tactile properties, as well as having a tactile physicality of its own.

12 These are commonplace notions that appear across the centuries and across disciplinary boundaries. Within philosophy, compare Maurice Merleau-Ponty (who resisted the rigidity of such distinctions): "In visual experience, which pushes objectification further than does tactile experience, we can, at least at first sight, flatter ourselves that we constitute the world, because it presents us with a spectacle spread out before us at a distance, and gives us the illusion of being immediately present everywhere and being situated nowhere. Tactile experience, on the other hand, adheres to the surface of our body ..." (*Phenomenology of Perception* [1945], trans. Colin Smith [London, 1962], p. 316).

13 Harold Rosenberg, "The Concept of Action in Painting," in *Artworks and Packages* (Chicago, 1969), p. 217.

14 Although the issue remains controversial, perceptual psychologists often distinguish terminologically between active and passive touch, referring to the former with the words "tactual" and "haptic" and to the latter with

171

the more familiar and general term "tactile" (cf. William Schiff and Emerson Foulke, eds., *Tactual Perception: A Sourcebook* [Cambridge, 1982], p. xi). In this essay, I will confine myself to "tactile," using it in all circumstances.

15 Concerning the significance of authorship for modernist practice, Pierre Bourdieu refers concisely to the "professional ideology of the uncreated 'creator' [natural producer of the authentic mark] which was developed during the nineteenth century" ("The Historical Genesis of a Pure Aesthetic," *Journal of Aesthetics and Art Criticism*, 46 [special supplementary issue, 1987], p. 204).

16 Gustave Geffroy, "Paul Cézanne" [1895], in *La Vie artistique*, 8 vols. (Paris, 1892–1903), vol. VI, p. 215.

17 Geffroy, "Salon de 1901" [1901], in *La Vie artistique*, vol. VIII, p. 376. Geffroy's argument is consistent with pantheistic sentiments he expressed elsewhere; see, e.g., "Le Symbolisme" [1892], in *La Vie artistique*, vol. II, p. 388.

18 Harold Rosenberg, "The American Action Painters" [1952], in *The Tradition of the New* (3rd edn, New York, 1965), p. 26.

19 Meyer Schapiro, *Paul Cézanne* (New York, 1962 [1952]), pp. 9–10. For Cézanne to occupy such a historical position involved a certain irony that was indicated by a number of earlier critics; they noted that the painter's awkwardness of form, assumed to result from his struggle to capture the reality of an object, was imitated by other artists who thus arrived at "abstractions" referring to no object whatsoever. Maurice Denis's comment is typical: "The fate of Cézanne is to have been the slave of nature and the model, and at the same time to have authorized every audacity, every abstraction, every looseness, every schematism [*tous les systèmes*), and to have fathered generations of improvisers who believe irrationally in a lack of finish" ("L'Aventure posthume de Cézanne," *L'Amour de l'art*, 20 [July 1939], p. 196).

20 Meyer Schapiro, "The Liberating Quality of Avant-garde Art," *Art News*, 56 (Summer 1957), p. 38.

21 Schapiro, *Cézanne*, p. 29.

22 At issue is the very fact that objects do appear in Cézanne's paintings and appear in a certain way, not the artist's selection of one type of object or genre over another. Concerning the significance of the choice of a still life in particular, Schapiro has argued that because its component objects are "freely disposable in reality" they are "connate with an idea of artistic liberty" (Meyer Schapiro, "The Apples of Cézanne: An Essay on the Meaning of Still-life" [1968], in his *Modern Art, 19th and 20th Centuries* [New York, 1978], pp. 20–21). Schapiro relies on the value of spontaneity (associated with a painter's arranging things freely, arbitrarily, expressively) to legitimize his analysis.

23 Schapiro, *Cézanne*, p. 10. Schapiro's reference to blindness evokes a long history of observations and arguments concerning relations between the senses, issues generally associated with seventeenth- and eighteenth-century thought (see Michael J. Morgan, *Molyneux's Question: Vision,*

Touch and the Philosophy of Perception [Cambridge, 1977]). Rather than exploring the historical origins of such questions, I wish to consider their intersection with Cézanne's painting practice and the tradition of its reception. I will therefore generally cite only those who had some involvement with Cézanne's art. For examples of comprehensive statements on vision and touch coincident with the artist's life, see Hippolyte Taine, *De l'intelligence*, 2 vols. (Paris, 1888 [1870]), esp. vol. I, pp. 191–202, 215–230, and vol. II, pp. 125–196; and Charles Dunan, "L'Espace visuel et l'espace tactile," *Revue philosophique de la France et de l'étranger*, 25 (1888), pp. 134–169, 354–386, 591–619. Like many others, Taine (vol. II, pp. 155–157) notes the effect of the previous experience of touch on blind persons who see for the first time; to such observers all visible objects seem to touch the eye, as if it could function only by analogy to the hand. For German thinking on touch and vision in relation to painting, see Margaret Olin, "Validation by Touch in Kandinsky's Early Abstract Art," *Critical Inquiry*, 16 (Autumn 1989), pp. 144–172. On blindness in relation to Cézanne specifically, see the odd, presumably fictionalized, account in Vollard, *Cézanne*, pp. 56–57.

24 Henri Ghéon, for instance, wrote that Cézanne's painting offered a purified formal order yet retained the feeling of the represented object itself, "its solidity, its volume, its profound truth" ("A propos des Indépendants," *Nouvelle Revue française*, 1 [May 1909], pp. 391–392). Adrian Stokes linked Cézanne's organization of discrete areas of color to what he called a "carving" mode of painting, associated with the capacity of Renaissance masters to reveal the inner nature of an object; such organization also established the absolute integrity of the painting surface ("in conjunction with extreme rotundity [Cézanne] insisted upon a certain flatness"; from "Colour and Form" [1937], in *The Critical Writings of Adrian Stokes*, ed. Lawrence Gowing, 3 vols. [London, 1978], vol. II, pp. 35–36). Clement Greenberg stated it this way, reversing the usual emphasis: "Cézanne got 'solidity,' all right; but it is as much a two-dimensional, literal solidity as a representational one" ("Cézanne" [1951], in *Art and Culture* [Boston, 1961], p. 54); he thus judged the paintings' formal construction "solid." Art historians sometimes associate the problem of pictorial physicality with Bernard Berenson, who spoke of an artist's capacity to "live" the form of an object. Throughout his career (beginning in the 1890s), Berenson referred to the perception of "tactile values"; Schapiro's sense of "solidity" evokes the same sort of experience, although the parallel does not hold for Greenberg or Stokes. According to Berenson, "tactile values occur in representations of solid objects when communicated ... in such a way that stirs the imagination to feel their bulk, heft their weight, realize their potential resistance, span their distance from us, and encourage us, always imaginatively, to come into close touch with, to grasp, to embrace, or to walk around them." Berenson included Cézanne among artists adept at representing "tactile values" (*Aesthetics and History* [Garden City, N.Y., 1954 (1948)], pp. 69–71, 73).

25 On related issues, see Richard Shiff, "Performing an Appearance: On the Surface of Abstract Expressionism," in *Abstract Expressionism: The Critical Developments*, ed. Michael Auping (New York, 1987), pp. 94–123.

26 Geffroy, "Paul Cézanne" [1894], in *La Vie artistique*, vol. III, p. 259. Schapiro himself alluded to this effect: "there is little difference between the textures of the near and far objects, as if all were beheld from the same distance" (*Cézanne*, p. 19).

27 See Wayne V. Andersen, "Cézanne, Tanguy, Chocquet," *Art Bulletin*, 49 (June 1967), p. 138 and note 18.

28 For detailed discussion of Cézanne's technique (in relation to a nineteenth-century project of representing originality), see Shiff, *Cézanne and the End of Impressionism*, esp. pp. 99–123, 199–219. The insistent repetitiveness of Cézanne's pattern of marks distinguished his technique from that of predecessors known for accentuating the visuality of the painting surface (Frans Hals in the seventeenth century, Gustave Courbet in the nineteenth century). But the judgment as to when a surface pattern actually interfered with representation was always relative to the historical moment. Throughout the nineteenth century, French art critics commonly faulted painters for applying a uniform touch that rendered diverse objects and subjects too much alike, eliminating the beauty of variety; see, e.g., Gustave Planche, *Salon de 1831* (Paris, 1831), p. 68. There were four possible implications to such a uniformity of painted surface: (1) the artist – like a scientist or a philosopher (Planche himself cited the case of Leibniz) – was asserting that all material things are in essence alike; (2) all things merely look alike because vision renders them so (a natural, universalizing iconicity); (3) all things look alike because technique renders them so (a conventional iconicity); (4) all things look alike when they have been transformed by the vision and touch of an individual artist (a particularizing indexicality). It was the last possibility, linked to notions of originality in expression, that became most significant for the Impressionist painters and their critics; but the other three were never entirely ignored.

29 Several scholars have commented on this aspect of Cézanne's works, which comes into play in many of his paintings that exhibit other paintings within them. Describing a work similar to *Wine Glass and Apples*, Schapiro himself (misleadingly, I believe) characterizes the depicted wallpaper pattern as "the shadow of a shadow, an echo of [Cézanne's] own art" (*Cézanne*, p. 54). On the broad range of works involving analogous kinds of pictorial tension, see Robert William Ratcliffe, "Cézanne's Working Methods and Their Theoretical Background," unpublished PhD dissertation, Courtauld Institute of Art, University of London, 1961, pp. 50–52, 400–402; and Theodore Reff, "The Pictures within Cézanne's Pictures," *Arts*, 53 (June 1979), pp. 90–104.

30 Roger Fry, "Acquisition by the National Gallery at Helsingfors," *Burlington Magazine*, 18 (February 1911), p. 293; Roger Fry, *Cézanne: A Study of His Development* (Chicago, 1989 [1927]), pp. 77–78.

31 Analogy (comparison with respect to some property) can be regarded as a form of metaphor (cf. Aristotle, *Poetics*, 1457b 15–30), but metaphor normally lacks the kind of reciprocity attributed to pictorial analogy.

32 If, as several scholars have argued, Cézanne's crouching figure derives from the artist's drawing of an antique sculptural fragment, the *Venus de Vienne* in the Louvre, its odd form might be explained by the fact that the source image had no head at all. In this case, the painter's hand was free to respond exclusively to what was found already lying on the canvas surface, the adjacent bathers. Concerning the source image, see Alfred Neumeyer, *Paul Cézanne: Die Badenden* (Stuttgart, 1959), p. 16.

33 Cf. statements recorded by the artist's son and published in Léo Larguier, *Le Dimanche avec Paul Cézanne* (Paris, 1925), p. 135. During Cézanne's lifetime linearity was commonly related to a tactile sense of objects and a primitivistic application of vision. Jules Laforgue argued that before man's understanding of color developed, the eye relied on tactile probing; this caused the sense of form to pass "from the fingers to the eye" ("L'Impressionnisme" [1883], in *Jules Laforgue: textes de critique d'art*, ed. Mireille Dottin [Lille, n.d. (1987)], p. 169).

34 Modeling could be established by gradations of a single hue (from black to gray or from red to pink) or by a sequence of hues that establish a passage from dark to light (from blue to green, to yellow-green, to yellow). Modeling is such a familiar and accommodating device that critics persist in "discovering" versions of it even where Cézanne employed its antithesis, repetitive sequences of abruptly contrasting colors (for instance, green, orange, and violet). The interpreter's discourse converts dissimilarity into similarity through selection of the standard of comparison. It is as if any variation in hue can become an instance of modeling, with the case of non-modeling assigned only to the extreme of a single hue applied uniformly. When in 1864 the critic and historian Ernest Chesneau recognized that painters were eliminating subtle tonal gradations for the sake of an effect of immediacy, he speculated that someone would eventually exhibit a "landscape" consisting of nothing but a broad field of gray or blue above one of green (*L'Art et les artistes modernes en France et en Angleterre* [Paris, 1864], p. 195). Given the complexity of the historical and discursive context, the interpreter is quite free to decide whether Cézanne's relatively abrupt color transitions should count as (1) an instance of modeling (perhaps abbreviated to "capture the moment"), (2) the "essence" of a structure, or (3) an assertion of the independence of painting from modeling and other illusionistic devices.

35 Cf. Shiff, "On Criticism Handling History," esp. pp. 83–84, note 2.

36 It should be recalled that during the artist's lifetime his style also succeeded in symbolizing (in a general way) the immediacy of direct, naive vision. The fragmentary quality of his surface contributed to this interpretation because incompleteness was associated with spontaneity. Cf. Shiff, *Cézanne and the End of Impressionism*, esp. pp. 111–123.

37 Charles Blanc, *Grammaire des arts du dessin* (Paris, 1880 [1867]), p. 574.

38 This is by no means the only possible description of Cézanne's surfaces.

For an alternative analysis informed by a notion of "atmospheric flatness," see Shiff, *Cézanne and the End of Impressionism*, pp. 172–173.

39 Cf. Roland Barthes, "The Reality Effect" [1968], in *The Rustle of Language*, trans. Richard Howard (New York, 1986), pp. 141–148; "The Photographic Message" [1961], in *Image–Music–Text*, ed. and trans. Stephen Heath (New York, 1977), pp. 15–31.

40 Photographs can, of course, be constructed in terms of pictorial analogy; when they are, they tend to be seen as "artistic." Cf. the discussion of Lee Friedlander's *New York City* (1965), in Shiff, "Performing an Appearance," pp. 99–100.

41 Henri Matisse, as quoted in Gaston Diehl, "Avec Matisse le classique," *Comoedia*, 12 June 1943, p. 1.

42 Geffroy, "Paul Cézanne" [1894], in *La Vie artistique*, vol. III, p. 257.

43 Thus the rhetorical figure at work might well be catachresis, as discussed below (see note 50). Concerning "solidity," cf. note 24 above.

44 Joachim Gasquet, *Cézanne* (Paris, 1926 [1921]). pp. 136, 196.

45 The gestural and even the aesthetic features can be attributed to either conscious intention or its lack. Modern connoisseurship often depends on the presumption that the most characteristic markings of an artist are the least controlled. But knowledge of such theory itself tends to make one aware of and attempt to control ever more minute aspects of artistic technique.

46 Schapiro, *Cézanne*, p. 10.

47 Schapiro, *Cézanne*, p. 20. The observation is commonplace; cf. Jean Helion, "Seurat as Predecessor," *Burlington Magazine*, 69 (July 1936), p. 10; "[With Cézanne] each touch of the picture [is] associated with a definite glance at a definite point of the model." A common turn of phrase – to "cast the eye" – metaphorically offers vision the probing, fragmented, and personal features of touch; cf. Shiff, "Performing an Appearance," p. 104.

48 D. S. MacColl, *Nineteenth Century Art* (Glasgow, 1902), p. 68.

49 For a characteristic Romantic statement linking idiosyncratic pictorial organization to notions of temperament and personal development, see Alfred Johannot, "Du point de vue dans la critique," *L'Artiste*, 1 (1831), pp. 109–110.

50 A traditional example of catachresis is "arm" of a chair. If one assumes that metaphor plays on, or figures, a more accepted "literal" usage, here "arm" is not a metaphor because this part of the chair has no other name. On catachresis, see Pierre Fontanier, *Les Figures du discours* (Paris, 1977 [1821–1830]), pp. 213–219.

51 It can be found also in the writings of Jacques Lacan, which include commentary on the relevant texts of Merleau-Ponty (cited below); see Jacques Lacan, *The Four Fundamental Concepts of Psycho-Analysis*, ed. Jacques-Alain Miller, trans. Alan Sheridan (New York, 1981), pp. 67–119. Lacan explores the extent to which viewing an object from a distance entails being affected – touched, so to speak – by that object, with the consequent emergence of one's own status as a thing to be

viewed and represented in language. As a further consequence of Lacan's mode of analysis, the body becomes more of a sign than a thing, whereas for Merleau-Ponty it retains its materiality.

52 Merleau-Ponty, *Phenomenology of Perception*, p. 93. Cf. also p. 315; "When one of my hands touches the other, the hand that moves functions as subject and the other as object." James J. Gibson offers a closely related analysis: "It is as if the same stimulating event had two possible poles of experience, one objective and the other subjective" (*The Senses Perceived as Perceptual Systems* [Boston, 1966], p. 99). On this matter both Merleau-Ponty and Gibson express indebtedness to the perceptual psychologist David Katz; Katz describes the sense of touch (in contrast to vision) as "bipolar" and distinguishes degrees of bipolarization affecting different parts of the body (*Der Aufbau der Tastwelt* [Leipzig, 1925], pp. 19–20).

53 Maurice Merleau-Ponty, *The Visible and the Invisible*, ed. Claude Lefort, trans. Alphonso Lingis (Evanston, Ill., 1968), p. 255 (working note, May, 1960).

54 Maurice Merleau-Ponty, "Eye and Mind" [1961], *The Primacy of Perception*, ed. James M. Edie, trans. Carleton Dallery (Evanston, Ill., 1964), p. 164 (emphasis eliminated).

55 Maurice Merleau-Ponty, "Cézanne's Doubt" [1945], *Sense and Non-Sense*, trans. Hubert L. Dreyfus and Patricia Allen Dreyfus (Evanston, Ill., 1964), p. 19 (original emphasis). An earlier, abridged translation of "Cézanne's Doubt" (by Juliet Bigney; lacking the section on Leonardo) appeared in *Partisan Review*, 13 (1946), pp. 464–478.

56 Gasquet, a poet and native of Aix-en-Provence who spoke frequently with Cézanne during the late 1890s, was an especially important factor in determining Merleau-Ponty's sense of the artist. He argued that Cézanne's painting expressed a classical Mediterranean heritage, achieving union with universal Nature. Gasquet's text contains numerous images of reciprocity; for instance, he reports Cézanne as saying: "We should live in harmony, my model, my paints and myself, blending together in the very moment that passes" (Gasquet, *Cézanne*, p. 195). For an example of Merleau-Ponty's use of Gasquet, see "Cézanne's Doubt," p. 17, and compare Gasquet, *Cézanne*, pp. 129–132. The leftist Merleau-Ponty and the rightist Gasquet (who lectured in a school run by Action Française) would have been at odds politically; but I have found no evidence that the philosopher took any interest in the motivations of his favored source of information.

57 Merleau-Ponty, "Cézanne's Doubt," p. 9.

58 *Ibid.*, p. 20.

59 Maurice Merleau-Ponty, "Introduction" [1960], in *Signs*, trans. Richard C. McCleary (Evanston, Ill., 1964), p. 16.

60 Schapiro, *Cézanne*, p. 19 (emphasis added).

61 Merleau-Ponty, *Phenomenology of Perception*, p. 261.

62 Merleau-Ponty, "Eye and Mind," p. 165.

63 *Ibid.*, p. 167.

64 In other words, we ignore the usual metonymy that allows the "thing" painted to become the thing seen in the distance, the object-model.

65 Maurice Merleau-Ponty, *Adventures of the Dialectic*, trans. Joseph Bien (Evanston, Ill., 1973 [1955]), p. 51.

66 Gibson uses the phrase "social touch" to describe such reciprocal tactile relationships as that of mother and child or of sexual partners – "each touches when touched" (*The Senses Considered as Perceptual Systems*, p. 132).

67 It is tempting to argue that such comprehension must precede the corresponding experience, but that is another matter; see Richard Shiff, "Remembering Impressions," *Critical Inquiry*, 12 (Winter 1986), pp. 439–448.

68 Henri Matisse, "Notes d'un peintre sur son dessin" [1939], in *Ecrits et propos sur l'art*, ed. Dominique Fourcade (Paris, 1972), p. 163.

69 Barnett Newman, "The 14 Stations of the Cross, 1958–1966," *Art News*, 65 (May 1966), p. 26.

70 Walter Benjamin, *Moscow Diary*, ed. Gary Smith, trans. Richard Sieburth (Cambridge, Mass., 1986), p. 42 (entry for 24 December, 1926).

71 In conventional painting, spatial distinction is especially apparent when there are suggestions of overlap; but even without overlap, variation in color can indicate spatial difference and aid in the achievement of a desirable "unity in variety" (concerning this traditional aim, see, e.g., Blanc, *Grammaire*, p. 555).

72 Cézanne believed the plaster cast to be of a work by Pierre Puget, an illustrious seventeenth-century predecessor from Provence, with whom the painter may have identified in some capacity; the sequence of works represented from right to left thus establishes a lineage from Michelangelo, a presumed source for the flayed figure, to Puget, to Cézanne himself. The French term for a flayed figure is *écorché*, which can also refer colloquially to a hypersensitive person; there is indirect evidence that Cézanne's acquaintances sometimes applied this word to him (see Gasquet, *Cézanne*, p. 19). It may also be significant that the Cupid has no arms, and hence no hands (just as the flayed figure has no skin). I will suspend these and other related observations that contribute to iconographical and psycho-biographical readings of *Still Life with Plaster Cupid*, to concentrate instead on the play of the artist's touch and vision. For standard comprehensive accounts of this painting, see Theodore Reff, "The Pictures within Cézanne's Pictures," pp. 99–100; and Dennis Farr and John House, *Impressionist and Post-Impressionist Masterpieces: The Courtauld Collection* (New Haven, 1987), cat. no. 28. Schapiro analyzed *Still Life with Plaster Cupid* twice: initially, stressing its formal (visual) peculiarities while also associating eroticism and passion with the Cupid and the flayed man respectively (*Paul Cézanne*, p. 98), and later, linking these elements to the still-life theme of apples ("The Apples of Cézanne," p. 11). For a critique of Schapiro's analysis, see Stephen Bann, *The True Vine: On Visual Representation and the Western Tradition* (Cambridge, 1989), pp. 75–78. Wayne Andersen comes closest to my

own concerns with the observation that the exaggerated *tactile* quality of Cézanne's art might be a result of the painter's well-documented fear of eroticized looking (letter to Kenneth Robson [1 May, 1973], *My Self* [Geneva, 1990], p. 482). It could be argued that Cézanne's act of painting displaces another kind of reciprocal touching-and-being-touched, namely, the autoerotic masturbatory touching of one's own body, often linked with a voyeuristic vision that has its origin in autoeroticism (cf. Sigmund Freud, "Instincts and Their Vicissitudes" [1915], in *The Standard Edition of the Complete Psychological Works of Sigmund Freud*, ed. and trans. Alix and James Strachey, 24 vols. [London, 1953–74], vol. XIV, pp. 127–133). Using some of Andersen's early observations, Theodore Reff developed the theme of masturbation in Cézanne's visual imagery, regarding the repetitive brush stroke as a device to control the visualization of fantasies, more a sublimated looking than sublimated touching ("Cézanne's Bather with Outstretched Arms," *Gazette des beaux-arts*, 59 [March 1962], pp. 173–90; "Cézanne's Constructive Stroke," *Art Quarterly*, 25 [Autumn 1962], pp. 214–226; "Cézanne's *Dream of Hannibal*," *Art Bulletin*, 45 [June 1963], pp. 148–152). Michel Artières approaches present concerns by referring to painting as a "sublimation of the desire to touch," as well as to the assertive materiality of Cézanne's representations and the evocation of "tactile imagination"; yet Artières fails to explore the actual practices of Cézanne's hand beyond the most conventional, visually oriented observations ("Menace d'objet et saisie du motif: Essai psychanalytique sur l'œuvre de Cézanne," *Topique: revue freudienne*, 33 [September 1984], pp. 7–33). This lack of particularized analysis of the painter's manual habits is typical of the psychoanalytic literature, even when it raises the issue of touch.

73 Theodore Reff ("Painting and Theory in the Final Decade," in William Rubin, ed., *Cézanne, The Late Work* [New York: Museum of Modern Art, 1977], pp. 30–32) remarked on the oddity of this effect and called it a "visual paradox." It is not, however, a *tactile* paradox.

74 The support for *Still Life with Plaster Cupid* is paper mounted on board. Despite the distinct physical properties of canvas and paper as resistant supports, the tactile quality and the pattern of distribution of Cézanne's paint do not vary consistently in relation to this difference.

75 Note also the analogy established between the rounded belly of the Cupid and the large fruit (a field apple?) lying on the studio floor "behind" to the right.

76 Compare the account I offer in a different interpretive context (*Cézanne and the End of Impressionism*, p. 303, note 40). There works of the type of *Still Life with Plaster Cupid* are related to the artist's presumed concern to merge his technique (signified by a previously painted painting appearing within the context of a new still life) and his sensation (the same painting observed as an integral part of a set of "real" objects being painted *as* a still-life composition).

77 Certain compositional orders characteristic of Cézanne are especially suggestive of lateral (tactile) movement as opposed to (visual) movement

into depth: for instance, the triple-banded type of composition seen in *Pommes et biscuits* (Collection Walter-Guillaume, Musée de l'Orangerie, Paris; c. 1879–1882) or *Mont Sainte-Victoire seen from Les Lauves* (Nelson-Atkins Museum, Kansas City; c. 1902–1906). In both paintings, despite differences in what is depicted, the various zones or compositional bands relate to one another ambiguously with regard to spatial order; any single zone can be imagined to project forward, asserting its material physicality as paint marks on a surface.

78 A number of similar linear marks lie along edges of foliage as if to reassert material and spatial distinction; these are more easily seen than the marks along the tree trunk.

79 William Rubin, citing statements by Picasso and Braque as well as other evidence, speaks of "a depersonalization of the act of painting that apparently played a role in Braque's and Picasso's thinking for several years" (*Picasso and Braque: Pioneering Cubism* [New York, 1989], p. 19). Picasso often signed his name to paintings and collages with a very regular cursive script like that of printed calling cards. He thus gave his personal mark a commonplace form, presumably conscious of the irony that such mechanically reproduced cursive lettering had itself been designed to connote "personal touch."

80 *Papier collé* is a type of collage that retains a certain integrity of medium, analogous to that of painting, by restricting its collaged elements to pieces of paper, usually adhering to a paper or cardboard support. Rubin (*Picasso and Braque*, pp. 36–39) emphasizes the need to distinguish the heterogeneity of collage (in its more disjunctive forms) from the homogeneity of the species *papier collé*. Like other recent commentators on Cubism, Rubin notes differences in visual effect and in conceptualization related to vision but does not allude to touch. If, however, the viewer attends instead to tactile relationships and conceives of the artist's physical manipulation of materials, differences between *papier collé* and collage fade. This is not to deny the significance of the variety of physical qualities that collage materials (other than paper) introduce into pictorial representations, but to stress, in the present context, the play of certain tactile effects common to painting and collage.

81 The surfaces that offer a hand its initial experiences and induce it to acquire habits and practices are, of course, neither canvases, nor panels, nor papers. We encounter the surfaces of human bodies and domestic environments long before developing the specific manipulative practices that pictorial representation involves.

82 See notes 11 and 16, above.

83 Maurice Merleau-Ponty, "The Experience of Others" [1951–52], trans. Fred Evans and Hugh J. Silverman, *Review of Existential Psychology and Psychiatry*, 18 (1982–1983), p. 38.

84 For all these reasons, Cézanne's paintings, when analyzed through a tactile mode of description, are especially suited to the development of feminist allegories and interpretations (which, to my knowledge, have not been applied to works of this artist).

9

Conditions and conventions: on the disanalogy of art and language

DAVID SUMMERS

I

In the introduction to his *Absorption and Theatricality* Michael Fried summarizes and extends the conclusions of the arguments he is about to make in the book by stating that each of the great French painters of the later eighteenth century "may be shown to have come to grips with one *primitive condition* of the art of painting – that its objects necessarily imply the presence before them of the beholder." In the second chapter of the book, entitled "Toward a Supreme Fiction," Fried remarks that in critical writing from around the middle of the eighteenth century the demand is frequently made that painting stand in a strong and definite relation to the viewer. This demand indicates, Fried argues, that just at that time the relation between painting and beholder was emerging as a problem in a way it had not been before: "The existence of the beholder, which is to say the *primordial convention* that paintings are made to be beheld, emerged as problematic for painting as never before."[1] It may be coincidental that the words "condition" and "convention" are used in two contexts as if they were more or less equivalent. Fried might possibly have meant that paintings are always made under the condition of conventionality, that is, paintings *must* be conventional, in which case the two terms cannot be equivalent since on this reading paintings are conditional *only* insofar as they are conventional; but the words "condition" and "convention" are used in parallel, and the modifiers "primitive" and "primordial" also suggest more than the relativism implied by this reading. The two terms are in fact not easily reconcilable and I may begin to define the problem I wish to explore by noting that they usually command quite different and even contradictory connotations. "Condition" suggests something without which there could be no painting at all, whereas "convention" implies that, although paintings have been accommodated to beholders from time immemorial, this is merely a possible state of affairs, one to which there are any number of possible historical alternatives. In fact Fried argues that something epochal took place in eighteenth-century painting, a deep transformation equally deeply altering the relation between painting and its beholder, and his argument in effect fuses the meanings of conventions and conditions, neither term in itself being altogether appropriate to what he wishes to characterize. That is, Fried seems to wish to argue that there are conditions under which paintings must be realized, but that these conditions are like conventions in that they are historical and subject to change; he wishes to say that a painting's being beheld is more than what we usually mean by a convention but that it is also more than what we usually mean by a condition.

In this chapter I am going to try to sort out the differences between conventions and conditions, both of which are, as Fried's use of the term suggests, fundamentally important for art historical interpretation.[2] In order to do that it will be necessary to examine and finally to reject one of the prevailing notions of convention in the contemporary discussion of art, which is based upon the analogy of images to the arbitrary signifier of language. Once this argument has been made, I will suggest ways in which the history of art might be recast as an open system of histories of conditions.

Convention, the more generally familiar of the terms I will consider, undoubtedly takes much of its currency and authority from the twentieth-century success of linguistics, from which the force of the analogy of art to language largely derives. In the following pages I will review some of the most general principles of linguistics that have found a place in recent art historical writing, as they have found places in the general discourse of the humanities. The importance to the history of art of the linguistic analogy in the last twenty-five years or so is not simply the consequence of the "influence" of a vigorous field of inquiry upon a more somnolent neighbor. Not only did the analogy of language provide a potent tool for the investigation and understanding of culture in general, but, in the history of art itself, certain ideas were very compatible with the analogy to language, so that the linguistic metaphor slipped smoothly and easily into the practical language of the history of art. Most generally, the modern notion of form, which made the non-imitative side of art paramount, has had the effect of identifying that which is historically essential about art with the conventional, at least with the conventional in the sense of that which is opposed to the natural, with which the arts were linked when they were believed to be essentially imitative.[3] Even though "form" itself is usually presented as having a "spiritual" or perceptual psychological basis, and therefore as in a sense natural, it is in another sense opposed to nature and is thus again like language. Both art and language are opposed to nature as that which shapes our interpretation of the natural world in culturally specific ways. From such a standpoint both language and art "determine" our world; the Eskimos "see" twenty-one kinds of snow, for which they have twenty-one words, and the forms of their art show us their "vision of reality." The idea of style, which pushes this understanding of form to its widest historical definitions, permits the inference easily to be drawn that the non-natural component of art distinguishes each style – each *Kunstwollen*, or each "world-view" – as different from every other, again much in the way languages differ. Even before linguistics and the structuralist and post-structuralist interpretation stemming from linguistics began to affect art historical interpretation, writers on art history and criticism often referred to the "language" of the visual arts. Sometimes this meant that art was a system of formal characteristics able to be "read" in meaningful ways once the "grammar" and "syntax" had been learned.[4] But it could also mean – and, if art was being considered historically, usually *did* mean – that art presented reality to us, or mediated or articulated reality for us, in a way unique to a time, place, or group of people. The idealist-historicist-relativist tenets of modern art history, to which the ideas of form and style are central, are thus very largely consistent with the idea of convention based on the conventionality of languages. (It might be noted that the examples of the twenty-one words for snow may be understood in two quite different ways. The more usual understanding seems to be that the twenty-one words are in effect categories of experience which *constitute* experience. This might be called the idealist view of the matter. The alternative, which might be called pragmatist, is that the twenty-one words articulate the effective truth of snow for those who live and work with snow as the Eskimos do. It will become clear that I am much more sympathetic to this second pragmatist view of language, which points outside language itself but at the same time does not involve any simple relation of word and object. It will also become clear that I wish to locate the significance of art within the region of praxis toward which language points.[5])

In the following pages I will not only examine some commonly current linguistic ideas, I will also raise a number of objections to the usual version of the linguistic analogy and to the notion of conventionality it undergirds. I will argue that the linguistic metaphor when applied to art conceals all-important issues of conditionality (that is, issues of what I shall call real spatiality and embodiment) which are constitutive and therefore meaningful for images (and for what we call art in general, although I will be most concerned with images, or, in semiotic terms, with icons) in ways that they are not for verbal signs. All works of art, I will argue, are embodied under certain *conditions*, and these are only *secondarily* conventional. To return to Fried's example, orientation with respect to a beholder is a condition for the actual presentation of any painting, but it is always realized as *that* orientation to a particular kind of viewer in *those* circumstances, a specifically historically configured orientation suited to the purposes of the time and place for which the image was made. Orientation – like conditions in general – is thus conventional in the sense that it always assumes specific historical form, but it is not *primarily* conventional; that is, there is no alternative in the making of an image to there being some orientation or another. Even when, as in Fried's argument, the painting becomes independent of the viewer, this independence is still a variant of the same elements and takes significance in opposition to preceding articulations of the condition. The problem is to establish the status within significance as a whole of such conditions.

The distinction I am going to draw between conventions and conditions preserves the positive and desirable social and historical features of the idea of convention – perhaps the deepest contribution of the analogy of language to the study of human institutions – but departs from the understanding of convention based on the linguistic analogy in rejecting the notion that the kind of arbitrariness associated with the verbal sign bears in any determinative way upon images (or icons) considered in themselves. It will become clear in what follows that I believe sufficient resemblance is possible (that is, that icons are not radically arbitrary, as most words are) and it will also become clear that I believe the extension of the idea of the arbitrariness of words to icons is a massive confusion of categories. Making a distinction between conventions and conditions does not mean that conditions are simply present or that they somehow escape the historicity and constitutive social affiliation entailed by the notion of convention. Rather it means that history and social affiliation reach even more deeply than the linguistic analogy allows us to suppose into our experience and behavior. What is shaped in art, the real and virtual spaces[6] given specific historical definition by art, cannot be reduced to the kind of neutrality implied by the comparison of images (and everything else we call art) to linguistic signs. The "grammar and syntax" of art are not just the "composition" revealed to us by "formal analysis"; rather what parallels "grammar and syntax" is the construction of real and virtual space consequent to patterns of human use. To make the assumption that the conditions of images are simply neutral vehicles – literal semaphors – is to presuppose from the outset that images signify in the main as written language does, or, more ethnocentrically still, that, as in the case of western naturalism, images may be adequately understood in separation from the conditions and circumstances of their own real spatiality. This assumption, I will argue, denies the sense not only of much non-western art, it also denies the meaning of many of the determinative aspects of western art as well.

In order to begin to get at the distinction between conventions and conditions, I am going to examine two texts by Ferdinand de Saussure on verbal signification. Both of these texts have been influential far beyond the borders of linguistics and the vocabulary and issues raised in each text will be familiar to many art historians. The first of these texts provides a more or less traditional foundation for the understanding of the conventionality of language based on the principle of the arbitrariness of the signifier. I will argue that, although in this first definition the relation between signifier and signified is arbitrary, that of signifier to referent is presumed *not* to be arbitrary, but rather that the signified is thought of at least in part as an *image* of the referent, and that this image relationship finally guarantees the signifier. This account of signification introduces one of the themes of this chapter and is paralleled by very common psychological explanations of images made by art according to which the percept – an image formed in the eye – is supposed to provide the basis for naturalistic, optical images and the concept – an image or quasi-image produced by the mind mostly out of visual experiences – is supposed to provide a basis for so-called "conceptual images," the non-naturalistic, planar images of which I shall write presently.

In these parallel views of verbal and iconic signification both words and images are validated by internal, mental images, by literally putative icons. It will be necessary to question these almost truistic assumptions in order to raise some of the issues I wish to raise. This

185

investigation will be facilitated by Saussure's second text, the famous definition of language as a system of differences, which is much less traditional, and which is to my mind not consistent with the first account. Certainly the role of the mental image is much more problematical in Saussure's second telling, and I shall try to consider the consequences for art historical description and interpretation of rejecting the common explanations of representation corresponding to Saussure's first account of the sign. I shall then consider the implications of his second discussion, which will eventually lead back around to the question of conditions.

In his first version of signification, Saussure defined a linguistic sign as "not a thing and a name, but a concept and a sound-image"; the latter is not a material sound but the "psychological imprint of the sound, the impression that it makes on the senses." The sound-image is merely "material" relative to the concept, which is more "abstract."[7]

The problematic and crucial term here is "concept." Concepts are more "abstract" because they are mental, whereas the "sound-image" is "material" or sensory in actually being uttered and heard. The "sign" is the union of these two, word and concept, signifier and signified. "One tends to forget [in mistakenly considering the word alone to be the sign] that *arbor* [as an example of any signifier] is called a sign only because it carries the concept "tree," with the result that the idea of the sensory part implies the whole."[8] To illustrate this relation Saussure uses the famous diagram:

Fig. 2

Here the ovals divided horizontally in half stand for the unity of the sign, divided equally between signifier and signified. The arrows at the side mean that each implies the other, the signified the signifier and vice versa. The two components of the sign are not simply equal, however, and the relationship of "carrying" as well as the hier-archical relation – mental vs. material – is stated by the simple placement of the mental or abstract signified above the "material" signifier.

A crucial ambiguity of the term "concept" is also simply stated by this diagram, which couples the word "tree" in quotation marks with the *shape* of a tree, a shape specifically "abstracted" by taking the irregular silhouette of a naturalistically described tree, what might almost have been taken from a *contre-jour* photograph of a more or less generic tree, some maple or sycamore. The quotation marks around the word "tree" seem to mean that *arbor* signifies *what we understand* by the word "tree"; and the silhouette seems to signify what we would recognize as a tree, or "think of" as a tree. Both aspects of the concept are carried by the sound-image, and Saussure's diagrams taken together make up a digest of the basic philosophical problems surrounding the term "concept." Straightforward and representative definitions of what we usually mean by "concept" are provided by P. L. Heath in the *Encyclopedia of Philosophy*.[9] These definitions by no means exhaust the problem, but rather afford a clear formulation from which we may work. Heath writes that, in general, to say we have a concept of *x* is (1) to know the meaning of the word, by which he must mean that we are able to give some kind of definition of an *x*, a migrating waterfowl, or whatever; (2) to be able to recognize an *x* or to distinguish *x*'s from non-*x*'s, or to be able to think of, have images or ideas of *x* or *x*'s when they are not present; and (3) "to know the nature of *x*, to have grasped or apprehended the properties (universals, essences, etc.) which characterize *x*'s and make them what they are."

The second of these definitions is most relevant to the present discussion. Being able to recognize something as an *x*, or being able to distinguish *x*'s from other things implies (at least) an image-making faculty in the mind; that is, it implies that on the basis of the comparison of an image we have in our minds to what we see we are able to recognize or distinguish. And this image-making faculty further allows us to have images or ideas of *x*'s *when they are no longer present*. That is, the mind is capable in some way of making substitutes. In a scheme familiar at least since Aristotle's *Parva naturalia*, sensation, which is a kind of reflection of external things, yields images which become memories of these things.[10] These images are cumulative and generic and are more or less abstract relative to sensations.[11] Memory thus may be viewed as storing sensations and also as modifying them. This modification *is* abstraction and is closely related to language and naming; to be able to recognize and distinguish things is perhaps inseparable from the ability to name them.

At the level of the concept, then, which is post-sensationary and pre-intellectual, word and image are already tightly intertwined. As we have seen, Saussure's diagram can be taken to show that the mental image of a tree, presumably corresponding to something like a "memory image" of a tree, is certainly derived from the perception of a tree or trees and is practically interchangeable with or complementary to "what we understand" when the word "tree" is uttered.

Some of the consequences of the ambivalence of the notion of the concept as both image and word may be gathered by taking up once again the so-called "conceptual image" introduced a few paragraphs ago. This idea has exerted a powerful if somewhat shadowy force on art historical thinking.[12] We have already seen that according to psychological explanations of images in art, all those that are not "perceptual" (that is, simply imitative or naturalistic) must be "conceptual." Given only these two alternatives, each category must be very capacious, and an indication of the reach of the idea of the conceptual when applied to the *history* of images is provided by Meyer Schapiro's observation that the polar oppositions used to describe certain general schemes of style (Wölfflin's "linear–painterly," Riegl's "haptic–optic," for example) are in fact "descriptions of the stages in the development of representation." Schapiro cites the example of Emmanuel Loewy's *The Rendering of Nature in Greek Art* of 1900 (a book that, as we shall presently see, is an immediate ancestor of E. H. Gombrich's *Art and Illusion*) in which the representation of nature in early art is plotted as a change in the "development of representation," moving between the poles of the conceptual and the perceptual, deeper psychological poles which, Schapiro observes, are capable of incorporating the polarities of the other writers on the development of style, polarities already based on principles of a very high degree of generality.[13]

Conceptual images – the frontal, planar, non-spatial, hierarchically proportioned images widely associated with non-western, archaic, and children's art in art historical writing – are, at least by implication, images of mental concepts, as optical images are images of percepts. But it requires only a moment's reflection to realize that we do not actually have mental images of concepts that are like what we call conceptual images; we do not form images in our mind that are frontal, planar, non-spatial, and hierarchically proportioned out of what we see (unless we happen to remember a conceptual image we have seen). The discrepancy between supposed model and image – very different from that between perceptual images and the presumed retinal image to which they are thought to correspond – is usually explained by arguing that conceptual images more nearly correspond to the verbal definition of a thing, and is finally rooted in the ambiguity already discussed of the verbal-visual notion of concept evident in Saussure's diagram.

The flatness or non-spatial character of conceptual images is presumably explained by a negative comparison to optical images, which, although they themselves supposedly correspond to images on the surface of the retina, are after-configurations determined by the actual spatial configurations of the object seen. Perceptual images are thus filled with the optical incidents of the particular, whereas conceptual images are generalized and typical. In being general or typical they are thus like memory images (as opposed to the necessarily particular images of sensation) and they are at the same time more like verbal definitions in showing what is basic to a thing, what makes it complete. (A person has a head, trunk, two arms, and two legs, and so on). At the same time that they most clearly show x and thus make x maximally (or most simply) possible to recognize (etymologically, to "know again"), the conceptual image also displays the "nature" of x, or the definition of x, or of *an* x. This "nature" tends toward the level of the verbal, again, the level of the general as opposed to the particular. Considered as an image – which it paradigmatically is in a fundamental aspect – the concept is not just an index, a trace of sensation; it is more permanent than that, a truer icon or substitute, truer in the sense that it is higher than any percept and truer in the sense that it is like things that can be said about what it represents.

I have lingered over Saussure's first, more traditional discussion of signification, and over the problem of the "conceptual image," which springs from the same philosophical ground, in order to make the point that this definition is fundamentally iconic in that the concept itself is treated as a mental icon. The example of the "conceptual" image suggests that the icon also functions at a crucially important metaphorical level in that the concept in its verbal aspect may be regarded as the "higher" icon. In old philosophical language it made perfect sense to talk about "intelligible form," that is, to describe the essential and invisible in metaphorical terms of the visible "forms" to be "seen" by a higher faculty of the mind, and these habits of thought have a clear analogue in western classicism, which drew on the same philosophical language to justify its project of making higher reality visible.[14] At a simpler but still related level, an obvious and centrally important characteristic of conceptual images is their tendency to be substantive or "nominative," to show us things that in language are nouns, and even to show the parts, attributes, and modifiers of things as if they were nouns in that they are given the same kind of definition. Conceptual images (or planar images, as I have called them in another essay[15]) are in fact immediate to substitutive images and have much of the same value as substitutive images. But the most important point to be made here is that the concept as an image in the mind has a similar substantive function, substantiating the signifier and thus guaranteeing the sign.

In the arguments just examined, which represent a long tradition of opinion, the word is established and validated by a mental icon, the concept. This conclusion points far beyond bare semiotic argument. According to Aristotle's millennial formulation of the matter at the beginning of the *De interpretatione*, spoken words are symbols (or signs) of *pathemata*, what in the Middle Ages were called "impressions," and written words are symbols (or signs) of spoken words.[16] The impression (whatever Aristotle might have thought it to be) is in effect an icon, standing in a relation of resemblance to its object, and serving as a substitute for it. At the same time, it is also in a certain sense a natural sign – what we might now call an index – since it is *after* its object and stands in a causal or at least sequential relation to it and – precisely because in being an image it is *not* its object – stands in a more or less symptomatic relation to its object, which is to say that something of the nature of the object may be inferred from the image. In being natural signs, impressions were opposed by Aristotle to words, which are conventional signs. These natural icons (as they might be called) are rooted in nature and are therefore universal, available to all persons much as the external world is in some way available to all. As various authors wrote in commentary upon the arguments of Aristotle still echoing in those of Saussure, the Greek and the Indian (for example) although they do not understand one another's languages (which are made up of conventional signs) *do* share the same concepts of the same things since they have had similar experiences, and, more specifically, similar sensations of the same things, and therefore are able to translate their respective languages.[17] At its simplest level the concept is a mental image, but it is an image that also provides access to the "nature" of the thing of which it is an image (which is more like the concept considered verbally, as we have just seen) in the same way that visual "form" was thought by Aristotle – and countless others after him – to provide the best access to that about things which is intelligible.

Before modern times a natural sign was defined not so much in terms of correspondence to its referent as in terms of its practical universality, its being potentially interchangeable or shared.[18] Most of us infer fire from smoke, or a foot from a footprint, regardless of what we might call them. Leonardo da Vinci's arguments in defense of painting over poetry were fully within the tradition of this understanding of the natural sign. Painting, he insisted, appeals to more people, and appeals to them differently, than does poetry. This appeal is possible, he argued, because painting is like sensation.[19] (The question of how sensation is like the external world is of course another question, demanding other kinds of answers; at the same time answers to this second question have exerted the strongest and most persistent pressure upon the question of the similarity of painting to the world. For a long time the question of whether sensation was like the external world seems simply to have been answered by saying – or assuming – that sensation is an *image* of the natural world.) In general, western naturalistic painting – and beyond painting, much of our understanding of the representation of the world not only by art, but also by the mind itself – has been based on the assumption of a relation between image and thing represented comparable in one way or another to that between word and concept. That is to say, the image is guaranteed not by its relation to the thing itself but rather by its relation to the *mental image* of the thing, to its percept or concept. At whichever end of the critical spectrum, "sensations" or "impressions" at one end, "ideal forms" at the other, the debate about what art is or should be has moved for centuries over the same terrain covered by the concept (which runs from a point immediately above sensation to some relation or another to imagination or intellection). As in the case of words as their signification has been traditionally understood, the relation of an image to that to which it refers in any specific instance is a relation of three terms rather than two. And the most problematical and mooted term has been the least obvious one (and the most deeply historical one): the understood nature of the percept or concept.

The problem of the clarification of the connection between perception, conception, and images is complicated by the fact that the metaphorical language used to characterize both perception and conception has for many centuries been itself set in terms of images. In general, the idea of visual images has exerted the strongest pull on theories of knowledge. According to the Platonists we are born in possession of ideas (in non-philosophical use "idea" meant the look or appearance of things) of which the forms delivered by sensation are inadequate lower versions. And again, if these ideas are not sensible (or visible) it is significant that they are called "ideas" in that they are at least in a metaphorical sense iconic. According to the Aristotelians, our senses (especially sight) give us the form (*eidos*, from the verb meaning "to see" and also "to know") of things, forms are then abstracted so that higher, less sensible (if not invisible) "forms" become known to the mind, subject in some way to the mind's "eye." Mental images have not only done heavy duty in the explanation of cognition but also in explanations of the operation of the faculties of memory and imagination. From Plato and Aristotle onwards, both sensation and memory were compared to painting, and more precisely to *imitative* painting.[20] Once this metaphor was established it changed in ways roughly parallel to the history of the technology of visual representation. Late-medieval optics deeply affected late-medieval accounts of cognition, John Locke compared the mind to a *camera obscura*, and the comparison of the eye to the cameras by which we are everywhere surrounded in the modern world is a commonplace. Visual metaphors of greater or less complexity thus contributed not only to accounts of sensation and elementary cognition; they also contributed to the formulation of what W. J. T. Mitchell has called "hypericons," the metaphors in terms of which mind itself is characterized.[21]

In sum, metaphorical "images" in the mind have no doubt been so indispensable and seem so "natural" because they serve the same purposes served by real images: they stand for what is not present, for what is distant in space or time in ways that words do not. Imagination and memory, language about which is filled with references to visual images, make it possible for us to live out of the past and into the future, to have experience. However images may be "manipulated" by "faculties" in mental "operations," these very metaphors of acting upon substantive forms are extensions of the idea that these forms themselves are substitutive and iconic. Mental images "stand for" the world; they "commemorate" it, and this primordial iconicity has not only determined the description of the workings of the mind; it has also deeply determined the characterization of representation in general.

Saussure imagined the emerging science of semiology as encompassing signs all the way from "completely natural signs, such as pantomime," to completely conventional signs, such as language.[22] If semiology finally admits natural signs, however, the major concerns of the science as he envisioned it must still always be semiotic systems based on the *arbitrariness* of the sign; "every means of expression used in society is based, in principle, on collective behavior ... on convention." By "arbitrary" Saussure means that in order to be of semiological interest the sign must be at least *as if* without intrinsic value, so that it may be described entirely in terms of relations, of context. Even though "polite formulas" often have "a certain natural expressiveness" (he gives the example of a Chinese who greets his emperor by bowing down to the ground nine times) it is nonetheless the contextual rule that demands the gesture, not anything intrinsic to the gesture itself. Systems of signs that are wholly arbitrary "realize better than the others the ideal of the semiological process," and that is why "linguistics can become the master pattern for all branches of semiology although language is only one particular semiological system."[23] Saussure is defining a radically *social* investigation of language in which signs function in conventional systems, systems which by implication must be mutually exclusive (even if they share certain structures in common).

Although it is of course the case that the bowing of the Chinese to his emperor is significant in the context of Chinese social practice taken altogether, and although the full meaning of the gesture is only to be understood in that context, it does not follow that the gesture is therefore utterly meaningless – that is, without something of the same meaning – if taken out of that context, as words taken out of the same context might be meaningless to speakers of another language. It is easy to imagine the same Chinese before the potentate of another land performing what was evidently an act of obeisance even though the act was just as evidently being done "in the Chinese manner," or in an alien or unfamiliar manner. But Saussure is not interested in such possibilities because the pursuit of his social investigation of language necessitates the redefinition of the signifier, a redefinition that in turn requires the separation – or at least suspension – of its vital connection to the iconic signified, to the concept as we have examined it. The opposition he makes between the natural and the conventional, the latter exemplified by language, thus entails an opposition between what might be called the ontological and the social, between what is simply "there" to be understood in itself and what has been given significant – that is, semiological – form. This opposition is simply a restatement of Saussure's argument that language is the fullest example of the semiological.

Saussure's second account of verbal signification, to which I now wish to turn, is consistent with his arguments about semiology in general and, as I have suggested, is in basic respects at odds with his first definition of the sign. In his second version Saussure deeply modified the traditional scheme and greatly expanded the importance of the social at the expense of the ontological by distinguishing what he now called "signification" from the new concept of "value." He reviewed the older notion of signification by using the example of money. Just as a coin can be exchanged for something different in kind, a loaf of bread, for example, so "a word can be exchanged for something dissimilar, an idea." In the use of the sign, in other words, the sound-image linked to a concept in the mind of the hearer who understands the language being spoken. It is thus once again the concept that guarantees communication. The equivalence (as its relation to the concept might be called) is to be distinguished from value, which is determined by the relation of the word to things with which it is comparable, that is, by its relation not to an idea or concept but to other words. This comparability makes visible differences, and brings language into view as a system of differences. Within this system words have different values, determined by their places in the system with which they are integral.[24]

In his second version Saussure presents both thought and the potential phonetic stuff of language as amorphous, as taking on definition only in the fact of the signs of language. This characterization has the effect of further undermining – or at least circumscribing – the simple exchange value of words implied by signification. The concept of value thus gives a new dimension and potency to the principle of the arbitrariness of the signifier; not only might any sound be coupled with any thing (dog, *Hund*, *chien*), as had been more or less agreed at least since Plato, but language as an autonomous system of differences carves out both conceptual *and* phonetic definitions. This argument might be taken to point in the direction of the absolute priority of language, to universalize language, to make it more than the master semiotic paradigm, since the interdependence of signifier and signified now means that changes in words themselves – which must be seen as changes *among* words themselves – can be seen as changes in the realities to which words are thought to refer. Saussure also saw other implications. He insisted upon the priority of value over simple signification, arguing that if a word is simply the union of a certain concept with a certain sound (his earlier definition of a sign), then value would be compromised, by which he seems to mean that the practical significance of the word would be determined by more than its position in the system to which it belongs, and again he seems to have seen this choice – between a kind of traditional signification and meaning determined by "entirely relative" value – as the choice between the ontological and the social. "The arbitrary nature of the sign explains ... why the social fact alone can create a linguistic system. The community is necessary if values that owe their existence solely to usage and general acceptance are to be set up; by himself the individual is incapable of fixing a single value." The notion that language is just a coupling of concept and sound "isolates the term from its system" precisely because it places reference above usage; it implies that language might simply be the sum of the addition of such references when for Saussure one must begin analysis from the "interdependent whole" of a functioning language.[25]

By means of the idea of value Saussure thus pries signification away from its presumed ontological moorings, moorings set in the presumed concrete of the reflective and iconic relation between the concept and that of which it is an image. He also wishes to pry signification away from any intrinsic property of the sign itself, again using the example of coinage, which has a "conventional value": "A coin nominally worth five francs may contain less than half of its worth of silver. Its value will vary according to the amount stamped upon it and according to its use inside or outside a political boundary." This is even truer of the linguistic signifier, which is not phonic but "incorporeal" – constituted not by its material substance but by the difference that separates its sound-image from all others.[26] This "incorporeality" is raised to the level of a principle, a corollary of the principle of the arbitrariness of the signifier. Just as there is no necessary connection between the sound of words and the things these sounds represent, so there is no relation between the letter "T" (for example) and the sound it designates. What is "incorporeal" is what is revealed as the principle of arbitrariness cuts more and more deeply, namely "system" (or what Saussure calls "form" as opposed to substance): "The means by which the sign is produced is completely unimportant, *for it does not affect the system* [emphasis mine]. Whether I make the letters in white or black, raised or engraved, with pen or chisel – all of this is of no importance *with respect to the signification*."[27]

In these last arguments, Saussure means to say that in order for language to be properly understood, it must not only be cut loose from the concept, it must also be rigorously separated from the conditions of its actual embodiment. This is not to say, of course, that for Saussure the actual embodiment of signs is not significant, but rather that its significance falls outside the range of linguistic significance he wants to identify and clarify. A number of important preliminary conclusions may be drawn: if linguistic structure is a separate realm of significance, then its application to other realms of significance must be approached with caution. It might be that Saussure in fact isolated relations in language applicable to other kinds of meaning, or it might be that relations of the kind he found to exist in language are also to be found in other areas of human enterprise, or neither might be the case. But, to anticipate my conclusion, I would like to argue that the category explicitly excluded by Saussure in order to reveal the system sustaining the values of words – namely the actual embodiment of the sign – is in fact something that, while it may lie outside the region of the central significance of language, is the primary region of significance of painting, sculpture, and architecture. I will argue that this region of significance from which Saussure wished to *separate* language is what must be insisted upon in order literally to flesh out – or complement – Saussure's notion of a theory of language which is not so much ontological (or substantial) as social. I believe in general that it is preferable to follow linguistics not in supposing that the ideas useful for the description of language are simply useful for the description of art (although some of them may very well be), but rather to follow linguistics by asking what the implications might be of considering images in light of the principle underlying the trans-formation of the notion of language in Saussurian linguistics. The appropriate question might be framed as follows: what would happen if images, like words, were cut loose from the assumption of validation by correspondence to an inner image, to a percept or concept? (Or, to put it in another way, what if the realization that the expectation of such a correspondence were peculiar to a specific tradition – the western tradition – made it evidently necessary to consider the possibility that all images are not so defined, that such expectations not only cannot account for many kinds of images, but that they even obscure the presentational character of western art itself?)

II

E. H. Gombrich viewed his *Art and Illusion* as a pioneering contribution to what he called "a linguistics of the visual image," and in the
course of his book he explored and adapted many of the themes I have
considered in the first part of this chapter.[28] As might be expected,
then, the book, both in the statement of its central problem and in the
solution of that problem, turns around the relation between the visual
arts and language. If paintings are "natural signs," as, Gombrich says,
has traditionally been believed, and if we all see the world with the
same optical apparatus, why are there many styles of visual representation? Gombrich's answer to this question is that art is never
immediate to nature or vision, but is always mediated by previous
representation. Art is, according to Gombrich, a kind of "conventional imitation," precisely comparable to onomatopoeia in language,
in which a given phonetic structure determines the imitation of
natural sounds, as in English we say "cock-a-doodle-doo" for the
crowing of a rooster, but the Chinese say "kiao-kiao."[29] We must
imitate sounds, and even other languages, with the phonemes of our
own language, and so the artist must approach the representation of
the visible world with what comes to hand, beginning from the forms
made available by tradition.

Gombrich modifies the traditional logical notions of both perception and conception and their relation to signification in ways that
call the status of mental icons into basic question. It has been
incorrectly believed, he argues, that, because translation is possible,
concepts exist independently of language – that they are in effect
icons in the terms of our earlier discussion. As we have seen,
Aristotle and many after him assumed that we all name the same
world, which is stored away in us as concepts, and it is because of this
common thesaurus of "natural signs" that translations may be made
from one language to another. Gombrich argues that such an understanding of the concept is untenable, that concepts are no more
available than is the supposed natural sign in perception, the retinal
image. Just as there is no "innocent eye" and the retinal image is
unavailable for inspection, so concepts are not to be experienced
except in realization, so that no "conceptual image" can be compared
to its supposed parent concept. Just as seeing is not an unbroken
gazing, but rather a temporal process of continual interpretation, so
the conceptual formation of perception is always governed by prior
habits of seeing and making. Art cannot simply depict sensation or

conception, the two of which are combined in Gombrich's notion of perception. And in this way art is again like language, which does not just name things, but actually shapes the world in one way or another: "Language does not give names to pre-existing things or concepts so much as it articulates the world of our experience."[30] So does art (or so does *naturalistic* art, with which Gombrich is concerned).

Although he rejects the psychological notion of the "conceptual image" as a sufficient principle of explanation, Gombrich retains and modifies the scheme of art historical development based upon it. His teacher Emmanuel Loewy, he writes, "taught us to appreciate the forces which have to be overcome by an art aiming at the illusion of reality," and *Art and Illusion* is an attempt to explain the same continuities explained by Loewy's theory of the development of ancient Greek art from conceptual to illusionistic.[31]

In fact, the idea of the conceptual image, with one or another inflection, recurs throughout Gombrich's book, and was already a theme in his earlier writing. In "Meditations on a Hobby Horse," the dense and brilliant prelude to *Art and Illusion*, Gombrich used the idea of the "conceptual image" to explain how naturalism works, and it is essential to his account of recognition and of what would come to be called "the beholder's share." In naturalistic traditions, painters, who must start with the "man-made, the conceptual image of convention, try to rid themselves of conceptual knowledge" and they do this by "stepping back and comparing" image to impression, and achieve their aim "by shifting something of the load of creation onto the beholder."[32] How is this done? The painter abandons the conceptual image and instead learns to make marks that trigger the concept in the mind of the viewer. The recognition of a naturalistic image is thus rather like the recognition of a word according to Saussure's first account. Visual representation in a certain sense begins and ends with the conceptual image; it is from such images that naturalism departs, and it is to such mental images that skillful marks must address themselves in being recognized and completed as what they represent.

In "Meditations on a Hobby Horse" the difference between "conceptual" and illusionistic images is linked to function at the same time that it continues to demarcate a fundamental difference in kinds of representation. Conceptual images (or the simplest of them, such as hobby horses) are not, according to Gombrich, examples of representation as we usually understand it. We in the western tradition understand an image to be something that first of all refers to something else by resemblance and may "therefore be the record of a visual experience." The simplest conceptual images, on the other hand, are primarily substitutive and do not refer by resemblance. Naturalism begins to develop when the notion of the image as a "record of visual experience" is separated from the substitutive, magical image; then, Gombrich argues, "the rules of primitive art" – such as planar completeness and hierarchical proportion and order – "can be transgressed with impunity," and optical accidents may begin to be incorporated into forms understood to be in virtual spaces. The earlier substitutive image has become the schema adjusted by progressive comparison to appearances of things. Making comes before matching.[33]

In *Art and Illusion* Gombrich eliminates the distinction between "conceptual" and illusionistic images maintained in the earlier essay, as we shall see. But the "conceptual image" has by no means disappeared in the later book and itself provides a "schema" that continues to be used and modified as the book unfolds. It is also clear that the "conceptual image" retains some of its old connotations. As explained in "Meditations on a Hobby Horse," the demand for substitution, to which "making" first responds, arises from deeper demands than those moving a child at play to make a stick serve as a hobby horse, and, beyond such simple substitution, the ease with which we recognize "minimal images" – schematic faces, smile buttons, for example – is for Gombrich proportional to the depth of the basic biological need to find such things in our world.[34] Something of this primordiality of images survives in *Art and Illusion*, in the chapter on the "power of Pygmalion," or in the comparison of the Greek "conquest of space" to the invention of flying: "The pull of gravitation that the Greek inventors had to overcome was the psychological pull toward the distinctive 'conceptual' image that had dominated representation heretofore and that we all have to counteract when we learn the skills of mimesis."[35]

Such survivals notwithstanding, much of *Art and Illusion* is in effect a critique of the older idea of the conceptual image. Sensation and conception, as we have seen, are combined by Gombrich in the active process of perception, so that the concept is now the hypothesis taken from past to present experience, integral with the interpretation of that experience, constantly changing rather than fixed like the old static abstract concept. In the chapters on the "beholder's share" (which increases with the development of naturalism), Gombrich writes of "projection" and "mental set." "It is the power of expectation rather than the power of conceptual knowledge that molds what we see in life no less than in art."[36] And it is finally ambiguity and not "completeness of essentials" (one of the "rules of primitive art" in "Meditations on a Hobby Horse") that triggers interpretation, the work not only of vision but of imagination and memory, and that make up "the conditions of illusion," as chapter 7 of *Art and Illusion* is called. Recognition is much more dynamic in the retelling of the "concept," at once more tentative and creative. The implicitly incomplete and hypothetical character of such a concept is consistent with the principles of Gombrich's Popperian "searchlight theory of perception" and with his own explanation of the development of naturalistic styles as a progress of "making and matching." And in terms of the discussion in the first part of this chapter, this view goes a long way toward freeing iconicity from the mental icon, from the substantive image in the mind. It also pushes the definition of iconicity firmly in the direction of the concrete function of images.

In the course of his arguments Gombrich resolves the "conceptual image" into two components, "schemata" and "relational models." Schemata, the prior representations from which any interrogation of appearances must begin, in effect displace the conceptual image into history, and, more specifically, into the history of representation. Since the tacit assumption of most discussion seems always to be that art imitates nature, and since nature is thought to be the opposite of history (or culture), imitation, insofar as it yields a "natural sign," is also unhistorical; but Gombrich's arguments mean that memories (the basis of the old "conceptual images") are never just memories of natural objects considered as objects of contemplation. They are more properly memories of artifacts, of culturally specific objects in culturally and historically specific circumstances. Among these artifacts are *representations* of natural objects, natural objects which in any case are experienced and learned in relation to specific patterns of use and purpose. Seen in these terms, the "memory image," and thus the conceptual image, is again closely related to what Gombrich calls "projection" and "mental set." The conceptual image is now like Michael Baxandall's "period eye,"[37] a radically historical perceptual *Gestalt* or a culturally specific predisposition to shape ambiguity in certain ways. On such a view, it is difficult to determine whether images are based upon memories of other images (which still demands the postulation of a mental image) or whether they are instead simply based upon earlier images, actual models. Furthermore, it is difficult to distinguish knowing what to make from knowing how to make it, that is, to distinguish the imagination of things to be made from the again culturally specific skill of making images in certain ways, by means of certain techniques and habits. People who make artifacts are specialists who, rather than simply working from memory, or from actual prototypes, have been taught specific operations, as Gombrich presents the history of western naturalism in one basic dimension as a history of the invention and development of certain skills. I shall return to this question at the end of this chapter.

In *Art and Illusion* Gombrich also eliminates the distinction between "conceptual" and illusionistic images maintained in "Meditations on a Hobby Horse" by arguing that *all* art is conceptual because all art "originates in the human brain." All images are visual "relational models." The relatively crude map of visual reality provided by a child's drawing is not different in principle from the "richer map" presented by naturalistic images.[38] It must, however, be recognized that Gombrich's elimination of the distinction is accomplished at a cost, because the new definition cuts images entirely away from their substitutive origins, therefore from what Gombrich regards as their deepest psychological origins, even their *ultimate* origins. But when the "conceptual image" becomes a "relational model," and all visual representation becomes conceptual in the sense of being relational, all of the former values, the "basic rules," of the "conceptual image" are lost, or lost to sight, both for "primitive" art and for western naturalistic art.

Gombrich also cuts the "conceptual image" loose from its erstwhile magical moorings by placing the notion of the concept in a logical tradition at least as old as Aristotle's *De interpretatione*. Just as Aristotle's "goatstag," a fabulous creature fabricated in the mind's eye of the imagination, is not false until a predicate is added to it, until, for example, it becomes the subject of a statement – "goatstags live in Greece" – so according to Gombrich an image is not false until it is *said* to be or to describe something.[39] This argument has the effect once again of undercutting the authority of the mental icon as a natural sign, since the icon may as easily be a product of imagination as a trace of sensation. To use Aristotle's example again, a painter might make a painting of a goatstag, and make it seem to be "true" (as in fact much of the painting since the Renaissance is what was called in the Renaissance "verisimilitudinous" rather than "true" because fantastic images are painted in the same way as others that might record real events). Again, the image (or mental picture or thought, the concept) of a goatstag is only false if it is labeled as the picture of a creature that exists or as the inhabitant of a zoo. For Gombrich, it is significant to note, paintings – historical, concrete representations of the world – replace the mental image. In themselves, naturalistic images (whether imitative or fantastic) are inherently ambivalent as to their truth. I may paint apparent portraits of individuals I have never seen at all, or who have never even existed.

Gombrich's analogy of art to language may thus be followed to conclusions very like the principles to be extracted from Saussure's second definition of signification. He has eliminated both of the mental icons that have traditionally served to guarantee visual representation, the retinal image and the concept, to replace them with a more functionalist kind of representation, and he concludes his second chapter with the statement that the "form of representation cannot be divorced from its purpose and the requirements of the society in which the given visual language gains currency."[40] Gombrich does not complete the program implied by this conclusion. Still, the conclusion follows from the argument and shows Gombrich to have arrived at the distinction between what was earlier called the ontological and the social, and to have opted in favor of the latter as the preferred course for art historical interpretation. These implications may be extended. If the concept in effect becomes previous images in a tradition, necessarily integral with traditions of correlative skills as new images are made for new places and purposes within embracing traditions of use, then the notion of art may be expanded to include not just images but the spaces of use from which these images are inseparable. This in turn suggests a kind of "competence" involving not just the understanding of signs, but rather a constitutively *practical* competence according to which one knows what to do in social circumstances, in all the senses of that word. This competence is of course reciprocal in relation to the culturally specific configuration of those environments; there is, in other words, a fit between appropriate behavior and the culturally specific spaces and times within which it is performed. To make a last analogy to language with the intention of indicating the fundamental split between language and art, the syntax of art – the "same order" to which painting, sculpture, and architecture are subject – is the real space in which they are realized. In such a case, art is not simply illustrative of context, in an important, irreducible, and even literal sense of the term, it *is* context. And the real spatial context leads us back to the subject of what I mean by the conditions through which culturally specific articulations of space – that is, conventional articulation of space as the basis of conventional constructions of behavior – are realized.

III

I wish now to return to two points touched on in the earlier sections, Saussure's notion of "incorporeality" and Gombrich's of the "relational model." Both of these ideas run almost exactly counter to what I mean by conditions and I may begin to conclude this chapter by explaining why this is so.

In order to be adequately defined by "difference," and in order for the proper inferences to be drawn from this definition, it is necessary, according to Saussure, for the words of a language to be utterly divorced from their material and sensual basis. It is incidental to the system within which words are significant that they are one or another sound or that these sounds have one or another character or quality. In the case of images, it is not simply the aesthetic or expressive character of their realization that is significant (as it also is for words, in poetry, for example) but it is the *fact* of the realization itself that points to the real (and virtual) spaces within which they possess their own modes of significance. (I mean "fact" in the etymological sense of something evidently done, that is, of something different from what it had been as a consequence of agency. On such a definition facts might be included in the larger category of events, which must be explained in terms other than those of agency.) Such factuality implies that which was already there to be encountered, and which was moved by actual effort, transformed by actual movements of the hand, and used in a determinate space for specific purposes by specific groups of people. Such real spatiality has its own coordinates and decorums, which, although they are again culturally specific, are not *radically* culturally specific, that is, not utterly conventional, any more than the basic categories of spatial experience for people in many cultures are not in important ways fundamentally the same. Images do not just represent, they place and replace, put what we want to face, realized by materially definite means with equally definite results, in determinative collective spaces. The significance of all this must elude our understanding if it is assumed from the outset that real spatial relations do not in themselves constitute irreducible meaning.

203

The real spatial value of images, their distinctive corporeality, leads around to Gombrich's category of "relational models." To define all images, as Gombrich does, as "relational models" is to define them, not merely in terms of resemblance, but in terms of various relations analogous to those to be found in what is represented. Here is a simple example: given a planar surface as the condition of representation, a smile button provides an adequately recognizable image by putting three marks in a circle in a way that corresponds to the order of eyes and mouth on a human face. A portrait by Jan van Eyck might be considered a more complex model, set in the virtual dimension, thus describing many more relations of visible surfaces, so that both faces may be placed near either end of the same scale of the description of relations. Gombrich then argues that the differences in complexity of the models are determined by the uses to which images are made to be put. As I have observed, this attachment to use indicates the path I have been trying to clear, as does the insistence on the mediation of all images. At the same time, the idea of the relational model in my view is a major impediment to the realization of Gombrich's goal of an understanding of images based upon use and mediation since, like Saussure's "incorporeality," it implies that pure relation rather than conditions of realization are essentially important for all images. It thus explicitly separates relations from conditions of realization, defining use simply in terms of kinds and degrees of informativeness, and in so doing cuts images off from the substitutive values at the core of their embracing real spatial values.

Insofar as it is a sign, an icon (as Gombrich would agree) signifies through its similarity; this similarity may be slight, or consist only of a few characteristics, as in the case of Gombrich's stick that serves as a hobby horse. As C. S. Peirce wrote, "anything is fit to be a Substitute for anything it is like."[41] The stick is like a horse only in salient ways that make it useful in the game of which it is part; in other ways it is overwhelmingly unlike a horse, and might in fact be less useful in the game if it *were* more like a horse. The same may be said of images, that is, icons similar by virtue of some degree of comparability of appearance. In general, similarity does not exhaust *any* icon, and, moreover, *any icon is in positive ways not that which it represents.* An image is at the same time a piece of worked stone, paint on a prepared canvas, paper with marks on it, the pattern made by a beam of electrons instantaneously scanning a screen. An image is similar only because it is dissimilar, dissimilar in the simple sense that it is borne, sustained, and related to persons, spaces, and other things by its actual physical unlikeness to what it represents. The statue resembles the general, but the general was not made of bronze. In general, unlikeness must not only be regarded as positive; it must also be seen as that which most clearly distinguishes the significance of images. The unlikeness of images, rather than being the passive vehicle of its resemblance, is an essential part of its use and meaning and provides myriad clues to its historical affiliations. The unlikeness is the specific *fact* of the image, which indicates operations by which the image came to be as it is and also indicates specific spaces of use.

The point I wish to make may now be illustrated by *contrasting* images to words. The "incorporeality" of the verbal sign is integral with its assumption of value from the rules of its combination with other verbal signs. If we think of the real spatial (and temporal) circumstances of language – what is analogous to conditions as I wish to define them – then it is evident that its formats (as opposed to the internal rules of the structure of language, the relation between format and these rules being yet another problem) are highly regimented, precisely in suppressing and channeling possible spatial variations, as in records, tapes, pages, and books. The spatial regimentation of texts also involves highly specific patterns of behavior (patterns of behavior easily distinguished from those appropriate to images, but distinctions lost, it may be noted, when we assume we are "reading" images). At the level I am trying to define and clarify, the significant relations for images are not the "formal" relations presupposing their incorporeality, but rather the real spatial relations in one way or another integral and continuous with their actual corporeality.

Meyer Schapiro made a distinction related to the one I am making in his essay on what he called "field and vehicle in image-signs." This treats "the non-mimetic elements of the image-sign and their role in constituting the sign."[42] By "non-mimetic" Schapiro means very nearly what I have called "unlikeness." "Field" and "vehicle" *are not* the image insofar as it is an icon, but they *are* the image considered as an actually embodied icon. Schapiro's arguments thus begin from the principle that bare iconicity is only a fraction – a small fraction – of the significance of an image, and that the conditions of the constitution of an image provide access to the larger fraction of significance. I have, however, generalized this principle to involve not simply formats and relations internal to them, but also the spaces with which their practical meaning is always integral.

The assumption that the meaning of images is exhausted by representation (or, as a corollary, by the manner of representation, the "unity of form and content," which of course subordinates form to content) is a major impediment to art historical interpretation and is perhaps itself a corollary of the deep-seated western assumption that images imitate the appearances of things or events, and that *all* images do these things either well or poorly, completely or incompletely, so that, as Aristotle wrote, the pleasure we take in imitation is the pleasure of recognition: *that* is a picture of a dog, or a horse.[43] On such a view, adequate imitation and word, image and label, are interchangeable. But the matter is not so simple. The bronze statue is an image of some man on some horse until it is labeled (a service often in effect performed by the art historical technique of iconography, the success and interest of which reinforces the erroneous notion that images are equivalent to texts). But I wish to indicate something more than such differences in signification, which themselves point to a presumed comparability that obscures the level of significance to which I mean to refer. Having encountered the bronze monument in the town square, we may infer much more than what we recognize, or what we might learn about it from reading a label. From the material of which it is made and the skill with which it has been worked we may infer technology and techniques as well as the importance of the person so conspicuously and honorifically commemorated; if we place the image in the historical series of bronze portraits or equestrian statues to which it belongs we begin to understand what kind of commemoration this is. From its location in a civic space, its size, centrality, and elevation, we may again safely conclude both the importance of the image of the person represented and of the incorporation of this image into a larger public order.

Not only must an image be made of *something* and placed *somewhere*, but these irreducible conditions, if necessarily therefore constant, are at the same time articulated in different ways in different cultures; moreover they are not, and cannot be, nugatory, or merely arbitrary choices determined by the prevailing demand for some means or another of illustration. These different articulations have continuities, histories, and it is not possible to understand artistic traditions without explaining these continuities. As for the problem of writing these histories, and making them part of historical interpretation, these conditions point to a level of interpretation quite apart from that suggested by the relation between images, recognition, and labels. Those who first used the artifacts and places we study *already understood* the values and ultimately the behavior demanded by the articulation of conditions. This understanding, finally rooted in the use of artifacts (including images) and places, is occluded for us simply because we already understand artifacts and spaces to have other significance, determined by other articulations of conditions. It is not simply that we do not know what artifacts and places mean, in the sense that we do not know that a woman holding a peach is an allegory of Veracity until we consult Ripa's *Iconologia*,[44] it is also the case that we do not know what to do, or why we should be expected to do it. No better example can be given than that of objects in a museum. Fourteenth-century Italian polyptychs or African dance masks, however we may be made to admire the formal characteristics of each of them by their installation, are objects we do not know how to use, and much less do we know the precincts, occasions, and rituals to which these objects and their uses were fitted. By the same token, as modern museum-goers, participants in the modern institution of the museum, we know other patterns of use in other spaces. Both of these are important for art historical interpretation. It is the spaces and uses we do not know that finally explain why these works were made the way they evidently were; at the same time, we must understand our own institutional spaces and uses, and the historical contingency of our own institutional spaces and uses, in order to try to understand the art of other times and places. The investigation of such meaning, I am arguing, demands the recognition of the prior significance of conditions and the further recognition that the conventional meanings of images and places, that is to say, the lost community of their meaning, is rooted in these conditions.

The lost or only partially surviving spaces to which all artifacts in so many ways belonged were once filled with individuals whose behavior in these spaces was more or less different from our own. Some of this behavior was the making of art, making still visible in the facture of the works themselves. Too little attention has been paid to Gombrich's principle that artistic traditions are traditions of skill and that changes in them are therefore to one degree or another modifications of skills. A fundamentally important inference may be drawn from this principle, that images do not (and cannot) have a simple precedent mental cause, that making an image in a certain way is not a matter of duplicating a mental image in material, but rather a matter of knowing what to do in order to make an image of a certain character. In principle no distinction may be drawn between duplicating a mental image and knowing how to make an image and, in fact, the insistence upon the precedence of the mental image simply continues the old idealist assumptions of the history of art as the history of imagination. This argument does not mean that mental images (or imagination) have nothing to do with the making of actual images, although it is to deny that mental images have *everything* to do with their making; it is rather to provide a better explanation, or part of a better explanation, for the conservatism and continuity of artistic traditions.

The foregoing argument might be summarized by saying that no icon is defined by its iconicity, and, insofar as it is (or is thought to be), positively conceals the conditions of its iconicity. Such concealment might be said to be implicit in the use of icons. That is, we take a certain kind of information from them ("that is the king") and pay little attention to the way the image is presented to us. But when we are users of images we pay little attention precisely because we already know the significance of the situation of which the icon is a part, a significance in fact constructed by the icon and by the space to which it belongs. Perhaps (as Roland Barthes might suggest) the icon "naturalizes" its conditions, makes them seem all to be of the same semiotic substance, as the photographic image in advertising – which has the value of the "real" – naturalizes the manifest contrivance of the organization in which it plays a part and thus conceals the whole level of ideological significance of that organization.[45] But if the conditions of images constitute the ground against which the icon is visible, then what was unconscious and "natural" for the user of images must be the object of conscious analysis on the part of the art historian if the world of the work of art is to be reconstructed, interpreted, and understood as an alternative human possibility.

NOTES

1 M. Fried, *Absorption and Theatricality. Painting and Beholder in the Age of Diderot* (Berkeley, Los Angeles, and London, 1980), pp. 4 and 93 (emphasis added).

2 I have treated these questions in a preliminary way in "Conventions in the History of Art," *New Literary History*, 13 (1981), pp. 103–125; and "Intentions in the History of Art," *New Literary History*, 17 (1985–1986), pp. 305–321.

3 See my "'Form', Nineteenth-Century Metaphysics, and the Problem of Art Historical Description," *Critical Inquiry*, 15 (1989), pp. 372–406.

4 In chapter 10 of this volume ("A minimal syntax for the pictorial"), Andrew Harrison goes over many of the same subjects I shall be treating.

The differences between the two arguments may perhaps be made clear by considering Harrison's notions of "symmetry" and "asymmetry," analogous to the distinction I shall make later in this paper between "likeness" and "unlikeness." As I understand his arguments, Harrison accepts with modifications Gombrich's definition of images as "relational models" (also to be discussed below) preferring the metaphor of a map for painting rather than that of a window. Pictures are "symmetrical" with what they represent in that they refer to their objects, but they are "asymmetrical" in that they are not their objects. Asymmetry thus begins to define the extrareferential about pictures, which Harrison explores as "syntax," called at one point the "syntactical condition of the pictorial" and compared to a "generative grammar" (p. 229). The simplicity of this syntax accounts for the fact that viewers of images have a much broader competence than listeners or readers (that is, more people recognize one anothers' images than understand one anothers' languages). It is important to note that Harrison does not compare pictures and language in point of arbitrariness; rather he argues, as I will, that images, and especially simple images (what I take him to mean by "demotic images") are sufficiently recognizable and points instead to what might be called structural analogies and disanalogies. Harrison himself writes that what he calls the "minimalism" of pictorial syntax "is the source of the most interesting disanalogies with [language]" (p. 227), and I would agree. I would question, however, whether it is desirable even to retain the linguistic metaphor of syntax. Harrison is concerned with what I will call "virtuality" (with our capacity to see three dimensions in two; see note 6 below, this chapter) and I would again agree that there is an extralinguistic structure of virtuality, which may be characterized as a kind of "syntax." But, as we shall see, I will argue that what corresponds at a deeper level to syntax is the real spatial basis of images, rooted in the simple fact that we always make images out of what was already there and from the modes of representation to be gathered from the exigencies of those conditions.

5 See my "This is not a Sign: Some Remarks on Art and Semiotics," *Art Criticism*, 3 (1986), pp. 30–45.

6 "Real space" is the space in which we find ourselves, with its own structures and decorums, which are, however, always culturally constructed; "virtual space" is the space we seem to see in surfaces, as in paintings and drawings. Real space is the prior category because we always have a real spatial relation to any illusionistic surface. I shall be concerned mostly with real space in this chapter.

7 F. de Saussure, *Course in General Linguistics*, ed. C. Bally et al. (New York, Toronto and London, 1966), p. 66.

8 *Ibid.*, p. 67.

9 P. L. Heath, "Concept," *The Encyclopedia of Philosophy*, ed. P. Edwards (New York and London, 1967), vol. II, pp. 177–180.

10 Aristotle, *On the Soul, Parva naturalia, On Breath*, trans. W. S. Hett (Cambridge and London, 1975). In the *De anima* (431a17) Aristotle states

the principle that "the soul never thinks without a mental image" (*phantasmata*); this is repeated in the *De memoria et reminiscentia* (449b32, 450a13) and elaborated with the example of an impression of a signet ring (also used in *De anima*, 424a15ff., to define sensation as the first apprehension by the soul of form without matter). The metaphor of this impression or mark is expanded as "a kind of picture," which in turn serves as the basis for an important discussion of memory.

11 D. Summers, *The Judgment of Sense. Renaissance Naturalism and the Rise of Aesthetics* (Cambridge, 1987), p. 209; also see J. Weinberg, "Abstraction in the Formation of Concepts," in *Dictionary of the History of Ideas*, ed. P. P. Weiner (New York, 1968), vol. I, pp. 1–9.

12 See E. H. Gombrich, "Art History and Psychology in Vienna Fifty Years Ago," *Art Journal*, 44 (1984), pp. 162–164. The idea of the "conceptual image" is a leitmotif in Gombrich's writing; in *Art and Illusion. A Study in the Psychology of Pictorial Representation* (Princeton, 1969), "primitive" and children's art are linked to "symbols of concepts" (p. 292).

13 M. Schapiro, "Style," in *Aesthetics Today*, ed. M. Philipson (Cleveland, 1961), p. 99.

14 See E. Panofsky, *Idea. A Concept in Art Theory*, trans. J. J. S. Peake (Columbia, 1968); and E. H. Gombrich, "Icones Symbolicae. Philosophies of Symbolism and their Bearing on Art," in his *Symbolic Images. Studies in the Art of the Renaissance II* (2nd edn, Chicago, 1985), pp. 123–234.

15 "Real Metaphor. Toward a Redefinition of the Conceptual Image," in *Visual Theory*, ed. N. Bryson, M. A. Holly, and K. Moxey (Oxford, 1991), pp. 231–259.

16 Aristotle, *De interpetatione* 16a1–9.

17 Summers, *Judgment of Sense*, p. 189, note 12.

18 On natural signs see B. E. Rollin, *Natural and Conventional Meaning. An Examination of the Distinction* (The Hague, 1976). The earliest writer I know to refer to *images* as natural signs is Roger Bacon (see K. M. Fredborg, L. Nielsen, and J. Pinborg, "An Unedited Part of Roger Bacon's 'Opus maius': 'De signis,'" *Traditio*, 34 [1978], p. 76). Having cited Augustine's *De doctrina christiana*, Bacon writes that there are natural signs "per configurationem, as the image of St. Nicholas is the sign of his configuration and conformation. And so all species are signs of things." Bacon could make this argument because Alhazen's theory of light made it possible to describe the transfer of a pattern of light points from one surface to another, so that the relation between object and sight had become clearly indexical. It may be suggested that it is the describability of this relation, fundamental to modern optics, that has given the retinal (and photographic) image the peculiar authority they have enjoyed in modern times. The species, the icon in sensation, was immediately seen as an unnecessary hypothesis (see K. Tachau, "The Problem of the Species in Medio at Oxford in the Generation after Ockham," *Medieval Studies*, 44 [1982], p. 400: "intuitive cognition does not require a representation or image; all that is required is an impressed quality.") This simple argument raised the very most fundamental questions about how

the mind knows the world and about the role of "form" in that process; it also became the progressive view of early modern science. See N. L. Maull, "Cartesian Optics and the Geometrization of Nature," *Review of Metaphysics*, 32:2 (1978), pp. 253–273.

19 Summers, *Judgment of Sense*, pp. 137–139.

20 Plato, *Philebus*, 39b; and, for Aristotle, see note 10 above.

21 W. J. T. Mitchell, *Iconology. Image, Text, Ideology* (Chicago and London, 1986), pp. 5–6.

22 Saussure, *Course*, p. 68.

23 *Ibid.* Saussure's presentation of linguistics as the purest form of semiology is very much extended by a writer such as R. Barthes, who states that "linguistics is not a part of the general science of signs, even a privileged part, it is semiology that is a part of linguistics" (*Elements of Semiology*, trans. A. Lavers and C. Smith [New York, 1968], p. 11). This highly questionable notion is to my mind essential both to structuralism and post-structuralism.

24 Saussure, *Course*, pp. 114–122.

25 *Ibid.*, p. 113.

26 *Ibid.*, pp. 118–119.

27 *Ibid.*, pp. 119–120.

28 Gombrich, *Art and Illusion*, pp. 8–9.

29 *Ibid.*, p. 362; see also p. 345: "All artistic discoveries are discoveries not of likenesses but of equivalences which enable us to see reality in terms of an image and an image in terms of reality."

30 *Ibid.*, pp. 89–90.

31 *Ibid.*, p. 23.

32 E. H. Gombrich, *Meditations on a Hobby Horse and Other Essays on the Theory of Art* (London, 1963), p. 10.

33 *Ibid.*, p. 9.

34 *Ibid.*, pp. 6–7 and *passim*.

35 *Art and Illusion*, p. 139.

36 *Ibid.*, p. 225.

37 M. Baxandall, *Painting and Experience in Fifteenth-Century Italy: A Primer in the Social History of Pictorial Style* (Oxford and New York, 1972), pp. 29–108.

38 Gombrich, *Art and Illusion*, p. 87.

39 *Ibid.*, p. 89.

40 *Ibid.*, p. 90. Interdependence of image and function is much more suggestively treated in "Meditations on a Hobby Horse." A restatement of the same principle in a more recent essay, Gombrich's "Mirror and Map: Theories of Pictorial Representation," in *The Image and the Eye. Further Studies in the Psychology of Pictorial Representation* (Oxford, 1982 [pp. 187–188]) extends the ideas of *Art and Illusion*.

41 C. S. Peirce, *Philosophical Writings*, ed. J. Buchler (New York, 1955), p. 104.

42 M. Schapiro, "On Some Problems in the Semiotics of Visual Art: Field and Vehicle in Image-Signs," in *Semiotics, an Introduction*, ed. R. E. Innis (Bloomington, Ind., 1985), p. 208.

43 Aristotle, *Poetics*, 1448b4ff.
44 The example is from E. Panofsky, "Iconography and Iconology. An Introduction to the Study of Renaissance Art," in *Meaning in the Visual Arts. Papers in and on Art History* (Garden City, N.J., 1955), p. 29.
45 R. Barthes, "Rhetoric of the Image," in his *Image–Music–Text*, ed. and trans. S. Heath (New York, 1977), pp. 32–51.

10

A minimal syntax for the pictorial: the pictorial and the linguistic – analogies and disanalogies

ANDREW HARRISON

INTRODUCTION

Since pictures are "about" what in various ways they depict, it is in the first instance trivially true that at least in this respect there is an *analogy* between "the pictorial" and "the linguistic": language without reference, or an account of language without some concept or concepts of reference, would be absurd, and so, equally, would be an account of the pictorial. But, on the other hand, what also seems to be trivially true is that there must be radical *disanalogies* between the use of pictures as devices of communication and any corresponding uses of language: we do not learn to read pictures as we do words. We seem to recognize them if not quite directly then by a process that seems to be far more intimately bound up with how we come to recognize visible things around us. In no clear and obvious sense does the pictorial seem to have a syntax at all like that of language, and (apart from cases of more or less stereotypical iconography) nothing in our coming to understand the pictorial seems to correspond remotely to what it is to learn the words of a dictionary. Pictures do not inherit the curse of Babel: pictorial art reaches across national and temporal boundaries easily and naturally. The drawn bison of cave art are as recognizable by us as the drawings of our contemporaries. No cave artist, and few of our contemporaries, speak a natural language which we know. So whereas language is, the use of pictures is not, "conventional."

Positively put, then, whatever can be visually recognized can be visually pictured, given the required skill, and whatever can be visually recognized, or visually imagined, can be recognized as it may be visually depicted.[1] There are many varieties of ways in which we do visually recognize things around us, and many interesting ways in which we may fail to do so. Reasons for all this must clearly have to do with cultural conditioning, or with conventions. Such conditioning and conventions will correspond exactly to the varieties of ways in which we may come to recognize what it is that is represented in a picture. Pictorial recognition and the recognition of common objects do not really raise different issues.

These claims for analogies and disanalogies of the pictorial with language are clearly not in conflict. For if the first corresponds to pictorial "reference" the second corresponds to pictorial "sense," or to what in the case of pictures plays the same role as sense does in language. Two pictures each representing the same object, but in different ways, have the same pictorial reference by a different pictorial sense. Together they make the "pictorial identity claim" that one and the same pictorial referent may be regarded (i.e., visually recognized) differently. This should set an agenda for an inquiry, an agenda tantamount to the thesis that the analogy between pictures and language is that two pictures, very different in content, may be about the same thing, while the disanalogy (left to be explored) has to do with what it is to recognize the different content of the two pictures.

How far, then, is understanding pictures radically different from the task of understanding the sense of a word or phrase. Do pictures have "sense?"

Perhaps the concept of "sense" for pictures smacks too much of the linguistic. A different terminology for this adopted by Wolterstorff from Walton refers to "q-representation" and "p-representation."[2] "When applying the [former] concept we are making a claim to the effect that some existent entity was represented. When applying the other we are making no such claim."[3] Thus, regarding "q-representation," a sentence may be about X in just the same way as a picture is of X, or a sentence and a picture together may refer to X: for example, "This [holding up a picture] is how she looked as a young girl" is about Great-aunt Mary, so that the whole is true or false of her depending on how she did in fact look at that age, or, alternatively, fictional if we are invited to suppose, or fictionally imagine, her thus. On the other hand "p-representation" seems to be very unlike language. To make a picture of Great-aunt Mary, or of a unicorn, in this sense is to produce "some visual design in a certain context ... What is also necessary," says Wolterstorff, "is that the design in question look like a unicorn – that it be capable of being seen as a unicorn. Only with a visual design that can be seen as a unicorn can one p-represent a unicorn." Clearly sentences do not have to look like unicorns to be descriptive of unicorns. I suspect that the claim that pictures are not "conventional" and that language is says no more of interest than this.

It might be objected that no visual design could possibly look like a unicorn, since nothing at all looks like a unicorn, so there can be no way of recognizing one visually, unicorns being non-existent. So let's say that the design must look like, be "capable of being seen as" how a unicorn is fictionally supposed to look (i.e. as part of our common stock of fictions, of mythical or imaginary beasts to be "found in our culture"). If it looks like a parrot with a horn on its behind and not like a horse with a horn like a narwhal's tusk on its forehead it fails to be a picture of a unicorn. Rectal-horned parrots are not part of our common fictional stock. But they could easily be; incorporating them as standard, "recognizable" fictions would not be difficult. Lack of standardization can pose a problem, but not an insuperable one. Dragons seem to be very generally available as fictions though they are more mythically variable in appearance: a child's drawing of a dragon can be quite firmly, and not at all incorrectly, asserted by its author to be just how her dragon, her very own invented dragon, really does look in imagination, or she may even say with perfect propriety that it would do if only she could manage to draw the feet right. Such complications are important, yet it is indeed to something like "p-representation" that a concept of "recognizably looking like" must apply to pictorial depiction in just that way in which it cannot apply to descriptive expressions in any non-pictographic language. This is, however, a pretty dull claim to make as a doctrine that pictures are not "like language": obviously "cat on mat" in no way looks like a cat on a mat, whereas a picture of a cat on a mat in some way should. Who in their right mind would deny it?

AN AGENDA

But what should we really want of a philosophical exploration here? I suggest we need answers to the following questions: first, and most vaguely, can we get any sort of focus on the very idea of pictorial, non-linguistic, thought and its expression and understanding? Second, how far can such a concept illuminate the idea of the aesthetics of the visual and its place in the depictive strategies of visual art? Third, how does such artistic depiction stand with respect to all those forms of visual depiction that lie outside the context of visual art, especially, and I think most importantly, what we might call the "demotic" of drawing?

In general, I suspect, there is at present no real consensus about how these different questions relate to one another, nor about how we might discover such relationships. But they are clearly linked. My suggestion in what follows is that to explore these issues fully we need to look rather more seriously at the idea that the pictorial has a specific, though strictly limited, analogy with the linguistic. We should not be put off by any initial uncertainty about the extent to which the relationship may turn out to be merely analogous. A clear analogy would be good enough to be getting on with.

My first suggestion is, however, quite depressingly unoriginal.[4] This is that any picture, whether found in art or anywhere else, has the logical form of a map, a complex such that to grasp its structure in a certain way – which way amounts to "understanding" it – is to see how elements within that structure correspond to properly sorted elements in its topic, what it is a map of. The idea of a map here is, of course, more general than popular, or familiar, examples of cartography suggest (such as Ordnance Survey maps, schematic maps of the London Underground and the like). It can embrace both those sorts of depictions which require considerable study of the mapping "conventions" and rules before they can be seen to depict what they do as well as those that may be virtually instantaneously recognized. For instance the sign * on its own, or the signs --- or ¶ have no recognizable depictive force; on the other hand

does so and, insofar as it can be seen to have a depictive force, is more or less instantly recognizable as what it depicts – as a face. That it should be instantly recognizable is a familiar fact of some importance both for psychology and for the philosophy of perception. The general sort of explanation that seems both natural and required is that for such a face-like object to be both as familiar as faces are and familiar in the way in which faces are implies our being firmly equipped with a pattern schema of faces to which such depicting devices conform, or our being equipped with a more or less well-stocked repertoire of such schema. This is a rich and complex matter with rather obvious, as well as less obvious, implications both for perception and for the nature of the pictorial. However, recognizability as such, especially the recognizability of such "conventional" or "stereotypical" depicting patterns clearly cannot demonstrate that they are not mapping devices in this general sense. Clearly they are. It is often supposed that it must follow from the idea that our pictorial recognitions are in this sense "conventional" or "stereotypical" that they are either open to optional abandonment (as if we could "choose" to see such arrays as non-face-depictors, or not as depictors at all, if we wished) or that they are open to learning or to learned study as (say) the "conventions" of the Ordnance Survey are. But this is simply a mistake. Richard Wollheim tells us, for instance, that we learn to read a map; we do not learn to read pictures, but to recognize them.[5] The implication is that therefore pictures are not maps (or perhaps that pictures in "art" are not). Yet nothing of the sort follows. It could be concluded equally that pictures, or pictures of these sorts, belong to that category of maps which just do invite more or less instant recognition, while it should be borne in mind that others obviously do not. It would then follow that the interesting questions will be about the conditions of such recognition.

This may suggest that the concept of mapping survives in this context at the price of triviality. This is, however, far from the case. For instance, this concept of a picture was assumed by the early Wittgenstein in the *Tractatus*[6] to enable a picture to provide a model for language, rather than the other way about, and the kind of "meaning theory of pictures" that would correspond to a picture theory of meaning is by no means without interest.[7] Our initial prejudices against such an idea are symmetrical. To tell anyone that a sentence, or a sentence-content, is "like a picture," that is, that "the cat sat on the mat" or "cat on mat" is pictorial, naturally invites the response that such sentences cannot by any stretch of imagination look like a cat on a mat, just as it might be objected that pictures are not "read" as the outcome of grasping a convention. Each objection involves a ground-floor misunderstanding of what the theory claims. The claim is not concerned with the experiences we may have of recognizing or understanding such systems of signs, but with the very simple concept of a minimal syntax for such sign systems. To comprehend such surfaces as depicting is essentially to be able to distinguish between a mark that indicates a relation between discriminable parts of the object and a mark that indicates the parts themselves.

This may need explaining. It ought, perhaps, to be taken far less for granted than it usually is that (however easily or "directly" recognized) drawings in outline in which cross-hatching is employed to produce the "effect" of shadow or changes in surface tonality and at the same time to indicate the direction of the planes of the object depicted are making use of these linearities in quite radically different ways. It ought to astonish us more than it does how ready we are to construe the depicting surface in the appropriate way. For example, we very rarely see a portrait in pen and ink, or an engraving, as a picture of a face encased in a net, or a landscape similarly constructed as crossed by fissures and paths. But such construals are possible. Often they would be simple mistakes. Sometimes they might be recognized (perhaps on the basis of other information) as correct, if disturbing, ways of regarding the picture, sometimes (more interestingly and, I suspect, more often) as uneasy and "expressive" possibilities lurking in the wings of our pictorial understanding. Quite rarely, I suspect, people very new to a medium may make such a simple mistaken misconstrual: a syntactic mistake.

The same point may be made more positively: children, and often adults in interestingly different ways, produce drawings in which quite distinct sorts of shapes, crude circles, blobs, sometimes – less often and oddly – triangles, and so on seem to be standardly used to indicate body-parts, connected or disconnected in equally interesting ways. The put-together pictorial constructions are, moreover, often quite standardized, and very readily recognizable. Yet none of these unit shapes (block visual "concepts," we might call them) have any claim to recognition in isolation from the ordered structures in which they can be found (just as the asterisks for eyes, above, do not). It is, I think, not at all misleading to think of such unit forms as "visual/ pictorial concepts," since they carry something like a semantics of depiction – concepts of what "goes to make up" a pictured body (say). Then it is the underlying syntax of how they must be ordered that permits such "concepts" – and permits the possibility of the "generation'" of innumerably more pictures being produced and recognized in comparable ways.

Significantly, however, in outlining these facts one is inclined to adopt as natural a range of expressions for the beholder's response to the depiction that runs from what can seem to be the "causal" concept of an "effect" to the far more obviously cognitive concepts of construing, interpreting, and understanding. What we have to do with here are more or less "natural," more or less learned or acquired, ways of seeing, or of understanding, the depicting surface as depiction. In pictures as in language, syntax is what makes semantics possible. The idea of the *Tractatus* that a sentence "hooked onto the world" like a picture – that in essence language pictured the world in describing it – was that names (signs for relata) can only succeed in naming insofar as they are articulated within a depicting structure of relationships which is the "structural" analogue of the state of affairs that is depicted, or described.

The *Tractatus* need not concern us here, except to note that it does provide a revealing (and, I think, instructively deficient) account of language. Its first implication might be seen to be that the ground-floor logical error in understanding a piece of language rich enough to count as the sense content of a proposition is to construe a form "a R b" (the standard logical shorthand for one thing to be related to another) as a three-object projection (perhaps having been confused by seeing three letters in a row) rather than a projection of two "objects" in a relation to one another. On this reading, getting the very idea of a relational symbolism is where the core of linguistic understanding lies. This, as it were, undercuts a subject-predicate grammar (which we might well suppose to be fundamental to language) by what is supposed to be a more fundamental account of how "things stand to one another" in ways that can be picked out by the projection.[8] That "normal" pictures certainly do not seem to have a subject-predicate form can seem to provide the strongest basis for an objection to the pictorial-linguistic analogy. But if both language and pictures are projections the objection falls: we have a "picture theory of meaning" for language. In effect such a doctrine trades on the fact that pictures have a non-subject-predicate syntax. It seems to me, however, that while this is essentially right about pictures it is mistaken about language, and radically reduces the concept of what we can say, if not of what we can depict.

What would correspond, if at all, to a subject-predicate distinction for pictures, paintings, drawings, and so on is the distinction we might draw between what it is that the picture is a picture of and what descriptions would be true of that subject if we are to suppose the picture to be reliable – as we might both know that P is a portrait of A yet show A to be quite different from how he really is. A portrait in oils may be as much a misdescription in this sense as any portrait in words. But that distinction lies not within the system of significant marks on the surface of the canvas, but in what we may say about it, having construed it as a portrait.[9]

Andrew Harrison

Mirrors and maps

In a well-known paper,[10] Gombrich contrasted a theoretical conception of a picture (a picture in "art") as a mirror with that of a picture as
a map. Both have deep historical roots, and neither is, on the face of it,
very convincing. On the one hand the idea that a painting or a
drawing could intelligibly aspire to mirror the world as we see it, that
is, to be a sort of perceptual replicator, seems to be manifestly absurd.
This is in spite of, or perhaps even because of, the central role that
something very like this idea has had in the history of painting. On
the other hand pictures really do not, perhaps cannot, either visually
resemble or phenomenologically resemble those familiar items of
cartography we normally think of as maps. But the opposition gets
the problem out of focus. The modest thesis of projection can apply
equally well to both sides of the opposition. A mirror image, understood in terms of its optics, can well serve as a standard case of
projection: manifestly, slightly modified, this is the role of optical
theory as applied to such things as ground-glass screens, cones of
vision, and so on as it is carried over into perspective theory.

Often this is regarded as a basis for the construction of visual replication (i.e. a causal variant in the system of perception such that the
"bundle of light rays" reaching the eye remains under certain controlled circumstances qualitatively unchanged). The history of perspective theory of the required kind is continuous with the history of
optics, whether in an observational science, such as astromomy, or
painting. It cannot be stressed too strongly that this tradition of
inquiry committed its protagonists to no particular theory as to
whether, metaphysically, there was a way the real world really looked
which might be uniquely mirrored in art (for in fact it set the stage for
considerable disagreement on that matter[11]) or to whether, phenomenologically, it need "feel" that way to the beholder. For the concept of
projection as such can at best set the frame within which such matters
can be discussed. It must itself be neutral on such matters.

However, while neutral, it is not powerless. It rules out what might
be called misplaced phenomenology which tells the story, as it were
the wrong way about, by attempting to start with the experience of
depiction without first asking what depiction is (i.e., asking how it is
that a picture could in principle stand for – "fit," in the right way –
what it depicts).

For instance, Richard Wollheim, in *Painting as an Art*, strongly
opposes the view that the capacity of the depicting surface to depict is

based on "conventions" in the way in which language is.[12] Perhaps the best clue to how he understands this doctrine can be found in his objection to what he calls the "semiotic" theory. For Wollheim, "it cannot account for . . . 'transfer' . . . that if I can recognise a picture of a cat, and I know what a dog looks like, I can be expected to recognise a dog . . . on the Semiotic view this ought to be baffling . . . as if knowing the French word 'chat' means a cat and knowing what dogs look like, I should, on hearing it, be able to understand what the word 'chien' means." But the analogy that matters is precisely with that aspect of language that does involve something like what Wollheim calls "transfer," namely that central fact of any language that a finite input of "learning data" can permit the speaker to understand and produce an unlimited set of further sentences. It is precisely with the idea of grammar as "generative" that the analogy is concerned, not with the morphological "arbitrariness" of individual words. Wollheim clearly does think that the pictorial is in some central sense "generative" – to be accounted for simply in terms of the fact that recognizing a picture of A must go along with "knowing what A looks like." This, as he also (rightly) sees cannot be a mere matter of visual resemblance: that concept either applies trivially (since anything visual in some way resembles any other visual thing) or else is question-begging, since it must, if used in a narrower sense, presuppose just the kind of visual resemblance (the sort involved when we see a picture as depicting what it does) that it seeks to explain. He turns, therefore, to the concept of "seeing-in," and the associated concept of "twofoldness."[13]

"Twofoldness"

The history of these concepts of "seeing-in" and "twofoldness" is instructive. Suppose we think of recognizing a painted surface as a picture of A as "seeing it as A." Then the immediate difficulty is obvious enough, namely that we are now in danger of assimilating that recognition to the quite different case of "mis-recognition," of taking it to be A, or even (less bad, but bad enough) of thinking it looks just as A does. (The latter can occur but is notoriously deviant from normal picture recognition.) And this would be to assimilate the recognition not to a perceptual mistake, *simpliciter*, but a specific kind of illusion. Normal illusions conflict with the beliefs we have, often dramatically, as with the stick we know to be straight that looks bent in water or the stage illusion of the lady being sawn in half whom we know could not possibly be being treated that way. Recognizing pictures really is not like that. (Equally, it is even less like those quite opposite cases where what we see is a consequence of the power of our beliefs, as where we see someone whom we believe to be unfriendly as threatening, because of our thoughts about him. Both sorts of responses have their place in our response to pictures, but in every case that is secondary to our recognition that they are indeed pictures.) However, this thought, or something like it, does seem to have been behind the choice of title, as well as many of the arguments of Gombrich's splendid *Art and Illusion*.[14] And clearly that assimilation needs to be resisted, not because it carries the manifestly false idea that (say) we mistake landscape pictures for landscapes when we see them to be landscape pictures, for it need not imply this at all, but because it implies the much subtler error that in responding to the depictive authority of a surface we see it as we know, or believe, it not to be.

Crucially, we need to believe that the surface before us is a picture insofar as we can begin to accept its depictive implications, and come under its sway as a depiction. Hence we cannot suspend judgment about, nor attention to, the depicting surface in favor of an attention to its subject matter. But the concept of "seeing-as" seems to lead Gombrich in precisely the opposite direction, to deny that we can, let alone that we do, attend both to the picture's surface at one and the same time as we attend to what we take the picture to depict. As an account of our experience as beholders this is quite clearly false. It does indeed seem to be crucial that there are what can seem to be two types of attention involved and, moreover, involved together as we respond to the pictorial.

Projective seeing

Part of Wollheim's strategy for reaching an account of this "twofold-ness" is to replace the Gombrichian (and popular) concept of "seeing-as" by what does certainly seem to be the more idiomatic "seeing-in." We see things "in" clouds, fires, crumbled walls; we do not – it would be absurd if we did – see fires, clouds, and crumbled walls "as" castles, camels, whales, landscapes, or battles. Thus far I would strongly agree with Wollheim. But then something goes wrong.

What goes wrong is that Wollheim then grounds the concept of depiction itself in the concept of projective seeing. Much of Gombrich's account of pictorial creativity very appropriately had centered around the example of Leonardo's advice to young painters, stuck for subject matter, to attend to such things as stained walls or stones of an uneven colour and to see there battles, landscapes, and the like: "an infinity of things which you will be able to reduce to their complete and proper forms ... as in the sound of bells in whose stroke you may find every named word which you can imagine."[15] "Representation arrives, then," writes Wollheim,[16] "when there is imposed upon the natural capacity of seeing-in something that so far it had been without: a standard of correctness and incorrectness. This standard is set – set for each painting – by the intentions of the artist in so far as they are fulfilled." But it must be clear here that something has gone wrong. What Leonardo wanted added to "seeing-in" was more work, "reducing" such objects of fancy "to their complete and proper forms." It is surely from the outcome of this work, which will be painting or drawing, that the "additional" account must come. But while that might well provide some content to the idea of "criteria of correctness" it would then assume the very account of the pictorial that we are seeking. Suppose, following Leonardo's own example, we thought that what it was to hear words was to hear them "in" the sounds of bells; then the answer to what words were heard, and to what would have been "correctly" heard, outside the realm of such fanciful imagining, had there been a "correct" way of hearing-in, would simply be a lesson in Leonardo's Italian. "Hearing-in" would fall away to be replaced by an account of what it was to understand a language.

The battle scenes Leonardo invites us to see in the wall are about as good an example as we might wish of a fully intentional object outside a propositional context, and unconstrained by anything comparable to such a context: there are no battle scenes or land-scapes "beyond" the agent's fanciful attention to the wall. So here there is no question of attending differentially to what is seen in the wall and to the wall. What is seen in the wall is how the wall is attended to. The whole is a single, if complex, form of experience. There can be no question about the relation between one thing – the surface – and another. What masquerades as a "relational" question is really a matter of an adverb qualifying a certain sort of attention to the wall. For, as Leonardo well saw, there is as yet no picture in the story, only a wall attention to which may, perhaps, prompt a picture. To go beyond such free fancy to true pictorial imagination we need the picture.

To attend to a picture is to attend from the start to what is recognized as a depicting surface. To be sure, we can attend to a marked surface, find that we see something, perhaps (as Leonardo suggests) many things "in" it. We may then come to the conclusion that it is indeed a picture and so, perhaps following Wollheim's train of thought, conclude that a certain way of seeing something in the surface is correct. But this train of thought is not that of recognizing a depiction *simpliciter*, but of following a certain sort of inductive argument which has as its conclusion that it is indeed a picture that we have before us and not merely a "picture" such as we may see in the fire. The conclusion that then follows is that it is not a natural object, such that it is a mere accident of its configuration and of our imaginative capacities that we can see whatever we do "in" it, but that it is something intended to be seen in that way. However, this condition of intention must not lead us to seek for some psychological state "still," as it were, located in the maker's mind. Rather its recognition is constitutive of what it is to acknowledge a depiction – a pictorial artifact already, as it were, in the public domain, as language must be.

No purely phenomenological story of the beholder's experience of "seeing-in" could possibly be adequate for this – hence concepts of "criteria of correctness" cannot be simply added on to such a "basic beginning." Indeed, in the case of certain pictures, perhaps in a difficult or unfamiliar style, we may not even begin to see anything "in" the differentiated surface until we have first construed it as a depiction. To be sure one may be able to see almost anything in almost any differentiated surface, but equally one may fail to. Whether or not we do may, on occasion, be quite independent of our powers of seeing-in. This is manifestly true of maps and diagrams (that is why Wollheim and others see them as radically opposed to the pictorial), but it is equally true of many children's drawings as well as of many drawings in a comparable style, often from quite sophisticated sources, which Wollheim also sees as radically opposed to the pictorial in art.[17]

The "symmetry" and "asymmetry" of the pictorial

We can, here, be seduced by the recognizable: to be sure, the dramatic recognizability of (say) cave paintings that show us what they depict across the millennia where we can have no independent knowledge of their makers' thought, apart from their paintings, is no illusion. But it does not follow that it is recognizability that grounds the nature of depiction. What is needed is an account of depiction that will explain recognizability – and its occasional absence – and which can connect these facts with their often, but not always, having a powerful and essential aesthetic content. For all this the "syntax" of depiction must come first. An account of this must require that we attend not to two things but to one significant object of visual depiction.

Is there not an obvious objection to this? There are, of course, two things: the sitter and her portrait, the landscape and the painting, the imaginary dragon and the non-imaginary drawing of a dragon. Of course this is true. The point is, however, that pictorial representation poses two logical questions that can easily seem to be at variance with one another if they are not properly distinguished. The first has to do with the asymmetry of "A pictorially represents B," the second with what can seem to be a kind of symmetry. Neither way of putting the matter is quite satisfactory. To take the first of these: notoriously, any account of "A pictures B" that relies on resemblance, either of visual appearance, *simpliciter*, or of being seen as having a common "mapping structure," must invite the immediate objection that if A resembles B, B resembles A in the same respect, whereas quite obviously, if A depicts B it does not follow (often is inconsistent with) the proposition that B depicts A. A standard way of dealing with this is to say something like "A is intended to depict B whereas B is not similarly intended to depict A." This is true, of course, but hardly meets the point since, obviously, if depiction were a symmetrical relation it would have to follow from the fact that A was intended to depict B that the converse was intended at least as a side-effect. Why that normally cannot be the case, intentionally or otherwise, is what has to be explained. The concept of intention on its own simply cannot do the relevant work for us.

What certainly can do the work, however, is the fact that any depiction may always be used – does not have to be used, but is necessarily available for use – to show how things are or how they might be. Maps, and pictures too, can always be used to express the proposition that "that is how things stand," where "that" refers to the content of the map (or picture). It is this "fact of semantics" that is the source of the fact that from "A depicts B" one may not ever infer that "B depicts A." The reason is straightforward enough. It is that maps, and all other picture representations and also descriptions and reports, can and normally must be true, so long as they tell the truth but do not tell the whole truth. A map that included everything in its landscape (right down to the last atom) would have to be at least as big as its landscape. Normally, of course, they radically simplify. But a map that included more item-referring or relation-indicating information than its topic actually contained would of necessity be false. The world, in other words, as we can map or picture it, is virtually always richer than our depictions of it. Depiction of the world, or a selected part of the world, is always a selection, a structured, organized aspect of what might equally well have been the source of another selection for an alternative depiction of the same thing.[18] Hence there cannot be an inference from "A depicts B" to "B depicts A" and normally the contrary follows. Hence it must be that to any state of affairs there must correspond an indefinite number of equally "correct," but non-equivalent, ways of depicting it.

However, to that asymmetry there also corresponds a symmetry, for "twofoldness" expresses a further fact about visual depiction as it is recognized in our experience of what we might call the "authority" of the depictive surface. That fact is: how we are shown that aspect of the world presented by the depiction is just how the depiction itself is to be seen. A successful picture, properly understood, presents us with how its maker thereby requires us to regard the depicted object. We are not presented with a "sight of" a real or imagined world, of which we see an aspect "through" the picture. Rather, we are presented with an object, real or imagined, as visually conceived in terms of the depicting surface. Pictures are not windows through which we peep at a corner of the world, not even a corner of a real or imagined world as through a glass darkly.

These two conditions of asymmetry with regard to the object depicted and symmetry with respect to how it is to be seen as depicted, are, despite appearance to the contrary, quite compatible. Indeed they go together, for the "asymmetry" of picturing corresponds to the fact that pictures may refer to the world, and thus, fictionally, refer to an imagined world. Meanwhile the "symmetry" of the pictorial to something that might naturally be called "pictorial sense" corresponds to what might be better called the projective symmetry of visual imagination.

This distinction is close to, but not quite identical with, that between p-representation and q-representation, and is at least analogous to that between sense and reference in language, though it would be well not to assume that we have established more than that analogy.

PICTURES IN ART AND NON-ART

Thus pictorial "sense" – in a slightly different analytic mode, "p-representation" – is the domain of "twofoldness" and of whatever minimal "syntax" the pictorial may have, that is, that pictures are a species of map, even if a species which, among other things, makes psychological claims of recognizability on us. Pictorial "sense" is also the domain of how our capacities for the play of visual imagination link to the aesthetic content of pictures. The "syntax" is both non-trivial and minimal. The non-triviality makes an analogy with language; the minimalism is the source of most of the interesting disanalogies. These differences and similarities have, I suggest, essentially to do with how our capacities for the play of visual imagination link to the aesthetic content of pictures.

Features of depicting surfaces do not depict *simpliciter*. They depict in terms of how the patterning they present to us can be construed in one way or another as an organized whole. Significantly, any depicting surface, sketch, painting, or photograph, has what may be called a "pictorial mesh." This means that while we may always up to a point divide up a picture to show details of the whole – a figure from a crowded landscape, an eye within a face, and so on – there must come a point beyond which we cannot go. Beyond this point the complexity of the marked surface is too minimal, too out of touch with the original organization to provide a clue to what is depicted. Here the organization has been broken down below the level of recognizability (as in good jig-saw puzzles). Without sufficient "structure" an area of a marked surface cannot be construed as an object-indicator or as a relation-indicator. It remains as a non-depicting mark. Variation in the "mesh" of any picture constitutes one of the central components of depictive style, for it relates the textural variety of the surface to how we are to regard the object as depicted. It controls "twofoldness" – how we see the depicting surface in terms of how we see the object as depicted.

Nothing in any specific mark on the surface can by itself indicate whether it is a relation sign or a relatum (object) sign. The world might be, or might be imagined to be, such that people do have perceivable black borders to their bodies in space much as tigers may be striped. This is what we would perceive to be depicted were we to misconstrue the linearities of an outline drawing as indicating relata, rather than relations in the object as seen depicted. (Similarly we might misconstrue a drawing which by a rich use of hatching indicates the direction of planes in a solid – such as a face – as signs for marks on the solid – such as wrinkles or a net veil.) Such mistakes, essentially "syntactical" mistakes, are perhaps not very common, but are very possible. It is even possible that they may be deliberately invited by the painter as a sort of visual "trope."[19] And just as a grammatical mistake in language may lead to a mistaken belief about what one is being told, so such misconstructions can lead to similar mistakes, but they derive from misunderstanding how the picture "works," not from directly mistaking what is represented.

Pictures, perception, and photographs

It might be objected that these facts could not apply to mechanically produced pictures such as photographs where the graphic exploration by a draftsman of the "abstraction" of more or less simplified, or interpretive, structural features in the object-as-depicted is not an option.[20] But in fact it applies equally in this case, though in ways that are much closer to how we tend to attend to our "normal" perceptions in the world around us. We may see the white of an area of sky either as an object in its own right or as a gap between objects. We may, to be sure, do either or both; what is equally certain is that such perceptions are different, just as it is equally certain that below a given level of complexity we do not recognize familiar objects. What photographs can exploit, via precisely what is popularly thought of as a photograph's "naturalism," is the analogy between the structural nature of depiction and our skills of recognition in normal perception. There, too, a percept may be notoriously too unstructured in its context to provide clues to recognition. Certain sorts of early Impressionism seem to exploit the same fact, so that we can easily be led to think of each brush-marked dab of paint as "corresponding" to a "sense-datum" – or "impression," or equally easily read classical exponents of sense-data theory as just like instructions for seeing the world as that sort of Impressionist painting. (These sorts of painterly styles provide no evidence for that specific philosophical theory, but rather evidence that what the theory calls "data" can well belong to a "style" of visual attention. Then all that is shown is that we can be encouraged to see the actual visual world as an object-as-depicted in terms of a particular sort of depicting surface. The philosophical theory is then not unlike the – clearly false – claim that this is the only, or only proper, way of seeing the world.) None of these facts would be intelligible if we supposed that Gombrich's contrast between a picture as mirror or as map were a genuine theoretical option. The former turns out to indicate merely some sorts of mapping styles, those that "fit" those of our recognition habits that may well be more natural to us in recognizing the un-depicted world.

Yet, for all that, since syntax is not content, the structure of depiction permits us to depict and to recognize as-depicted, in an astonishingly rich variety of ways. The pictorial is free from the curse of Babel far more radically than is often supposed. We possess a skill to construe quite sophisticated drawings that we could not have the skill to make. This apparent discrepancy, far from posing a barrier to our recognition of work well beyond our powers of execution, seems to enable it. What can seem to be the greatest contrast with language, that recognition runs far ahead of competence, would seem to be intelligible only on the assumption that deeper than such differences of skill and style lies something like a "generative grammar" common to all and thus of great simplicity.

The limits of the pictorial

Should we therefore think of the pictorial as a universal syntax? (Even, perhaps, as part and parcel of the "structure" of perceptual recognition itself?) The ideal of a universal language is less fantastic than that of the Philosophers' Stone and perhaps haunts us as much or more. I would make no such claim, but would claim only that the flexibility of the syntactical condition of the pictorial derives merely from its minimal nature. It is astonishingly minimal. For any idea of a pictorial syntax can in principle only be an idea of a system of perceptual sense-contents, sense-contents construed merely as structural analogues of visually understood states of affairs. A picture shows how things can be seen to stand in relation to one another. It is a form of communication that is in effect "bracket-free." In other words, with a picture one can show how things can be (visually) imagined to be, but one can show no more than that in purely pictorial terms. External to the picture one may say that "that," where "that" refers to the depiction-of-A and at the same time to A-as-depicted, is how something is, might be, could be, and so on, but neither the assertion of fact nor of modality can be made within the picture. So, for instance, no assertion of conditional modality like "If A were possible, B might be more likely than it seems now to be" could be encompassed by pictorial form unaided by a linguistic addition. A picture may indeed show that some state of affairs is (visually) conceivable as far as it may be pictured, but unaided by overt or tacit language it can do more.

Specifically, this means that unaided the pictorial cannot render what it cannot project. Possibility, reiterated conditionality, causal or moral responsibility, the concept of the self, values, hopes, and fears, can none of them be pictured, depicted pictorially, as such. Neither can quantification with modality: one may picture a horse, but not that these are all the horses there are or might be. Any language that was in this sense merely pictographic would run out of its capacity to communicate in all these areas. For what strictly lies outside the competence of the strictly pictorial is more or less precisely what within the tradition of classical empiricism is not open to direct perception, the topics of Humean and later Positivist skepticism. It is as if classical empiricism construes the concept of "what can be perceived" as "what may be seen" in just this sense of what can be visually recognized and depicted.

This is indeed a far narrower use of "see" than in most ordinary idioms in which we can say quite straightforwardly "I saw him insult her" or "I saw that she could not possibly have done that." Notoriously, "see that . . ." constructions have no place in the "data base" of radical empiricism.[21]

But here it might be strongly objected that pictures – certainly any pictures which we value in "art" – convey thought that essentially has to do with what I claim is beyond the power of visual depiction. (This is essentially Wollheim's objection to what he takes to be Lessing's thesis in *Laocoon*.[22]) There must be more to seeing than (simply) meets the eye, and thus more to painting and drawing than is confined to the minimal syntax of relata in bracket-free relations. What is needed, if I am right, is an account of how the "merely" pictorial is reinforced, and interrelates with, what are essentially non-pictorial modes of graphic communication. Just as an error of empiricism was to suppose that perception as such was limited to what can be simply drawn or photographed (so, as it were, since one cannot photograph a value, or a self, we can have no experience of such things), so neither should we limit painting and drawing to the merely pictorial. To our understanding of most pictures, whether in "art" or elsewhere, we bring, normally, a whole galaxy of knowledge and belief that essentially requires linguistic expression, and which essentially attaches to "q-representation." In this sense the Sistine Chapel ceiling, no less than illustrations to Dickens, cannot be understood except and insofar as we can bring to our interpretation of it some (perhaps very rich) knowledge of mythic narrative and belief. Most trivially, for instance, a picture of Tom grasping the knife in the back of Jerry can be depictively identical (in terms of "p-representation") with Tom's stabbing Jerry or his pulling the knife out. We require, in other words, that most serious uses of the pictorial be in the widest sense "illustration."

Yet "pure" depiction (pictorial "sense" as such) has powers of its own that do not belong to the linguistic, capacities to communicate in ways not expressible in unaided language. The exploration of receding planes, of horizons, of relations between figure and ground, of what can be seen as objects within the relations of the pictorial space (the very idea of pictorial space), and thus of visually imagined rhythms and patterns of balance or imbalance, are all things that can be drawn and which can be linguistically alluded to only via reference to pictures or via a recollection of drawings, paintings, and sketches. It is these elements that are pregnant with the possibilities of visual aesthetic interest, which belong essentially to pictorial "sense" and require a concept of the underlying syntax.

The aesthetics of pictures

Then what of the matter of "art," of aesthetics, of painting "as an art" as opposed to all those uses of the pictorial that do not belong to art?

The "minimal syntax" of the pictorial makes it a necessary truth that a picture of any sort gives to the beholder a pattern of visual salience: what the information is that a picture contains is not simply that things can be ordered (and sorted) in a determinate way, but that a certain kind of ordering is significant as a way of regarding the topic of the picture.[23] This is why the mere idea that a picture conveys information will not do, as a simple counter-example will make clear. A weak view of information here might be that A carries the same information as B if it is possible uniquely to determine A from how B is ordered. So consider a Fax machine that can reproduce pictures "down a wire." If we "break into" the process at the halfway stage there will be an ordered set of numbers that just fits (will uniquely cause) both B and what adequately resembles A. However, in no sense other than this is a print-out of those numbers a picture, neither picture A nor picture B, any more than a similar set of numbers for reproducing the surface appearance of a page of print can be said to constitute a set of sentences. For here "information" need only refer to a recipe for producing a given marked surface. Only when the marked surface can be construed in a certain way do we have either a picture or a page of print. Therefore, those types of pictures that capture aesthetic salience (by no means all types) do so via this capacity they have for pattern-presentation.

All pictures, whether used in "art" or in any other field, derive their depictive force on us from their capacity to draw our attention simultaneously to the ordered patterns we can see in the depicting surface and, thereby, to an object or state of affairs presented to us in terms of an analogous ordered pattern. This is then conceived as a structure in terms of which the depicted object can be regarded, a regard rooted in our visual imagination. (Model-making, of which the visually pictorial is a species is, of course, a wider concept.) Visual interest is not, therefore, a goal of the pictorial, as a number of writers, for example both Richard Wollheim and Michael Baxandall,[24] wish to argue. For visual interest is constitutive of the pictorial itself: to speak of "intentional visual interest" (as Baxandall does) as a goal of depictive painting or drawing is comparable to claiming that communication is a goal of language, or that ingesting food is a primary goal of eating. Eating does not count as eating unless food is ingested; using language does not count as speaking or writing unless communication occurs, and similarly the painting or drawing does not count as visual depiction unless the appropriate sort of visual interest is engaged. However, within that very general fact we can make distinctions. Distinctions regarding the type of depictively successful visual interest can direct us to the differences between varieties of visual depiction in "art" on the one hand and varieties of successful visual depictions that do not make an essential claim on our aesthetic response on the other.

Most of us can recall being coached by school science teachers in how not to draw flowers or other biological subjects. The point was not to be "arty" about the business, but to show just those structures and connections that mattered from the point of view of the curriculum. It might have been that we were told not to pay attention to the light and shade of the texture of the petals, but to attend rather to their manifest connections with the other significant parts of the flower, say from the point of view of plant morphology. Clear lines (perhaps) mattered, not subtle shadings or texturings. Rebelliously, I can recall thinking of Leonardo, who could be permitted all of what I was denied and still do a "scientific" drawing. But my rebellion missed the point. The point was not to suppress any visual interest in the depicting surface I was supposed to produce, for in a "good" drawing of the type required the salient record was indeed to be communicated via the visual interest of the line. And, of course, I was not Leonardo. The wrong type of exploration of the fascination of the marked surface (especially if inexpertly done) would necessarily obscure the communication. The aim was to pursue the discipline of prose, not of poetry, in drawing. Yet, as we all know, the discipline of prose can lie at the heart of writing's aesthetic power. We might set such recollections as these against other bad memories from school, memories of over-enthusiastic teachers of "self-expression" in the art room who may equally have been infuriated by a child's failure to handle paint or crayon freely and fluidly in a misplaced urge to get the thing right. That such battles and stresses can occur over ways of depiction – almost exactly comparable to battles and confusions over the place of art and imagination in the use of words – may itself help us to understand where we might begin to place the role of aesthetics in the pictorial.

Pictorial aesthetic interest begins with the celebration of the power of aspect-selection present in depiction itself. It is as if the aesthetic power of depiction begins to develop when the picture (sketch, painting, or drawing) makes on us what can seem to be two conflicting claims. On the one hand, the "authority" of the depicting surface demands that the way in which it presents itself to us is the only way (as long as we attend to the picture) we can attend to the *object-as-depicted*. However, as we regard the picture we must take it for granted that this is, and is inevitably, just one of an indenumerable number of possible ways in which the *object-that-is-depicted* might have been attended to, and with equal aptness. Outside the arena of "art," or of something very close to art, this distinction between the *object-as-depicted* and the *object-that-is-depicted* makes few, if any, claims on our understanding as beholders.

Art, I suggest, is essentially concerned with two issues that set it apart from other activities. The first derives from the relationship of art with a developing, changing cultural history. That is, the "seriousness" of artistic concerns is not merely to do with the production of aesthetically attractive or engaging products, but rather with the posing and resolving of predicaments over time and within a community of makers and beholders. All sorts of people may with varying degrees of skill make attractive objects, produce attractive sounds, but, for instance, the serious problems of the composition of nineteenth-century symphonies would have been unintelligible had Haydn not gone before, just as the serious problems inherent in the making and beholding of Cézanne's mature painting would have been unintelligible in isolation from a prior history of painting. The second applies to those forms of art that are about a real or fictional world, namely, a correspondingly systematic interest in the forms of imagination involved. It would, I think, be an exaggeration to suppose, as Arthur Danto seems to for all modern forms of art, that art systematically questions its own status, and is virtually a form of philosophy in the recursive nature of its self-consciousness.[25] But both pictorial and literary art must inevitably invite our attention not only to *what* is represented or described, but also to *how* the presented forms of communication do this. Thus we are inevitably obliged to attend to the fact that objects of art, whether naturalistic or otherwise, are artifacts with qualities in their own right that cannot be divorced from that fact.

In the case of visual art this is to say far more than that our invited attention to the qualities of the depicting surface is crucial. Many of the simpler, perhaps primary, aesthetic qualities, or aspects of things that engage our imaginative attention, belong to those marked surfaces that depict in their own right and for this reason have conventionally been referred to as "formal" qualities. These include qualities of balance, gracefulness, awkwardness, the relaxed or frenetic quality of a drawn line, and so on. I have argued elsewhere[26] that such features, despite attracting "psychological" predicates, do not take such predicates metaphorically, nor elliptically. I have further argued that their role in our understanding cannot be reduced either to concepts of the pictorial or the linguistic, even though (as any qualities capable of communication, of being "meaning-like," must be) they must in some ways be present in our public understanding. Briefly, if we think of such qualities as "gestural" qualities, deriving from the emotionally appropriate gesture involved in their making, they are essentially neither causally construable symptoms of the maker's state of mind nor construable as causally productive of a corresponding state of mind in the beholder. One does not have to be relaxed to be able to draw a relaxed line, nor relaxed to recognize one. Such qualities are "detached" from their "original" symptomatic occurrence by certain cultural capacities we possess. These are related to our ability to act in a manner dissociated from how we may feel (much as an actor performs) and to do so without lying to, or misleading, one another. But if such qualities belong to the depicting surfaces in their own right it must be that it is in attention to that fact together with attention to the object-as-depicted that its distinction from, and at the same time reminder of, the object-that-is-depicted derives. Our aesthetic interest, in other words, both distinguishes and interlinks not a duality but an essentially tripartite distinction between the object that is depicted, the object as depicted, and the depicting surface. Therefore the aesthetic power of the pictorial must go beyond twofoldness to a kind of threefoldness of response; hence the importance of something like a "minimal syntax" theory.

Art and the "demotic" of picturing

While these considerations may help us to understand a quite deep difference between depiction in "art" and the use of the pictorial in other, more mundane, contexts, they can demonstrate why we could not in principle give an account of one without reference to the other. Most "ordinary" non-artists in our society firmly believe that in any "serious" sense they cannot draw. Indeed, it seems to be quite firmly embedded in the cultural institutionalization of "art" in our society that (unlike language) the gap between competence and comprehension is for most people too wide to be bridgable. This sense has traditionally been reinforced by the post-medieval search for better and better ways of exploring the rich resources of varieties of the replication and transfiguration[27] of visual experience. In immediately responding to, in recognizing, such work we at the same time know that we could not hope to attain to such a skill. We know that the skill of Titian, Rembrandt, Turner and so on and so on is so far beyond us that we could not attempt it – even badly. Most of us, by contrast, can imagine writing like Shakespeare – very badly: we can at least produce the relevant language. We have learned to stand before paintings as we might fully hear and understand a language we are ourselves unable to speak. Part of the shock of a certain strand of modern painting is the thought that here this is not so, that we might well be able to draw in the roughly handled simplified style of much of Matisse or Picasso et al. – even if very badly. For the naive or uninstructed public the reaction to that shock has always been (very understandably) the standard Philistine complaint that "anyone could draw like that, even I could." And in a rather important sense they are right, even if they derive quite mistaken critical conclusions. It is the responsibility of those who have a non-naive, instructed, understanding of this sort of work not to ignore those aspects of it that have in this way genuinely bewildered the uninformed public, but to see and to explain their real implications.

We need a theory that does not set this understanding in opposition to our reaction to other artistic traditions, but reinforces it. We still sometimes resent the demotic, and may even attempt to deny that it is presented to us. But the demotic of the pictorial does not attempt to replicate the content of visual experience: it rather maps it as far, and often only as far, as the need of the occasion requires. In this sense, and it is the fundamental sense, virtually all humans and certainly no other animal, can draw and do so frequently – on the backs of envelopes, split beer mats, as instructions to builders on half-painted walls, and as subversive eroticism on other walls, even with our hands in the air when asked the way by passing strangers. One of the central messages of liberation of twentieth-century art is that from such demotic resources limitless rich aesthetic power can spring, a power quite commensurate with the power of "traditional" painting, a power to see that it is possible to use the demotic not as we normally do, badly and stammeringly, but, if ever so rarely, well.

NOTES

Early versions of this paper have been given as pilot discussions to the Centre for Cognitive Issues in the Arts, University of Bristol, during 1990. I am most grateful for the help and interest received there.

1 The slogan here is Norman Freeman's, slightly adapted. I am indebted to him for his stimulation and encouragement in this project. See N. H. Freeman, "Drawing: the Representation of Public Representation", forthcoming in *The Development and Use of Representation in Children*, ed. C. Pratt and A. F. Garton (London, forthcoming); "Pattern-making and Pictographics: What Relations Should We be Looking For? A Discussion of Drora Booth's Research", *Journal of the Institute of Art Education*, 10 (1986), pp. 55–62; and *Strategies of Representation in Young Children: Analysis of Spatial Skill and Drawing Processes* (London, 1980). See also N. H. Freeman and M. V. Cox, *Visual Order: the Nature and Development of Pictorial Representation* (Cambridge, 1985).
2 See Nicholas Wolterstorff, *Works and Worlds of Art* (London, 1980).
3 *Ibid.*, p. 266.
4 The argument in what follows is at any rate not entirely new for me, and I have sketched much of it in outline elsewhere; see Andrew Harrison "Representation and Conceptual Change" in *Philosophy and the Arts*, ed. Godfrey Vesey (Royal Institute of Philosophy Lectures, 6 [1971–1972], London, 1973), pp. 106–131; *Making and Thinking: a Study of Intelligent Activities* (Sussex, 1978), esp. chapter 6; and "Dimensions of Meaning", in *Philosophy and the Visual Arts: Seeing and Abstracting*, ed. Andrew Harrison (Dordrecht, 1985), pp. 51–76.

5 Richard Wollheim, *Painting as an Art* (Princeton, N.J., and London, 1987), p. 61. I have slightly compressed his words in my indirect quotation.

6 Ludwig Wittgenstein, *Tractatus Logico-Philosophicus*, trans. D. F. Pears and B. F. McGuinness (London, 1961).

7 See my "Representation and Conceptual Change" (see note 4).

8 Commentators in this field are legion, many excellent, and it would be out of place here to review that extensive literature. An excellent recent study which gives due attention to the concept of propositions as pictures is David Pears, *The False Prison: A Study in the Development of Wittgenstein's Philosophy* (Oxford, 1987). Pears summarizes the Wittgensteinian picture-theory of meaning in a manner that may be illuminating in this context: "names are correlated with objects just as the flecks of paint in a pointillist painting are correlated with points in the scene that it depicts." He does not further note, but might well have done, that such painting, seen in such a way, then turns out to be that (rather unusual) sort of painting which contains no signs for relations, except tacit ones derived from the ordering of the "flecks." I suspect that no pointillist painting could ever be quite that "pure" in style. Certainly no drawing could be like that, nor any painting that incorporates drawing technique.

Relevant passages in the *Tractatus* are, among others, 4.01ff., especially:

> 4.011. At first sight a proposition – one set out on the printed page, for example – does not seem to be a picture of the reality with which it is concerned. But no more does musical notation at first sight seem to be a picture of music, nor our phonetic notation (the alphabet) seem to be a picture of our speech.
>
> And yet these sign-languages prove to be pictures, even in the ordinary sense, of what they represent.
>
> 4.012. It is obvious that a proposition of the form 'a R b' strikes us as a picture. In this case the sign is obviously a likeness of what is signified.

To many, of course, this is not obvious at all. But it is well worth attempting to capture that train of thought in which it might well begin to strike one as obvious.

9 Perhaps a better case for a pictorial communication having all the force of a subject-predicate proposition might be where a child is presented with an outline drawing of a cow and then invited to color it in. So then his cow is (shown to be) purple as another child might have made hers yellow. But, here, the presentation of a child with a drawing and then the invitation to add a further property indicator (a move which seems exactly to match the grammar of predicating something of an object) really belongs, I suggest, to the context of linguistic exchanges between the protagonists. Much the same will apply, by parity of reasoning, to those subtler cases where just one agent first draws an object and then adds further feature-indicators to that drawn-object. The "narrative" of

that compositional process conforms then (as all narrative must) to an essentially linguistic structure, as it were a debate with himself, following the patterns of linguistic thought, expressed in the action of painting or drawing. For an extended discussion of this sort of compositional thought, see my *Making and Thinking*.

10 E. H. Gombrich, "Mirror and Map: Theories of Pictorial Representation," *Philosophical Transactions of the Royal Society*, 270 (1975), pp. 119–149, reprinted in his *The Image and The Eye* (London, 1989).

11 It is a mistake to assume as Richard Rorty does (in his *Philosophy and the Mirror of Nature* [Oxford, 1980]) that the seventeenth century, for instance, assumed that the mind was a mirror of nature, though of course many did so (see Andrew Marvell's lines in "The Garden": "The mind, that ocean where each kind / Does straight its own resemblance find.") What seems, rather, to have been the case was that the issue remained challengingly unresolved; see Svetlana Alpers, *The Art of Describing* (Chicago, 1983), for an illuminating discussion of this with respect to the Keplerian tradition. For, among other good things, a compendium of criticism, especially of Rorty's historical interpretation, see the papers in *Philosophy, its History and Historiography*, ed. A. J. Holland (Dordrecht, 1983).

12 See esp. pp. 43–100. Wollheim's footnotes to this section are wonderfully extensive and both narrate the public debate on these matters in an exemplary way and fill out the arguments in the text, which should not, I suggest, be read without constant reference to the notes.

13 *Ibid.*, p. 77.

14 E. H. Gombrich, *Art and Illusion* (New York, 1960).

15 The quotation is in *Art and Illusion*, p. 188; see also the *Notebooks of Leonardo da Vinci*, ed. and trans. Edward McCardy (London, 1938).

16 *Painting as an Art*, p. 48.

17 *Ibid.*, p. 13.

18 The variability of depiction, it needs stressing, therefore by itself in no way implies the sort of anti-realist considerations associated with Richard Rorty, for example, or as put forward in the present context by Nelson Goodman (see *Ways of Worldmaking* [Sussex, 1978]). It does not strictly imply the contrary either, but it is for all that far more easily accounted for on the assumption that the central difference between the one and only world there is and our descriptive, or depictive, "versions" of it is that it is too rich and complex for any single account to exhaust the possibilities of truth; see my *Making and Thinking*, pp. 198ff. (see note 4).

19 A lot has been written, by, for example, Wollheim (*Painting as an Art*, pp. 305ff.), on visual metaphor – a topic of enormous importance, still too little explored – but this rather simple sort of example is not, perhaps significantly, discussed by him.

20 See Roger Scruton, *The Aesthetic Understanding* (Manchester 1983), pp. 102–136, and also Kendall Walton, "Transparent Pictures: On the Nature of Photographic Realism", *Critical Inquiry* 11:2 (December 1984), pp. 246–277.

21 See my "Dimensions of Meaning" (see note 4).

22 See Gotthold Ephraim Lessing, *Laocoon*, trans. Sir Robert Phillimore (London, 1874). In my view Wollheim misunderstands Lessing's argument which is not, I think, discussing "What we can see" (and thus render in visual art) but, despite his debt to empiricist discussions of perception, he is discussing, rather, what "logically" lies within the power of pictorial and sculptural, as opposed to linguistic, communication. This seems to be specially apparent in the uncompleted notes Lessing made for the final form of the never-to-be-completed work, where he in effect makes it perfectly clear that there is a real sense of "see" which goes far beyond that which is optically present.

23 See Kendall Walton, "Looking at Pictures and Looking at Things," in Harrison, ed., *Philosophy and the Visual Arts* (pp. 277–300). On information content in pictures see, for instance, J. J. Gibson's paper "The Information Available in Pictures," *Leonardo*, 4:1 (Winter, 1971), pp. 27–35, and also Nelson Goodman's reply, "Professor Gibson's New Perspective", *Leonardo*, 4:4 (Autumn 1971), pp. 359–360. The problem of defining a sound concept of "information content" for these purposes is far more extensive than my rather sketchy remarks in this chapter may seem to indicate.

24 See Michael Baxandall, *Patterns of Intention: On The Historical Explanation of Pictures* (New Haven and London, 1985), esp. in this context his chapter entitled "Intentional Visual Interest," and Wollheim, *Painting as an Art*, p. 22, note 359. Wollheim offers the concept of (pictorial) "meaning" as "that which we grasp when we understand a painting" and he proposes it as an overall end to which the agent's action in painting the picture is directed so that it may be intelligibly described as intentional action. This move seems to me to be an *ad hoc* solution to an unreal problem (for, as I argued in *Making and Thinking*, there is no reason why intentionality should require overall purposive goals in this way) and inevitably renders the account he offers of an artist's activity circular.

25 See Arthur Danto, *The Transfiguration of the Commonplace* (Cambridge, Mass., 1981), and also *The Philosophical Disenfranchisement of Art* (New York, 1986).

26 See "Dimensions of Meaning." I claim in that paper, and would still claim, that what I there call different "dimensions" of meaning, varieties of meaning systems that correspond to the pictorial (discussed in this chapter), the linguistic (the greatest power of which is, I believe, the power of narrative of agent responsibility), and the "gestural," correspond to, and thus express, quite different cognitive states, and that our normal ways of expression interrelate these as a solid might be located in a space of (here conveniently) three dimensions. This is, among other things, what is happening when the rich capacities of painting as a full and powerful art form engage us at many levels that must inevitably go far beyond the range of the "merely" pictorial. But there is not space to explore these large issues here, to which this chapter can, at best, be a mere prolegomenon.

27 The phrase is, of course, Danto's, in *The Transfiguration of the Commonplace*.

Index

Index

Buchler, J., 211
Budd, Malcolm, 66
Buren, Daniel, 1, 7, 11, 13–18, 28, 32, 34

caesura, 14, 29–30
Carnap, Rudolph, 51
catachresis, 4–5, 78–79, 150–151,
    158–159, 164–167, 169, 170. *See also*
    metaphor; touch
causality, 20, 30; and art history, 63–64,
    115, 139, 154–155; and touch,
    135–136. *See also* authority;
    catachresis; metonymy
Cavell, Stanley, 107, 127
Cézanne, Paul, 1–5, 11, 32–33, 98–108,
    118, 127, 129–180, 234; and
    modernism, 129–132, 138, 162. *See
    also* vision; touch
Chaput, Thierry, 34
Chardin, Jean-Baptiste-Siméon, 115, 119
Chesneau, Ernst, 175
chiasmus, 22, 151
chō, 33
Churchill, Sir Winston, 87
cinema, 12, 94
classicism, 16, 98
clinamen, 28, 152
cognition, 35–50, 101–103
collage, 162–166; and catachresis,
    164–166. *See also* Picasso, Pablo
Collingwood, R. G., 104
color, 13, 22–27, 33. *See also* blue;
    presence
commensurazione, 120–121
commerce, 12–13, 87, 89, 208. *See also*
    society
communication, 6–9, 207, 223, 233, 239
competence, 235
conceptual image, 5, 186–189, 191–192,
    199, 200, 201, 204, 205, 209, 211–212.
    See also analogy; Gombrich, Sir
    Ernst; language conditions, 181–184,
    190, 193, 203, 209. *See also*
    conventions
construction, 1–2, 46, 49, 102, 207, 209
consumer society, 13, 98, 129, 166, 135,
    207, 208. *See also* society, context
context, 105, 131, 149, 151;
    political-historical, 153–155; styles,
    113–114; uniqueness of, 183–196. *See
    also* conditions; society
conventions, 97–100, 129, 136, 155, 182,
    183, 193, 195, 197; linguistic, 84,
    182–183, 185, 193, 197–201, 211. *See
    also* conditions; interpretation;
    metaphor
Cooke, Deryck, 66

correspondence, 51–65. *See also*
    expressiveness; projection
Courbet, Gustave, 174
Cox, M. V., 236
creativity, 101, 102
criticism, 1–2, 197–203; inferential,
    73–74; literary, 25, 71–73, 111. *See
    also* metaphor
Cubism, 109, 127, 160, 180. *See also*
    painting
culture, 1–3, 6–7, 23–24, 119, 129–131,
    135, 138, 153, 170, 200. *See also*
    society

Dallery, Carleton, 177
Danto, Arthur, 234, 239
Davidson, Donald, 65
da Vinci, Leonardo, 39, 99, 124, 177,
    191, 223–224, 232–233
d'Azevedo, Warren L., 75
de Mazia, Violette, 169
Delacroix, Eugène, 74
demotic, 216, 235
Denis, Maurice, 172
Descartes, René, 46; Cartesian optics,
    211. *See also* optics
destiny, 19–20, 30
determinism, 103–105
de Vleeschauwer, H. J., 40, 49
de Vries, Jan Vredeman, 124
Dewey, John, 66
Dickens, Charles, 230
Diderot, Denis, 16, 31, 208
dídón, 69, 95–99
Diehl, Gaston, 176
discourse, 3–4, 12, 36, 39, 101; as
    exemplary, 123–124. *See also*
    language; metaphor
Dōgen, 33
Donatello, 75, 91, 93
Dottin, Mireille, 175
Drebbel, Cornelis, 123
Dreyfus, Hubert L., 177
Dreyfus, Patricia Allen, 177
Dryden, John, 90
Duchamp, Marcel, 11, 32
Dummett, Michael, 85, 99
Dunan, Charles, 173
Duret, Théodore, 171
Dutton, Denis, 126

écorché, 178
Edge, D. O., 179
Edie, James M., 177
Edwards, P., 209
Eliot, T. S., 97
Empson, William, 72

Index

Index

Ockham, William, 210
Olin, Margaret, 173
optics, 119, 146, 210, 220, 239. *See also*
Descartes, René

painting, 3–4, 14; and writing, 29–34,
35, 79, 140, 213, 227, 231
Panofsky, Erwin, 210, 212
pantomime, 192–193
paronymy, 132–148, 159–160. *See also*
catachresis; interpretation; vision
Passmore, John, 74–75, 126
Peake, J. J. S., 210
Pears, D. F., 237
Peirce, Charles S., 103, 126–127, 204, 211
perception, 12–22, 28, 36, 38, 45, 72,
129–130, 216, 228, 230; and scanning,
4–5, 72, 144, 151, 204. *See also*
photography
performance art, 7–8
Perkins, David, 127
Phaino-words, 50
Philipson, M., 210
photography, 26, 102, 147–148, 176,
187, 208, 210, 227, 238
Picasso, Pablo, 113, 116–118, 161–166,
180, 235; and *Guernica*, 96
Pinborg, J., 210
place, 16–18, 28, 29
Planche, Gustave, 174
Plato, 3, 35, 42–43, 50, 82–83, 92, 99,
192, 211
Pliny the Elder, 121
plot, 21–25, 28, 30
poetry, 29, 78, 83, 84, 90–91, 191, 203;
and poetics, 211, 233, 238
Pointillism, 237. *See also* style
politics, 169, 177; and political allegory,
137, 153, 162–163, 168–169
Pollock, Jackson, 84
Pope, Alexander, 90
Popper, Sir Karl, 200
Poussin, Nicholas, 31
Pratt, C., 236
Praus, Gerold, 37–46, 49
prediction, 5, 37–38, 40, 45, 52–53,
54–58, 184–186, 201, 234, 237. *See
also* correspondence; expressiveness;
metaphor; projection
presence, 1–2, 11–34, 44, 85, 181, 196,
232, 239. *See also* metaphor
primitive art, 3, 56, 60, 69, 188, 199,
201, 210, 224, 226
production, 1, 12, 170, 198, 201,
204–205, 234. *See also* image
projection, 3, 9, 51–66, 199, 226. *See
also* expressiveness; Freud, Sigmund

Proust, Marcel, 27
psychology, 3, 53, 151, 210, 216, 227,
234. *See also* image; meaning;
projection
Putnam, Hilary, 88, 100

Raphael, 11, 70
Ratcliff, Robert William, 174
reception, 1, 12, 132, 222
recognition, 60, 104, 111, 205, 206,
213–214, 222, 224, 228. *See also*
identification; memory
Reff, Theodore, 174, 178–179
reflection, 14, 27–30, 31, 76
Rembrandt, 123, 235
Renaissance, 122, 138, 201, 211–212
Renoir, Pierre-Auguste, 133, 165, 171
representation, 15–19, 28, 44, 117,
168–169, 174, 209, 210–211, 222, 225
retrieval, 206–208
Rewald, John, 170–171
rhetoric, 77, 155, 212; and visual trope,
228
Richards, I. A., 66, 110, 128
Riegl, Alois, 188
Ripa, Cesare, 207
Rivière, Georges, 171
Robson, Kenneth, 179
Rollin, B. E., 210
Romanticism, 17, 23–25, 102, 127, 149,
150, 176
Rorty, Richard, 238
Rosenberg, Harold, 66, 134, 137,
171–172
Rousset, Bernard, 40
Rubens, Peter Paul, 74
Rubin, William, 127, 179–180
rule, 39, 104, 201, 205. *See also*
conventions; linguistic convention
Ryman, Robert, 13

Saussure, Ferdinand de, 5, 96, 203, 209,
211
Savile, Anthony, 65
Sayre, Henry M., 8, 10
Schapiro, Meyer, 137, 140, 147, 149,
152, 171, 176–178, 205–211
Schiff, William, 172
Schönberg, Arnold, 33
science, 11, 80, 119, 199, 200, 201, 204;
and scientific knowledge, 43, 77,
191–192, 199, 202, 211
Scruton, Roger, 2, 9, 238
sculpture, 77, 196, 202, 205–206, 239
semantics, 218, 225. *See also* linguistic
convention; meaning
sense, 12, 85, 111, 112, 187, 189, 194,

Index